2024 EDITION

MODEL RULES OF PROFESSIONAL CONDUCT

AMERICAN**BAR**ASSOCIATION

Center for Professional Responsibility

Cover design by ABA Design.

The ABA Model Rules of Professional Conduct, including Preamble, Scope and Comment, were adopted by the ABA House of Delegates on August 2, 1983, and amended in 1987, 1989, 1990, 1991, 1992, 1993, 1994, 1995, 1997, 1998, 2000, 2002, 2003, 2007, 2008, 2009, 2012, 2013, 2016, 2018, 2020, and 2023.

Nothing contained herein is to be considered as the rendering of legal advice for specific cases, and readers are responsible for obtaining such advice from their own legal counsel. This book is intended for educational and informational purposes only.

© 2024 American Bar Association. All rights reserved.

No part of this publication may be reproduced, stored in a retrieval system, or transmitted in any form or by any means, electronic, mechanical, photocopying, recording, or otherwise, without the prior written permission of the publisher. For permission contact the ABA Copyrights & Contracts Department, copyright@americanbar.org, or complete the online form at http://www.americanbar.org/utility/reprint.html.

Printed in the United States of America.

28 27 26 25 24   5 4 3 2 1

ISBN: 978-1-63905-471-8
e-ISBN: 978-1-63905-472-5

Discounts are available for books ordered in bulk. Special consideration is given to state bars, CLE programs, and other bar-related organizations. Inquire at Book Publishing, ABA Publishing, American Bar Association, 321 N. Clark Street, Chicago, Illinois 60654-7598.

www.ShopABA.org

AMERICAN BAR ASSOCIATION
CENTER FOR PROFESSIONAL RESPONSIBILITY

The Center for Professional Responsibility is the American Bar Association's "home" for lawyers who are interested in professionalism, ethics, client protection, legal malpractice, discipline, and regulation. The Center has served as locus for many ABA initiatives, including those of the Commission on Multidisciplinary Practice, the Commission on Multijurisdictional Practice, the Commission on Evaluation of the Rules of Professional Conduct (Ethics 2000), the Joint Commission to Evaluate the Model Code of Judicial Conduct, and the Commission on Ethics 20/20. The Center comprises numerous committees and publishes various works relating to professional responsibility law. In addition, the Center:

- Develops rules of lawyer and judicial ethics, professional discipline, and client protection that serve as the model for jurisdictions throughout the country;
- Produces numerous publications including *Annotated Model Rules of Professional Conduct*, *Annotated Model Code of Judicial Conduct*, *The Paralegal's Guide to Professional Responsibility*, model lawyer, judicial, and client protection rules, and, together with Bloomberg Industry Group, the *ABA/Bloomberg Lawyers' Manual on Professional Conduct*;
- Issues formal opinions to resolve questions about applying ethics rules;
- Operates the National Lawyer Regulatory Data Bank, the only national repository of information relating to lawyers who have received public disciplinary sanctions;
- Offers on-site consultations to individual jurisdictions reviewing their discipline systems; and
- Presents the National Conference on Professional Responsibility, National Forum on Client Protection, National Legal Malpractice Conference, and numerous CLE webinars.

Center membership is open to ABA lawyer, associate, and law student members in all practice settings. Benefits include steep discounts on publications and CLE events.

Find out more about the Center at http://ambar.org/CPRHome or contact the Center at cpr@americanbar.org.

ABA Standing Committee on Ethics and Professional Responsibility
2023–2024

BRUCE A. GREEN, *Chair*
New York, NY

HILARY GERZHOY
Washington, DC

MARK A. ARMITAGE
Detroit, MI

WENDY MUCHMAN
Chicago, IL

MATTHEW CORBIN
Olathe, KS

HON. JENNIFER RYMELL
Fort Worth, TX

ROBINJIT K. EAGLESON
Lansing, MI

TIM PIERCE
Madison, WI

BRIAN FAUGHNAN
Memphis, TN

CHARLES J. VIGIL
Albuquerque, NM

Board of Governors Liaison
HON. JAMES HILL
Bismark, ND

American Bar Association
Center for Professional Responsibility

Director
TERESA SCHMID

Contents

Preface ix

Commission on Evaluation of Professional Standards xiii

Chair's Introduction xv

Commission on Evaluation of the Rules of Professional Conduct xix

Chair's Introduction xxi

Preamble and Scope 1

Rules

1.0 Terminology 7

Client-Lawyer Relationship

1.1 Competence 11
1.2 Scope of Representation and Allocation
     of Authority between Client and Lawyer 13
1.3 Diligence 17
1.4 Communication 19
1.5 Fees 21
1.6 Confidentiality of Information 25
1.7 Conflict of Interest: Current Clients 33
1.8 Conflict of Interest: Current Clients: Specific Rules 45
1.9 Duties to Former Clients 55
1.10 Imputation of Conflicts of Interest: General Rule 59
1.11 Special Conflicts of Interest for Former and
     Current Government Officers and Employees 62
1.12 Former Judge, Arbitrator, Mediator
     or Other Third-Party Neutral 66
1.13 Organization as Client 69
1.14 Client with Diminished Capacity 74
1.15 Safekeeping Property 78

v

1.16	Declining or Terminating Representation	80
1.17	Sale of Law Practice	84
1.18	Duties to Prospective Client	88

COUNSELOR

2.1	Advisor	91
2.2	(Deleted 2002)	93
2.3	Evaluation for Use by Third Persons	93
2.4	Lawyer Serving as Third-Party Neutral	95

ADVOCATE

3.1	Meritorious Claims and Contentions	97
3.2	Expediting Litigation	98
3.3	Candor Toward the Tribunal	99
3.4	Fairness to Opposing Party and Counsel	104
3.5	Impartiality and Decorum of the Tribunal	106
3.6	Trial Publicity	107
3.7	Lawyer as Witness	110
3.8	Special Responsibilities of a Prosecutor	112
3.9	Advocate in Nonadjudicative Proceedings	116

TRANSACTIONS WITH PERSONS OTHER THAN CLIENTS

4.1	Truthfulness in Statements to Others	117
4.2	Communication with Person Represented by Counsel	118
4.3	Dealing with Unrepresented Person	120
4.4	Respect for Rights of Third Persons	121

LAW FIRMS AND ASSOCIATIONS

| 5.1 | Responsibilities of Partners, Managers, and Supervisory Lawyers | 123 |
| 5.2 | Responsibilities of a Subordinate Lawyer | 125 |

5.3	Responsibilities Regarding Nonlawyer Assistance	126
5.4	Professional Independence of a Lawyer	128
5.5	Unauthorized Practice of Law; Multijurisdictional Practice of Law	130
5.6	Restrictions on Right to Practice	136
5.7	Responsibilities Regarding Law-Related Services	137

PUBLIC SERVICE

6.1	Voluntary Pro Bono Publico Service	140
6.2	Accepting Appointments	143
6.3	Membership in Legal Services Organization	144
6.4	Law Reform Activities Affecting Client Interests	145
6.5	Nonprofit and Court-Annexed Limited Legal Services Programs	146

INFORMATION ABOUT LEGAL SERVICES

7.1	Communications Concerning a Lawyer's Services	148
7.2	Communications Concerning a Lawyer's Services: Specific Rules	149
7.3	Solicitation of Clients	153
7.4	(Deleted 2018)	157
7.5	(Deleted 2018)	157
7.6	Political Contributions to Obtain Government Legal Engagements or Appointments by Judges	157

MAINTAINING THE INTEGRITY OF THE PROFESSION

8.1	Bar Admission and Disciplinary Matters	159
8.2	Judicial and Legal Officials	160
8.3	Reporting Professional Misconduct	160
8.4	Misconduct	162
8.5	Disciplinary Authority; Choice of Law	164

Appendices

Appendix A:
Subject Guide 169

Appendix B:
Correlation Tables 195

Appendix C:
ABA Standing Committee on
Ethics and Professional Responsibility:
Composition and Jurisdiction and Rules of Procedure 211

Appendix D:
ABA Special Committee on Implementation
of the Model Rules of Professional Conduct 215

Appendix E:
Amendments to the
Model Rules of Professional Conduct

    By Rule 217

    By Date 222

Appendix F:
Formal Ethics Opinions

    Formal Opinion 504:
    Choice of Law 225

    Formal Opinion 505:
    Fees Paid in Advance for Contemplated Services 237

    Formal Opinion 506:
    Responsibilities Regarding Nonlawyer Assistants 252

    Formal Opinion 507:
    Office Sharing Arrangements with Other Lawyers 258

    Formal Opinion 508:
    The Ethics of Witness Preparation 266

PREFACE

For more than one hundred years, the American Bar Association has provided leadership in legal ethics and professional responsibility through the adoption of professional standards that serve as models of the regulatory law governing the legal profession.

On August 27, 1908, the Association adopted the original Canons of Professional Ethics. These were based principally on the Code of Ethics adopted by the Alabama Bar Association in 1887, which in turn had been borrowed largely from the lectures of Judge George Sharswood, published in 1854 as Professional Ethics, and from the fifty resolutions included in David Hoffman's A Course of Legal Study (2d ed. 1836). Piecemeal amendments to the Canons occasionally followed.

In 1913, the Standing Committee on Professional Ethics of the American Bar Association was established to keep the Association informed about state and local bar activities concerning professional ethics. In 1919 the name of the Committee was changed to the Committee on Professional Ethics and Grievances; its role was expanded in 1922 to include issuing opinions "concerning professional conduct, and particularly concerning the application of the tenets of ethics thereto." In 1958 the Committee on Professional Ethics and Grievances was separated into two committees: a Committee on Professional Grievances, with authority to review issues of professional misconduct, and a Committee on Professional Ethics with responsibility to express its opinion concerning proper professional and judicial conduct. The Committee on Professional Grievances was discontinued in 1971. The name of the Committee on Professional Ethics was changed to the Committee on Ethics and Professional Responsibility in 1971 and remains so.

In 1964, at the request of President Lewis F. Powell Jr., the House of Delegates of the American Bar Association created a Special Committee on Evaluation of Ethical Standards (the "Wright Committee") to assess whether changes should be made in the then-current Canons of Professional Ethics. In response, the Committee produced the Model Code of Professional Responsibility. The Model Code was adopted by the House of Delegates on August 12, 1969, and subsequently by the vast majority of state and federal jurisdictions.

In 1977, the American Bar Association created the Commission on Evaluation of Professional Standards to undertake a comprehensive rethinking of the ethical premises and problems of the legal profession. Upon evaluating the Model Code and determining that amendment of the Code would not achieve a comprehensive statement of the law governing the legal profession, the Commission commenced a six-year study and drafting process that produced the Model Rules of Professional Conduct. The Model Rules were adopted by the House of Delegates of the American Bar Association on August 2, 1983.

Between 1983 and 2002, the House amended the Rules and Comments on fourteen different occasions. In 1997, the American Bar Association created the Commission on Evaluation of the Rules of Professional Conduct ("Ethics 2000 Commission") to comprehensively review the Model Rules and propose amendments as deemed appropriate. On February 5, 2002 the House of Delegates adopted a series of amendments that arose from this process.

In 2000, the American Bar Association created the Commission on Multijurisdictional Practice to research, study and report on the application of current ethics and bar admission rules to the multijurisdictional practice of law. On August 12, 2002 the House of Delegates adopted amendments to Rules 5.5 and 8.5 as a result of the Commission's work and recommendations.

In 2002, the American Bar Association created the Task Force on Corporate Responsibility to examine systemic issues relating to corporate responsibility arising out of the unexpected and traumatic bankruptcy of Enron and other Enron-like situations that had shaken confidence in the effectiveness of the governance and disclosure systems applicable to public companies in the United States. In August 11-12, 2003, the House of Delegates adopted amendments to Rules 1.6 and 1.13 as a result of the Task Force's work and recommendations.

In 2009, the American Bar Association created the Commission on Ethics 20/20 to perform a thorough review of the ABA Model Rules of Professional Conduct and the U.S. system of lawyer regulation in the context of advances in technology and global legal practice developments. On August 6, 2012 and February 11, 2013 the House of Delegates adopted a series of amendments to the Rules and Comments as a result of the Commission's work and recommendations.

In February 2016, the Section on International Law recommended amending Model Rule of Professional Conduct 5.5 and the ABA Model

Rule for Registration of In-House Counsel to include language specifying that the court of highest appellate jurisdiction may, in its discretion, allow foreign in-house lawyers who do not meet the ABA definition of foreign lawyer because they cannot be "members of the bar" to be able to practice as in-house counsel in the United States and to be so registered. On February 8, 2016, the House of Delegates adopted the suggested amendments with further revisions.

In August 2016, the Standing Committee on Ethics and Professional Responsibility brought to the House of Delegates amendments to Model Rule 8.4, Misconduct. Proposed new paragraph (g) prohibited lawyers from discrimination and harassment in conduct related to the practice of law. On August 8, 2016, the House of Delegates adopted the recommended amendments.

In 2018, the Standing Committee on Ethics and Professional Responsibility suggested amendments to the Model Rules regulating lawyer advertising with the goal of simplifying and making those rules more uniform. On August 6, 2018, the House of Delegates adopted the suggested amendments.

In 2020, the Standing Committee on Ethics and Professional Responsibility suggested amendments to Model Rule 1.8(e) to allow lawyers, representing someone on a pro bono basis, to provide limited financial assistance to that client. On August 12, 2020, the House of Delegates adopted the recommended amendments.

In 2021, the Standing Committees on Ethics and Professional Responsibility and Professional Regulation suggested amending the In-House Counsel Registration Rule so that lawyers who work as in-house counsel for a law firm could be registered as in-house counsel. This suggested amendment was adopted by the ABA House of Delegates in August 2021.

In 2023, the Standing Committees on Ethics and Professional Responsibility and Professional Regulation suggested amending Model Rule 1.16 to address a lawyer's responsibility to inquire into and assess a matter. This amendment was adopted by the ABA House of Delegates in August 2023.

The American Bar Association continues to pursue its goal of assuring the highest standards of professional competence and ethical conduct. The Standing Committee on Ethics and Professional Responsibility, charged with interpreting the professional standards of the Association and recommending appropriate amendments and clarifications, issues opinions interpreting the Model Rules of Professional Conduct and the Model Code of Judicial Conduct. The opinions of the Committee are published by the American Bar Association in a series of bound volumes containing opinions from 1924 through 2013 and as individual PDFs starting with the 1984 opinions.

Requests that the Committee issue opinions on particular questions of professional and judicial conduct should be directed to the American Bar Association, Center for Professional Responsibility, 321 N. Clark Street, Chicago, Illinois 60654.

ABA MODEL RULES

ABA Commission on Evaluation of Professional Standards (1977–1983)

ROBERT W. MESERVE, *Chair*
Boston, Massachusetts

MARVIN E. FRANKEL
New York, New York

RICHARD H. SINKFIELD
Atlanta, Georgia

ALAN BARTH
Washington, D.C.

LOIS C. HARRISON
Lakeland, Florida

WILLIAM B. SPANN, JR.
Atlanta, Georgia

ARNO H. DENECKE
Salem, Oregon

ROBERT O. HETLAGE
St. Louis, Missouri

SAMUEL D. THURMAN
Salt Lake City, Utah

THOMAS EHRLICH
Washington, D.C.

ROBERT B. McKAY
New York, New York

ROBERT J. KUTAK
Omaha, Nebraska
Former Chair

JANE FRANK-HARMAN
Washington, D.C.

L. CLAIR NELSON
Washington, D.C.

Liaisons

MICHAEL FRANCK
Lansing, Michigan
Standing Committee on Professional Discipline

JOHN C. DEACON
Jonesboro, Arkansas
Board of Governors

H. WILLIAM ALLEN
Little Rock, Arkansas
Standing Committee on Ethics and Professional Responsibility

THOMAS Z. HAYWARD, JR.
Chicago, Illinois

Consultants

BETTY B. FLETCHER
Seattle, Washington

L. RAY PATTERSON
Atlanta, Georgia

JOHN F. SUTTON, JR.
Austin, Texas

Reporter

GEOFFREY C. HAZARD, JR.
New Haven, Connecticut

Assistant Reporters

THOMAS J. McCORMICK
Washington, D.C.

DANIEL S. REYNOLDS
DeKalb, Illinois

COMMISSION ON EVALUATION OF PROFESSIONAL STANDARDS
CHAIR'S INTRODUCTION

The Commission on Evaluation of Professional Standards was appointed in the summer of 1977 by former ABA President William B. Spann, Jr. Chaired by Robert J. Kutak until his death in early 1983, the Commission was charged with evaluating whether existing standards of professional conduct provided comprehensive and consistent guidance for resolving the increasingly complex ethical problems in the practice of law. For the most part, the Commission looked to the former ABA Model Code of Professional Responsibility, which served as a model for the majority of state ethics codes. The Commission also referred to opinions of the ABA Standing Committee on Ethics and Professional Responsibility, as well as to decisions of the United States Supreme Court and of state supreme courts. After thoughtful study, the Commission concluded that piecemeal amendment of the Model Code would not sufficiently clarify the profession's ethical responsibilities in light of changed conditions. The Commission therefore commenced a drafting process that produced numerous drafts, elicited voluminous comment, and launched an unprecedented debate on the ethics of the legal profession.

On January 30, 1980, the Commission presented its initial suggestions to the bar in the form of a Discussion Draft of the proposed Model Rules of Professional Conduct. The Discussion Draft was subject to the widest possible dissemination and interested parties were urged to offer comments and suggestions. Public hearings were held around the country to provide forums for expression of views on the draft.

In the year following the last of these public hearings, the Commission conducted a painstaking analysis of the submitted comments and attempted to integrate into the draft those which seemed consistent with its underlying philosophy. The product of this analysis and integration was presented on May 31, 1981, as the proposed Final Draft of the Model Rules of Professional Conduct. This proposed Final Draft was submitted in two formats. The first format, consisting of blackletter Rules and accompanying Comments in the so-called restatement format, was submitted with the Commission's recommendation that it be adopted. The alternative format was patterned after the Model Code and consisted of Canons, Ethical Considerations, and Disciplinary Rules. In February 1982, the House of Delegates by substantial majority approved the restatement format of the Model Rules.

The proposed Final Draft was submitted to the House of Delegates for debate and approval at the 1982 Annual Meeting of the Association in San Francisco. Many organizations and interested parties offered their comments in the form of proposed amendments to the Final Draft. In the time allotted on its agenda, however, the House debated only proposed amendments to Rule 1.5. Consideration of the remainder of the document was deferred until the 1983 Midyear Meeting in New Orleans. The proposed Final Draft, as amended by the House in San Francisco, was reprinted in the November 1982 issue of the *ABA Journal*.

At the 1983 Midyear Meeting the House resumed consideration of the Final Draft. After two days of often vigorous debate, the House completed its review of the proposed amendments to the blackletter Rules. Many amendments, particularly in the area of confidentiality, were adopted. Debate on a Preamble, Scope, Terminology, and Comments, rewritten to reflect the New Orleans amendments, was deferred until the 1983 Annual Meeting in Atlanta, Georgia.

On March 11, 1983, the text of the blackletter Rules as approved by the House in February, together with the proposed Preamble, Scope, Terminology, and Comments, was circulated to members of the House, Section and Committee chairs, and all other interested parties. The text of the Rules reflected the joint efforts of the Commission and the House Drafting Committee to incorporate the changes approved by the House and to ensure stylistic continuity and uniformity. Recipients of the draft were again urged to submit comments in the form of proposed amendments. The House Committees on Drafting and Rules and Calendar met on May 23, 1983, to consider all of the proposed amendments that had been submitted in response to this draft. In addition, discussions were held among concerned parties in an effort to reach accommodation of the various positions. On July 11, 1983, the final version of the Model Rules was again circulated.

The House of Delegates commenced debate on the proposed Preamble, Scope, Terminology, and Comments on August 2, 1983. After four hours of debate, the House completed its consideration of all the proposed amendments and, upon motion of the Commission, the House voted to adopt the Model Rules of Professional Conduct, together with the ancillary material as amended. The task of the Commission had ended and it was discharged with thanks.

Throughout the drafting process, active participants included not only the members of the Commission but also the Sections and Committees of the American Bar Association and national, state, and local bar organizations. The work of the Commission was subject to virtually continuous scrutiny by academicians, practicing lawyers, members of the press, and the judiciary. Consequently, every provision of the Model Rules reflects the thoughtful consideration and hard work of many dedicated professionals. Because of their input, the Model Rules are truly national in derivation. The Association can take immense pride in its continued demonstration of leadership in the area of professional responsibility.

The Model Rules of Professional Conduct are intended to serve as a national framework for implementation of standards of professional conduct. Although the Commission endeavored to harmonize and accommodate the views of all the participants, no set of national standards that speaks to such a diverse constituency as the legal profession can resolve each issue to the complete satisfaction of every affected party. Undoubtedly there will be those who take issue with one or another of the Rules' provisions. Indeed, such dissent from individual provisions is expected. And the Model Rules, like all model legislation, will be subject to modification at the level of local implementation. Viewed as a whole, however, the Model Rules represent a responsible approach to the ethical practice of law and are consistent with professional obligations imposed by other law, such as constitutional, corporate, tort, fiduciary, and agency law.

I should not end this report without speaking of the Commission's debt to many people who have aided us in our deliberations, and have devoted time, energy, and goodwill to the advancement of our work over the last six years. It would probably be impossible to name each of the particular persons whose help was significant to us, and it surely would be unfortunate if the name of anyone were omitted from the list. We are, and shall remain, deeply grateful to the literally hundreds of people who aided us with welcome and productive suggestions. We think the bar should be grateful to each of them, and to our deceased members, Alan Barth of the District of Columbia, who we hardly had time to know, Bill Spann, who became a member after the conclusion of his presidential term, and our original chair, Bob Kutak.

The long work of the Commission and its resulting new codification of the ethical rules of practice demonstrate, it is submitted, the commitment of the American lawyer to his or her profession and to achievement of the highest standards.

Robert W. Meserve
September 1983

ABA COMMISSION ON EVALUATION OF THE RULES OF PROFESSIONAL CONDUCT (1997–2002)

HON. E. NORMAN VEASEY, *Chair*
Wilmington, Delaware

MARGARET C. LOVE
Washington, D.C.

LAWRENCE J. FOX
Philadelphia, Pennsylvania

SUSAN R. MARTYN
Toledo, Ohio

ALBERT C. HARVEY
Memphis, Tennessee

DAVID T. MCLAUGHLIN
New London, New Hampshire

GEOFFREY C. HAZARD, JR.
Swarthmore, Pennsylvania

RICHARD E. MULROY
Ridgewood, New Jersey

HON. PATRICK E. HIGGINBOTHAM
Dallas, Texas

LUCIAN T. PERA
Memphis, Tennessee

W. LOEBER LANDAU
New York, New York

HON. HENRY RAMSEY, JR. (Ret.)
Berkeley, California

HON. LAURIE D. ZELON
Los Angeles, California

LIAISONS

JAMES B. LEE
Salt Lake City, Utah
Board of Governors

SETH ROSNER
Greenfield Center, New York
Board of Governors

REPORTERS

NANCY J. MOORE
Boston, Massachusetts
Chief Reporter

THOMAS D. MORGAN (1998–1999)
Washington, D.C.

CARL A. PIERCE
Knoxville, Tennessee

CENTER FOR PROFESSIONAL RESPONSIBILITY

JEANNE P. GRAY
Chicago, Illinois
Director

CHARLOTTE K. STRETCH, *Counsel*
Chicago, Illinois

SUSAN M. CAMPBELL, *Paralegal*
Chicago, Illinois

COMMISSION ON EVALUATION OF THE
RULES OF PROFESSIONAL CONDUCT ("ETHICS 2000")

CHAIR'S INTRODUCTION

In mid-1997, ABA President Jerome J. Shestack, his immediate predecessor, N. Lee Cooper, and his successor, Philip S. Anderson had the vision to establish the "Ethics 2000" Commission. These three leaders persuaded the ABA Board of Governors that the Model Rules adopted by the ABA House of Delegates in 1983 needed comprehensive review and some revision, and this project was launched. Though some might have thought it premature to reopen the Model Rules to such a rigorous general reassessment after only fourteen years, the evaluation process has proven that the ABA leadership was correct.

One of the primary reasons behind the decision to revisit the Model Rules was the growing disparity in state ethics codes. While a large majority of states and the District of Columbia had adopted some version of the Model Rules (then thirty-nine, now forty-two), there were many significant differences among the state versions that resulted in an undesirable lack of uniformity—a problem that had been exacerbated by the approximately thirty amendments to the Model Rules between 1983 and 1997. A few states had elected to retain some version of the 1969 Model Code of Professional Responsibility, and California remained committed to an entirely separate system of lawyer regulation.

But it was not only the patchwork pattern of state regulation that motivated the ABA leaders of 1997 to take this action. There were also new issues and questions raised by the influence that technological developments were having on the delivery of legal services. The explosive dynamics of modern law practice and the anticipated developments in the future of the legal profession lent a sense of urgency as well as a substantive dimension to the project. These developments were underscored by the work then underway on the American Law Institute's *Restatement of the Law Governing Lawyers*.

There was also a strong countervailing sense that there was much to be valued in the existing concepts and articulation of the Model Rules. The Commission concluded early on that these valuable aspects of the Rules should not be lost or put at risk in our revision effort. As a result, the Commission set about to be comprehensive, but at the same time conservative, and to recommend change only where necessary. In balancing the need to preserve the good with the need for improvement, we were mindful of Thomas Jefferson's words of nearly 185 years ago, in a letter concerning the Virginia Constitution, that "moderate imperfections had better be borne with; because, when once known, we accommodate ourselves to them, and find practical means of correcting their ill effects."

Thus, we retained the basic architecture of the Model Rules. We also retained the primary disciplinary function of the Rules, resisting the temptation to preach aspirationally about "best practices" or professionalism concepts. Valuable as the profession might find such guidance, it would not have—and should not be misperceived as having—a regulatory dimension. We were, however, always conscious of the educational role of the Model Rules. Finally, we tried to keep our changes to a minimum: when a particular provision was found not to be "broken" we did not try to "fix" it. Even so, as the reader will note, the Commission ended up making a large number of changes: some are relatively innocuous and nonsubstantive, in the nature of editorial or stylistic changes; others are substantive but not particularly controversial; and a few are both substantive and controversial.

The deliberations of the Commission did not take place in a vacuum and our determinations are not being pronounced *ex cathedra*. Rather, they are products of thorough research, scholarly analysis, and thoughtful consideration. Of equal importance, they have been influenced by the views of practitioners, scholars, other members of the legal profession, and the public. All these constituencies have had continual access to and considerable—and proper—influence upon the deliberations of the Commission throughout this process.

I must pause to underscore the openness of our process. We held over fifty days of meetings, all of which were open, and ten public hearings at regular intervals over a four-and-a-half-year period. There were a large number of interested observers at our meetings, many of whom were members of our Advisory Council of 250-plus persons, to offer comments and suggestions. Those observations were very helpful and influential in shaping the Report. Our public discussion drafts, minutes, and Report were available on our website for the world to see and comment upon. As a consequence, we received an enormous number of excellent comments and suggestions, many of which were adopted in the formulation of our Report.

Moreover, we encouraged state and local bar associations, ABA sections and divisions, other professional organizations, and the judiciary to appoint specially designated committees to work with and counsel the Commission. This effort was successful, and the Commission benefitted significantly from the considered views of these groups.

In heeding the counsel of these advisors, we were constantly mindful of substantial and high-velocity changes in the legal profession, particularly over the past decade. These changes have been highlighted by increased public scrutiny of lawyers and an awareness of their influential role in the formation and implementation of public policy; persistent concerns about lawyer honesty, candor, and civility; external competitive and technological pressures on the legal profession; internal pressures on law firm organization and management raised by sheer size, as well as specialization and lawyer mobility; jurisdictional and governance issues, such as multidisciplinary and multijurisdictional practice; special concerns of lawyers in nontraditional practice settings, such as government lawyers and in-house counsel; and the need to enhance public trust and confidence in the legal profession.

At the end of the day, our goal was to develop Rules that are comprehensible to the public and provide clear guidance to the practitioner. Our desire was to preserve all that is valuable and enduring about the existing Model Rules, while at the same time adapting them to the realities of modern law practice and the limits of professional discipline. We believe our product is a balanced blend of traditional precepts and forward-looking provisions that are responsive to modern developments. Our process has been thorough, painstaking, open, scholarly, objective, and collegial.

It is impossible here to go into detail about the changes proposed by the Commission. The changes recommended by the Commission clarified and strengthened a lawyer's duty to communicate with the client; clarified and strengthened a lawyer's duty to clients in certain specific problem areas; responded to the changing organization and structure of modern law practice; responded to new issues and questions raised by the influence that technological developments are having on the delivery of legal services; clarified existing Rules to provide better guidance and explanation to lawyers; clarified and strengthened a lawyer's obligations to the tribunal and to the justice system; responded to the need for changes in the delivery of legal services to low- and middle-income persons; and increased protection of third parties.

The ABA House of Delegates began consideration of the Commission's Report at the August 2001 Annual Meeting in Chicago and completed its review at the February 2002 Midyear Meeting in Philadelphia.

At the August 2002 Annual Meeting in Washington, D.C., the ABA House of Delegates considered and adopted additional amendments to the Model Rules sponsored by the ABA Commission on Multijurisdictional Practice and the ABA Standing Committee on Ethics and Professional Responsibility. As state supreme courts consider implementation of these newly revised Rules, it is our fervent hope that the goal of uniformity will be the guiding beacon.

In closing, the Commission expresses its gratitude to the law firm of Drinker Biddle & Reath, whose generous contribution helped make possible the continued, invaluable support of the Commission's Chief Reporter. I also want to express personally my gratitude to and admiration for my colleagues. The chemistry, goodwill, good humor, serious purpose, collegiality, and hard work of the Commission members, Reporters, and ABA staff have been extraordinary. The profession and the public have been enriched beyond measure by their efforts. It has been a pleasure and a privilege for me to work with all of them.

Hon. E. Norman Veasey
August 2002

PREAMBLE AND SCOPE

PREAMBLE:
A LAWYER'S RESPONSIBILITIES

[1] A lawyer, as a member of the legal profession, is a representative of clients, an officer of the legal system and a public citizen having special responsibility for the quality of justice.

[2] As a representative of clients, a lawyer performs various functions. As advisor, a lawyer provides a client with an informed understanding of the client's legal rights and obligations and explains their practical implications. As advocate, a lawyer zealously asserts the client's position under the rules of the adversary system. As negotiator, a lawyer seeks a result advantageous to the client but consistent with requirements of honest dealings with others. As an evaluator, a lawyer acts by examining a client's legal affairs and reporting about them to the client or to others.

[3] In addition to these representational functions, a lawyer may serve as a third-party neutral, a nonrepresentational role helping the parties to resolve a dispute or other matter. Some of these Rules apply directly to lawyers who are or have served as third-party neutrals. See, e.g., Rules 1.12 and 2.4. In addition, there are Rules that apply to lawyers who are not active in the practice of law or to practicing lawyers even when they are acting in a nonprofessional capacity. For example, a lawyer who commits fraud in the conduct of a business is subject to discipline for engaging in conduct involving dishonesty, fraud, deceit or misrepresentation. See Rule 8.4.

[4] In all professional functions a lawyer should be competent, prompt and diligent. A lawyer should maintain communication with a client concerning the representation. A lawyer should keep in confidence information relating to representation of a client except so far as disclosure is required or permitted by the Rules of Professional Conduct or other law.

[5] A lawyer's conduct should conform to the requirements of the law, both in professional service to clients and in the lawyer's business and personal affairs. A lawyer should use the law's procedures only for legitimate purposes and not to harass or intimidate others. A lawyer should demonstrate respect for the legal system and for those who serve it, including judges, other lawyers and public officials. While it is a law-

yer's duty, when necessary, to challenge the rectitude of official action, it is also a lawyer's duty to uphold legal process.

[6] As a public citizen, a lawyer should seek improvement of the law, access to the legal system, the administration of justice and the quality of service rendered by the legal profession. As a member of a learned profession, a lawyer should cultivate knowledge of the law beyond its use for clients, employ that knowledge in reform of the law and work to strengthen legal education. In addition, a lawyer should further the public's understanding of and confidence in the rule of law and the justice system because legal institutions in a constitutional democracy depend on popular participation and support to maintain their authority. A lawyer should be mindful of deficiencies in the administration of justice and of the fact that the poor, and sometimes persons who are not poor, cannot afford adequate legal assistance. Therefore, all lawyers should devote professional time and resources and use civic influence to ensure equal access to our system of justice for all those who because of economic or social barriers cannot afford or secure adequate legal counsel. A lawyer should aid the legal profession in pursuing these objectives and should help the bar regulate itself in the public interest.

[7] Many of a lawyer's professional responsibilities are prescribed in the Rules of Professional Conduct, as well as substantive and procedural law. However, a lawyer is also guided by personal conscience and the approbation of professional peers. A lawyer should strive to attain the highest level of skill, to improve the law and the legal profession and to exemplify the legal profession's ideals of public service.

[8] A lawyer's responsibilities as a representative of clients, an officer of the legal system and a public citizen are usually harmonious. Thus, when an opposing party is well represented, a lawyer can be a zealous advocate on behalf of a client and at the same time assume that justice is being done. So also, a lawyer can be sure that preserving client confidences ordinarily serves the public interest because people are more likely to seek legal advice, and thereby heed their legal obligations, when they know their communications will be private.

[9] In the nature of law practice, however, conflicting responsibilities are encountered. Virtually all difficult ethical problems arise from conflict between a lawyer's responsibilities to clients, to the legal system and to the lawyer's own interest in remaining an ethical person while earning a satisfactory living. The Rules of Professional Conduct often prescribe terms for resolving such conflicts. Within the framework of these Rules,

however, many difficult issues of professional discretion can arise. Such issues must be resolved through the exercise of sensitive professional and moral judgment guided by the basic principles underlying the Rules. These principles include the lawyer's obligation zealously to protect and pursue a client's legitimate interests, within the bounds of the law, while maintaining a professional, courteous and civil attitude toward all persons involved in the legal system.

[10] The legal profession is largely self-governing. Although other professions also have been granted powers of self-government, the legal profession is unique in this respect because of the close relationship between the profession and the processes of government and law enforcement. This connection is manifested in the fact that ultimate authority over the legal profession is vested largely in the courts.

[11] To the extent that lawyers meet the obligations of their professional calling, the occasion for government regulation is obviated. Self-regulation also helps maintain the legal profession's independence from government domination. An independent legal profession is an important force in preserving government under law, for abuse of legal authority is more readily challenged by a profession whose members are not dependent on government for the right to practice.

[12] The legal profession's relative autonomy carries with it special responsibilities of self-government. The profession has a responsibility to assure that its regulations are conceived in the public interest and not in furtherance of parochial or self-interested concerns of the bar. Every lawyer is responsible for observance of the Rules of Professional Conduct. A lawyer should also aid in securing their observance by other lawyers. Neglect of these responsibilities compromises the independence of the profession and the public interest which it serves.

[13] Lawyers play a vital role in the preservation of society. The fulfillment of this role requires an understanding by lawyers of their relationship to our legal system. The Rules of Professional Conduct, when properly applied, serve to define that relationship.

SCOPE

[14] The Rules of Professional Conduct are rules of reason. They should be interpreted with reference to the purposes of legal representation and of the law itself. Some of the Rules are imperatives, cast in the terms "shall" or "shall not." These define proper conduct for purposes of professional discipline. Others, generally cast in the term "may," are

permissive and define areas under the Rules in which the lawyer has discretion to exercise professional judgment. No disciplinary action should be taken when the lawyer chooses not to act or acts within the bounds of such discretion. Other Rules define the nature of relationships between the lawyer and others. The Rules are thus partly obligatory and disciplinary and partly constitutive and descriptive in that they define a lawyer's professional role. Many of the Comments use the term "should." Comments do not add obligations to the Rules but provide guidance for practicing in compliance with the Rules.

[15] The Rules presuppose a larger legal context shaping the lawyer's role. That context includes court rules and statutes relating to matters of licensure, laws defining specific obligations of lawyers and substantive and procedural law in general. The Comments are sometimes used to alert lawyers to their responsibilities under such other law.

[16] Compliance with the Rules, as with all law in an open society, depends primarily upon understanding and voluntary compliance, secondarily upon reinforcement by peer and public opinion and finally, when necessary, upon enforcement through disciplinary proceedings. The Rules do not, however, exhaust the moral and ethical considerations that should inform a lawyer, for no worthwhile human activity can be completely defined by legal rules. The Rules simply provide a framework for the ethical practice of law.

[17] Furthermore, for purposes of determining the lawyer's authority and responsibility, principles of substantive law external to these Rules determine whether a client-lawyer relationship exists. Most of the duties flowing from the client-lawyer relationship attach only after the client has requested the lawyer to render legal services and the lawyer has agreed to do so. But there are some duties, such as that of confidentiality under Rule 1.6, that attach when the lawyer agrees to consider whether a client-lawyer relationship shall be established. See Rule 1.18. Whether a client-lawyer relationship exists for any specific purpose can depend on the circumstances and may be a question of fact.

[18] Under various legal provisions, including constitutional, statutory and common law, the responsibilities of government lawyers may include authority concerning legal matters that ordinarily reposes in the client in private client-lawyer relationships. For example, a lawyer for a government agency may have authority on behalf of the government to decide upon settlement or whether to appeal from an adverse judgment. Such authority in various respects is generally vested in the attorney

general and the state's attorney in state government, and their federal counterparts, and the same may be true of other government law officers. Also, lawyers under the supervision of these officers may be authorized to represent several government agencies in intragovernmental legal controversies in circumstances where a private lawyer could not represent multiple private clients. These Rules do not abrogate any such authority.

[19] Failure to comply with an obligation or prohibition imposed by a Rule is a basis for invoking the disciplinary process. The Rules presuppose that disciplinary assessment of a lawyer's conduct will be made on the basis of the facts and circumstances as they existed at the time of the conduct in question and in recognition of the fact that a lawyer often has to act upon uncertain or incomplete evidence of the situation. Moreover, the Rules presuppose that whether or not discipline should be imposed for a violation, and the severity of a sanction, depend on all the circumstances, such as the willfulness and seriousness of the violation, extenuating factors and whether there have been previous violations.

[20] Violation of a Rule should not itself give rise to a cause of action against a lawyer nor should it create any presumption in such a case that a legal duty has been breached. In addition, violation of a Rule does not necessarily warrant any other nondisciplinary remedy, such as disqualification of a lawyer in pending litigation. The Rules are designed to provide guidance to lawyers and to provide a structure for regulating conduct through disciplinary agencies. They are not designed to be a basis for civil liability. Furthermore, the purpose of the Rules can be subverted when they are invoked by opposing parties as procedural weapons. The fact that a Rule is a just basis for a lawyer's self-assessment, or for sanctioning a lawyer under the administration of a disciplinary authority, does not imply that an antagonist in a collateral proceeding or transaction has standing to seek enforcement of the Rule. Nevertheless, since the Rules do establish standards of conduct by lawyers, a lawyer's violation of a Rule may be evidence of breach of the applicable standard of conduct.

[21] The Comment accompanying each Rule explains and illustrates the meaning and purpose of the Rule. The Preamble and this note on Scope provide general orientation. The Comments are intended as guides to interpretation, but the text of each Rule is authoritative.

RULE 1.0: TERMINOLOGY

(a) "Belief" or "believes" denotes that the person involved actually supposed the fact in question to be true. A person's belief may be inferred from circumstances.

(b) "Confirmed in writing," when used in reference to the informed consent of a person, denotes informed consent that is given in writing by the person or a writing that a lawyer promptly transmits to the person confirming an oral informed consent. See paragraph (e) for the definition of "informed consent." If it is not feasible to obtain or transmit the writing at the time the person gives informed consent, then the lawyer must obtain or transmit it within a reasonable time thereafter.

(c) "Firm" or "law firm" denotes a lawyer or lawyers in a law partnership, professional corporation, sole proprietorship or other association authorized to practice law; or lawyers employed in a legal services organization or the legal department of a corporation or other organization.

(d) "Fraud" or "fraudulent" denotes conduct that is fraudulent under the substantive or procedural law of the applicable jurisdiction and has a purpose to deceive.

(e) "Informed consent" denotes the agreement by a person to a proposed course of conduct after the lawyer has communicated adequate information and explanation about the material risks of and reasonably available alternatives to the proposed course of conduct.

(f) "Knowingly," "known," or "knows" denotes actual knowledge of the fact in question. A person's knowledge may be inferred from circumstances.

(g) "Partner" denotes a member of a partnership, a shareholder in a law firm organized as a professional corporation, or a member of an association authorized to practice law.

(h) "Reasonable" or "reasonably" when used in relation to conduct by a lawyer denotes the conduct of a reasonably prudent and competent lawyer.

(i) "Reasonable belief" or "reasonably believes" when used in reference to a lawyer denotes that the lawyer believes the matter in question and that the circumstances are such that the belief is reasonable.

(j) "Reasonably should know" when used in reference to a lawyer denotes that a lawyer of reasonable prudence and competence would ascertain the matter in question.

(k) "Screened" denotes the isolation of a lawyer from any participation in a matter through the timely imposition of procedures within a firm that are reasonably adequate under the circumstances to protect information that the isolated lawyer is obligated to protect under these Rules or other law.

(l) "Substantial" when used in reference to degree or extent denotes a material matter of clear and weighty importance.

(m) "Tribunal" denotes a court, an arbitrator in a binding arbitration proceeding or a legislative body, administrative agency or other body acting in an adjudicative capacity. A legislative body, administrative agency or other body acts in an adjudicative capacity when a neutral official, after the presentation of evidence or legal argument by a party or parties, will render a binding legal judgment directly affecting a party's interests in a particular matter.

(n) "Writing" or "written" denotes a tangible or electronic record of a communication or representation, including handwriting, typewriting, printing, photostating, photography, audio or videorecording, and electronic communications. A "signed" writing includes an electronic sound, symbol or process attached to or logically associated with a writing and executed or adopted by a person with the intent to sign the writing.

Comment

Confirmed in Writing

[1] If it is not feasible to obtain or transmit a written confirmation at the time the client gives informed consent, then the lawyer must obtain or transmit it within a reasonable time thereafter. If a lawyer has obtained a client's informed consent, the lawyer may act in reliance on that consent so long as it is confirmed in writing within a reasonable time thereafter.

Firm

[2] Whether two or more lawyers constitute a firm within paragraph (c) can depend on the specific facts. For example, two practitioners who share office space and occasionally consult or assist each other ordinarily would not be regarded as constituting a firm. However, if they present themselves to the public in a way that suggests that they are a firm or conduct themselves as a firm, they should be regarded as a firm for purposes of the Rules. The terms of any formal agreement between associated lawyers are relevant in determining whether they are a firm, as

is the fact that they have mutual access to information concerning the clients they serve. Furthermore, it is relevant in doubtful cases to consider the underlying purpose of the Rule that is involved. A group of lawyers could be regarded as a firm for purposes of the Rule that the same lawyer should not represent opposing parties in litigation, while it might not be so regarded for purposes of the Rule that information acquired by one lawyer is attributed to another.

[3] With respect to the law department of an organization, including the government, there is ordinarily no question that the members of the department constitute a firm within the meaning of the Rules of Professional Conduct. There can be uncertainty, however, as to the identity of the client. For example, it may not be clear whether the law department of a corporation represents a subsidiary or an affiliated corporation, as well as the corporation by which the members of the department are directly employed. A similar question can arise concerning an unincorporated association and its local affiliates.

[4] Similar questions can also arise with respect to lawyers in legal aid and legal services organizations. Depending upon the structure of the organization, the entire organization or different components of it may constitute a firm or firms for purposes of these Rules.

Fraud

[5] When used in these Rules, the terms "fraud" or "fraudulent" refer to conduct that is characterized as such under the substantive or procedural law of the applicable jurisdiction and has a purpose to deceive. This does not include merely negligent misrepresentation or negligent failure to apprise another of relevant information. For purposes of these Rules, it is not necessary that anyone has suffered damages or relied on the misrepresentation or failure to inform.

Informed Consent

[6] Many of the Rules of Professional Conduct require the lawyer to obtain the informed consent of a client or other person (e.g., a former client or, under certain circumstances, a prospective client) before accepting or continuing representation or pursuing a course of conduct. See, e.g., Rules 1.2(c), 1.6(a) and 1.7(b). The communication necessary to obtain such consent will vary according to the Rule involved and the circumstances giving rise to the need to obtain informed consent. The lawyer must make reasonable efforts to ensure that the client or other person

possesses information reasonably adequate to make an informed decision. Ordinarily, this will require communication that includes a disclosure of the facts and circumstances giving rise to the situation, any explanation reasonably necessary to inform the client or other person of the material advantages and disadvantages of the proposed course of conduct and a discussion of the client's or other person's options and alternatives. In some circumstances it may be appropriate for a lawyer to advise a client or other person to seek the advice of other counsel. A lawyer need not inform a client or other person of facts or implications already known to the client or other person; nevertheless, a lawyer who does not personally inform the client or other person assumes the risk that the client or other person is inadequately informed and the consent is invalid. In determining whether the information and explanation provided are reasonably adequate, relevant factors include whether the client or other person is experienced in legal matters generally and in making decisions of the type involved, and whether the client or other person is independently represented by other counsel in giving the consent. Normally, such persons need less information and explanation than others, and generally a client or other person who is independently represented by other counsel in giving the consent should be assumed to have given informed consent.

[7] Obtaining informed consent will usually require an affirmative response by the client or other person. In general, a lawyer may not assume consent from a client's or other person's silence. Consent may be inferred, however, from the conduct of a client or other person who has reasonably adequate information about the matter. A number of Rules require that a person's consent be confirmed in writing. See Rules 1.7(b) and 1.9(a). For a definition of "writing" and "confirmed in writing," see paragraphs (n) and (b). Other Rules require that a client's consent be obtained in a writing signed by the client. See, e.g., Rules 1.8(a) and (g). For a definition of "signed," see paragraph (n).

Screened

[8] This definition applies to situations where screening of a personally disqualified lawyer is permitted to remove imputation of a conflict of interest under Rules 1.10, 1.11, 1.12 or 1.18.

[9] The purpose of screening is to assure the affected parties that confidential information known by the personally disqualified lawyer remains protected. The personally disqualified lawyer should acknowledge

the obligation not to communicate with any of the other lawyers in the firm with respect to the matter. Similarly, other lawyers in the firm who are working on the matter should be informed that the screening is in place and that they may not communicate with the personally disqualified lawyer with respect to the matter. Additional screening measures that are appropriate for the particular matter will depend on the circumstances. To implement, reinforce and remind all affected lawyers of the presence of the screening, it may be appropriate for the firm to undertake such procedures as a written undertaking by the screened lawyer to avoid any communication with other firm personnel and any contact with any firm files or other information, including information in electronic form, relating to the matter, written notice and instructions to all other firm personnel forbidding any communication with the screened lawyer relating to the matter, denial of access by the screened lawyer to firm files or other information, including information in electronic form, relating to the matter and periodic reminders of the screen to the screened lawyer and all other firm personnel.

[10] In order to be effective, screening measures must be implemented as soon as practical after a lawyer or law firm knows or reasonably should know that there is a need for screening.

CLIENT-LAWYER RELATIONSHIP

RULE 1.1: COMPETENCE

A lawyer shall provide competent representation to a client. Competent representation requires the legal knowledge, skill, thoroughness and preparation reasonably necessary for the representation.

Comment
Legal Knowledge and Skill

[1] In determining whether a lawyer employs the requisite knowledge and skill in a particular matter, relevant factors include the relative complexity and specialized nature of the matter, the lawyer's general experience, the lawyer's training and experience in the field in question, the preparation and study the lawyer is able to give the matter and whether it is feasible to refer the matter to, or associate or consult with, a lawyer of established competence in the field in question. In many instances, the

required proficiency is that of a general practitioner. Expertise in a particular field of law may be required in some circumstances.

[2] A lawyer need not necessarily have special training or prior experience to handle legal problems of a type with which the lawyer is unfamiliar. A newly admitted lawyer can be as competent as a practitioner with long experience. Some important legal skills, such as the analysis of precedent, the evaluation of evidence and legal drafting, are required in all legal problems. Perhaps the most fundamental legal skill consists of determining what kind of legal problems a situation may involve, a skill that necessarily transcends any particular specialized knowledge. A lawyer can provide adequate representation in a wholly novel field through necessary study. Competent representation can also be provided through the association of a lawyer of established competence in the field in question.

[3] In an emergency a lawyer may give advice or assistance in a matter in which the lawyer does not have the skill ordinarily required where referral to or consultation or association with another lawyer would be impractical. Even in an emergency, however, assistance should be limited to that reasonably necessary in the circumstances, for ill-considered action under emergency conditions can jeopardize the client's interest.

[4] A lawyer may accept representation where the requisite level of competence can be achieved by reasonable preparation. This applies as well to a lawyer who is appointed as counsel for an unrepresented person. See also Rule 6.2.

Thoroughness and Preparation

[5] Competent handling of a particular matter includes inquiry into and analysis of the factual and legal elements of the problem, and use of methods and procedures meeting the standards of competent practitioners. It also includes adequate preparation. The required attention and preparation are determined in part by what is at stake; major litigation and complex transactions ordinarily require more extensive treatment than matters of lesser complexity and consequence. An agreement between the lawyer and the client regarding the scope of the representation may limit the matters for which the lawyer is responsible. See Rule 1.2(c).

Retaining or Contracting With Other Lawyers

[6] Before a lawyer retains or contracts with other lawyers outside the lawyer's own firm to provide or assist in the provision of legal services to a client, the lawyer should ordinarily obtain informed consent

from the client and must reasonably believe that the other lawyers' services will contribute to the competent and ethical representation of the client. See also Rules 1.2 (allocation of authority), 1.4 (communication with client), 1.5(e) (fee sharing), 1.6 (confidentiality), and 5.5(a) (unauthorized practice of law). The reasonableness of the decision to retain or contract with other lawyers outside the lawyer's own firm will depend upon the circumstances, including the education, experience and reputation of the nonfirm lawyers; the nature of the services assigned to the nonfirm lawyers; and the legal protections, professional conduct rules, and ethical environments of the jurisdictions in which the services will be performed, particularly relating to confidential information.

[7] When lawyers from more than one law firm are providing legal services to the client on a particular matter, the lawyers ordinarily should consult with each other and the client about the scope of their respective representations and the allocation of responsibility among them. See Rule 1.2. When making allocations of responsibility in a matter pending before a tribunal, lawyers and parties may have additional obligations that are a matter of law beyond the scope of these Rules.

Maintaining Competence

[8] To maintain the requisite knowledge and skill, a lawyer should keep abreast of changes in the law and its practice, including the benefits and risks associated with relevant technology, engage in continuing study and education and comply with all continuing legal education requirements to which the lawyer is subject.

Definitional Cross-References

"Reasonably" *See* Rule 1.0(h)

RULE 1.2: SCOPE OF REPRESENTATION AND ALLOCATION OF AUTHORITY BETWEEN CLIENT AND LAWYER

(a) Subject to paragraphs (c) and (d), a lawyer shall abide by a client's decisions concerning the objectives of representation and, as required by Rule 1.4, shall consult with the client as to the means by which they are to be pursued. A lawyer may take such action on behalf of the client as is impliedly authorized to carry out the representation. A lawyer shall abide by a client's decision whether to settle a matter. In a criminal case, the lawyer shall abide by the client's decision, after consultation with the lawyer, as to a plea to be entered, whether to waive jury trial and whether the client will testify.

(b) A lawyer's representation of a client, including representation by appointment, does not constitute an endorsement of the client's political, economic, social or moral views or activities.

(c) A lawyer may limit the scope of the representation if the limitation is reasonable under the circumstances and the client gives informed consent.

(d) A lawyer shall not counsel a client to engage, or assist a client, in conduct that the lawyer knows is criminal or fraudulent, but a lawyer may discuss the legal consequences of any proposed course of conduct with a client and may counsel or assist a client to make a good faith effort to determine the validity, scope, meaning or application of the law.

Comment
Allocation of Authority between Client and Lawyer

[1] Paragraph (a) confers upon the client the ultimate authority to determine the purposes to be served by legal representation, within the limits imposed by law and the lawyer's professional obligations. The decisions specified in paragraph (a), such as whether to settle a civil matter, must also be made by the client. See Rule 1.4(a)(1) for the lawyer's duty to communicate with the client about such decisions. With respect to the means by which the client's objectives are to be pursued, the lawyer shall consult with the client as required by Rule 1.4(a)(2) and may take such action as is impliedly authorized to carry out the representation.

[2] On occasion, however, a lawyer and a client may disagree about the means to be used to accomplish the client's objectives. Clients normally defer to the special knowledge and skill of their lawyer with respect to the means to be used to accomplish their objectives, particularly with respect to technical, legal and tactical matters. Conversely, lawyers usually defer to the client regarding such questions as the expense to be incurred and concern for third persons who might be adversely affected. Because of the varied nature of the matters about which a lawyer and client might disagree and because the actions in question may implicate the interests of a tribunal or other persons, this Rule does not prescribe how

such disagreements are to be resolved. Other law, however, may be applicable and should be consulted by the lawyer. The lawyer should also consult with the client and seek a mutually acceptable resolution of the disagreement. If such efforts are unavailing and the lawyer has a fundamental disagreement with the client, the lawyer may withdraw from the representation. See Rule 1.16(b)(4). Conversely, the client may resolve the disagreement by discharging the lawyer. See Rule 1.16(a)(3).

[3] At the outset of a representation, the client may authorize the lawyer to take specific action on the client's behalf without further consultation. Absent a material change in circumstances and subject to Rule 1.4, a lawyer may rely on such an advance authorization. The client may, however, revoke such authority at any time.

[4] In a case in which the client appears to be suffering diminished capacity, the lawyer's duty to abide by the client's decisions is to be guided by reference to Rule 1.14.

Independence from Client's Views or Activities

[5] Legal representation should not be denied to people who are unable to afford legal services, or whose cause is controversial or the subject of popular disapproval. By the same token, representing a client does not constitute approval of the client's views or activities.

Agreements Limiting Scope of Representation

[6] The scope of services to be provided by a lawyer may be limited by agreement with the client or by the terms under which the lawyer's services are made available to the client. When a lawyer has been retained by an insurer to represent an insured, for example, the representation may be limited to matters related to the insurance coverage. A limited representation may be appropriate because the client has limited objectives for the representation. In addition, the terms upon which representation is undertaken may exclude specific means that might otherwise be used to accomplish the client's objectives. Such limitations may exclude actions that the client thinks are too costly or that the lawyer regards as repugnant or imprudent.

[7] Although this Rule affords the lawyer and client substantial latitude to limit the representation, the limitation must be reasonable under the circumstances. If, for example, a client's objective is limited to securing general information about the law the client needs in order to handle a common and typically uncomplicated legal problem, the lawyer and

client may agree that the lawyer's services will be limited to a brief telephone consultation. Such a limitation, however, would not be reasonable if the time allotted was not sufficient to yield advice upon which the client could rely. Although an agreement for a limited representation does not exempt a lawyer from the duty to provide competent representation, the limitation is a factor to be considered when determining the legal knowledge, skill, thoroughness and preparation reasonably necessary for the representation. See Rule 1.1.

[8] All agreements concerning a lawyer's representation of a client must accord with the Rules of Professional Conduct and other law. See, e.g., Rules 1.1, 1.8 and 5.6.

Criminal, Fraudulent and Prohibited Transactions

[9] Paragraph (d) prohibits a lawyer from knowingly counseling or assisting a client to commit a crime or fraud. This prohibition, however, does not preclude the lawyer from giving an honest opinion about the actual consequences that appear likely to result from a client's conduct. Nor does the fact that a client uses advice in a course of action that is criminal or fraudulent of itself make a lawyer a party to the course of action. There is a critical distinction between presenting an analysis of legal aspects of questionable conduct and recommending the means by which a crime or fraud might be committed with impunity.

[10] When the client's course of action has already begun and is continuing, the lawyer's responsibility is especially delicate. The lawyer is required to avoid assisting the client, for example, by drafting or delivering documents that the lawyer knows are fraudulent or by suggesting how the wrongdoing might be concealed. A lawyer may not continue assisting a client in conduct that the lawyer originally supposed was legally proper but then discovers is criminal or fraudulent. The lawyer must, therefore, withdraw from the representation of the client in the matter. See Rule 1.16(a). In some cases, withdrawal alone might be insufficient. It may be necessary for the lawyer to give notice of the fact of withdrawal and to disaffirm any opinion, document, affirmation or the like. See Rule 4.1.

[11] Where the client is a fiduciary, the lawyer may be charged with special obligations in dealings with a beneficiary.

[12] Paragraph (d) applies whether or not the defrauded party is a party to the transaction. Hence, a lawyer must not participate in a transaction to effectuate criminal or fraudulent avoidance of tax liability. Paragraph (d) does not preclude undertaking a criminal defense incident to a

general retainer for legal services to a lawful enterprise. The last clause of paragraph (d) recognizes that determining the validity or interpretation of a statute or regulation may require a course of action involving disobedience of the statute or regulation or of the interpretation placed upon it by governmental authorities.

[13] If a lawyer comes to know or reasonably should know that a client expects assistance not permitted by the Rules of Professional Conduct or other law or if the lawyer intends to act contrary to the client's instructions, the lawyer must consult with the client regarding the limitations on the lawyer's conduct. See Rule 1.4(a)(5).

Definitional Cross-References

"Fraudulent" *See* Rule 1.0(d)
"Informed consent" *See* Rule 1.0(e)
"Knows" *See* Rule 1.0(f)
"Reasonable" *See* Rule 1.0(h)

RULE 1.3: DILIGENCE

A lawyer shall act with reasonable diligence and promptness in representing a client.

Comment

[1] A lawyer should pursue a matter on behalf of a client despite opposition, obstruction or personal inconvenience to the lawyer, and take whatever lawful and ethical measures are required to vindicate a client's cause or endeavor. A lawyer must also act with commitment and dedication to the interests of the client and with zeal in advocacy upon the client's behalf. A lawyer is not bound, however, to press for every advantage that might be realized for a client. For example, a lawyer may have authority to exercise professional discretion in determining the means by which a matter should be pursued. See Rule 1.2. The lawyer's duty to act with reasonable diligence does not require the use of offensive tactics or preclude the treating of all persons involved in the legal process with courtesy and respect.

[2] A lawyer's work load must be controlled so that each matter can be handled competently.

[3] Perhaps no professional shortcoming is more widely resented than procrastination. A client's interests often can be adversely affected

by the passage of time or the change of conditions; in extreme instances, as when a lawyer overlooks a statute of limitations, the client's legal position may be destroyed. Even when the client's interests are not affected in substance, however, unreasonable delay can cause a client needless anxiety and undermine confidence in the lawyer's trustworthiness. A lawyer's duty to act with reasonable promptness, however, does not preclude the lawyer from agreeing to a reasonable request for a postponement that will not prejudice the lawyer's client.

[4] Unless the relationship is terminated as provided in Rule 1.16, a lawyer should carry through to conclusion all matters undertaken for a client. If a lawyer's employment is limited to a specific matter, the relationship terminates when the matter has been resolved. If a lawyer has served a client over a substantial period in a variety of matters, the client sometimes may assume that the lawyer will continue to serve on a continuing basis unless the lawyer gives notice of withdrawal. Doubt about whether a client-lawyer relationship still exists should be clarified by the lawyer, preferably in writing, so that the client will not mistakenly suppose the lawyer is looking after the client's affairs when the lawyer has ceased to do so. For example, if a lawyer has handled a judicial or administrative proceeding that produced a result adverse to the client and the lawyer and the client have not agreed that the lawyer will handle the matter on appeal, the lawyer must consult with the client about the possibility of appeal before relinquishing responsibility for the matter. See Rule 1.4(a)(2). Whether the lawyer is obligated to prosecute the appeal for the client depends on the scope of the representation the lawyer has agreed to provide to the client. See Rule 1.2.

[5] To prevent neglect of client matters in the event of a sole practitioner's death or disability, the duty of diligence may require that each sole practitioner prepare a plan, in conformity with applicable rules, that designates another competent lawyer to review client files, notify each client of the lawyer's death or disability, and determine whether there is a need for immediate protective action. Cf. Rule 28 of the American Bar Association Model Rules for Lawyer Disciplinary Enforcement (providing for court appointment of a lawyer to inventory files and take other protective action in absence of a plan providing for another lawyer to protect the interests of the clients of a deceased or disabled lawyer).

Definitional Cross-References

"Reasonable" *See* Rule 1.0(h)

Rule 1.4: Communication

(a) A lawyer shall:

(1) promptly inform the client of any decision or circumstance with respect to which the client's informed consent, as defined in Rule 1.0(e), is required by these Rules;

(2) reasonably consult with the client about the means by which the client's objectives are to be accomplished;

(3) keep the client reasonably informed about the status of the matter;

(4) promptly comply with reasonable requests for information; and

(5) consult with the client about any relevant limitation on the lawyer's conduct when the lawyer knows that the client expects assistance not permitted by the Rules of Professional Conduct or other law.

(b) A lawyer shall explain a matter to the extent reasonably necessary to permit the client to make informed decisions regarding the representation.

Comment

[1] Reasonable communication between the lawyer and the client is necessary for the client effectively to participate in the representation.

Communicating with Client

[2] If these Rules require that a particular decision about the representation be made by the client, paragraph (a)(1) requires that the lawyer promptly consult with and secure the client's consent prior to taking action unless prior discussions with the client have resolved what action the client wants the lawyer to take. For example, a lawyer who receives from opposing counsel an offer of settlement in a civil controversy or a proffered plea bargain in a criminal case must promptly inform the client of its substance unless the client has previously indicated that the proposal will be acceptable or unacceptable or has authorized the lawyer to accept or to reject the offer. See Rule 1.2(a).

[3] Paragraph (a)(2) requires the lawyer to reasonably consult with the client about the means to be used to accomplish the client's objectives. In some situations—depending on both the importance of the action under consideration and the feasibility of consulting with the client —this duty will require consultation prior to taking action. In other cir-

cumstances, such as during a trial when an immediate decision must be made, the exigency of the situation may require the lawyer to act without prior consultation. In such cases the lawyer must nonetheless act reasonably to inform the client of actions the lawyer has taken on the client's behalf. Additionally, paragraph (a)(3) requires that the lawyer keep the client reasonably informed about the status of the matter, such as significant developments affecting the timing or the substance of the representation.

[4] A lawyer's regular communication with clients will minimize the occasions on which a client will need to request information concerning the representation. When a client makes a reasonable request for information, however, paragraph (a)(4) requires prompt compliance with the request, or if a prompt response is not feasible, that the lawyer, or a member of the lawyer's staff, acknowledge receipt of the request and advise the client when a response may be expected. A lawyer should promptly respond to or acknowledge client communications.

Explaining Matters

[5] The client should have sufficient information to participate intelligently in decisions concerning the objectives of the representation and the means by which they are to be pursued, to the extent the client is willing and able to do so. Adequacy of communication depends in part on the kind of advice or assistance that is involved. For example, when there is time to explain a proposal made in a negotiation, the lawyer should review all important provisions with the client before proceeding to an agreement. In litigation a lawyer should explain the general strategy and prospects of success and ordinarily should consult the client on tactics that are likely to result in significant expense or to injure or coerce others. On the other hand, a lawyer ordinarily will not be expected to describe trial or negotiation strategy in detail. The guiding principle is that the lawyer should fulfill reasonable client expectations for information consistent with the duty to act in the client's best interests, and the client's overall requirements as to the character of representation. In certain circumstances, such as when a lawyer asks a client to consent to a representation affected by a conflict of interest, the client must give informed consent, as defined in Rule 1.0(e).

[6] Ordinarily, the information to be provided is that appropriate for a client who is a comprehending and responsible adult. However, fully informing the client according to this standard may be impracticable, for example, where the client is a child or suffers from diminished capacity.

See Rule 1.14. When the client is an organization or group, it is often impossible or inappropriate to inform every one of its members about its legal affairs; ordinarily, the lawyer should address communications to the appropriate officials of the organization. See Rule 1.13. Where many routine matters are involved, a system of limited or occasional reporting may be arranged with the client.

Withholding Information

[7] In some circumstances, a lawyer may be justified in delaying transmission of information when the client would be likely to react imprudently to an immediate communication. Thus, a lawyer might withhold a psychiatric diagnosis of a client when the examining psychiatrist indicates that disclosure would harm the client. A lawyer may not withhold information to serve the lawyer's own interest or convenience or the interests or convenience of another person. Rules or court orders governing litigation may provide that information supplied to a lawyer may not be disclosed to the client. Rule 3.4(c) directs compliance with such rules or orders.

Definitional Cross-References

"Informed consent" *See* Rule 1.0(e)
"Knows" *See* Rule 1.0(f)
"Reasonably" *See* Rule 1.0(h)

RULE 1.5: FEES

(a) A lawyer shall not make an agreement for, charge, or collect an unreasonable fee or an unreasonable amount for expenses. The factors to be considered in determining the reasonableness of a fee include the following:

(1) the time and labor required, the novelty and difficulty of the questions involved, and the skill requisite to perform the legal service properly;

(2) the likelihood, if apparent to the client, that the acceptance of the particular employment will preclude other employment by the lawyer;

(3) the fee customarily charged in the locality for similar legal services;

(4) the amount involved and the results obtained;

(5) the time limitations imposed by the client or by the circumstances;

(6) the nature and length of the professional relationship with the client;

(7) the experience, reputation, and ability of the lawyer or lawyers performing the services; and

(8) whether the fee is fixed or contingent.

(b) The scope of the representation and the basis or rate of the fee and expenses for which the client will be responsible shall be communicated to the client, preferably in writing, before or within a reasonable time after commencing the representation, except when the lawyer will charge a regularly represented client on the same basis or rate. Any changes in the basis or rate of the fee or expenses shall also be communicated to the client.

(c) A fee may be contingent on the outcome of the matter for which the service is rendered, except in a matter in which a contingent fee is prohibited by paragraph (d) or other law. A contingent fee agreement shall be in a writing signed by the client and shall state the method by which the fee is to be determined, including the percentage or percentages that shall accrue to the lawyer in the event of settlement, trial or appeal; litigation and other expenses to be deducted from the recovery; and whether such expenses are to be deducted before or after the contingent fee is calculated. The agreement must clearly notify the client of any expenses for which the client will be liable whether or not the client is the prevailing party. Upon conclusion of a contingent fee matter, the lawyer shall provide the client with a written statement stating the outcome of the matter and, if there is a recovery, showing the remittance to the client and the method of its determination.

(d) A lawyer shall not enter into an arrangement for, charge, or collect:

(1) any fee in a domestic relations matter, the payment or amount of which is contingent upon the securing of a divorce or upon the amount of alimony or support, or property settlement in lieu thereof; or

(2) a contingent fee for representing a defendant in a criminal case.

(e) A division of a fee between lawyers who are not in the same firm may be made only if:

(1) the division is in proportion to the services performed by each lawyer or each lawyer assumes joint responsibility for the representation;

(2) the client agrees to the arrangement, including the share each lawyer will receive, and the agreement is confirmed in writing; and

(3) the total fee is reasonable.

Comment

Reasonableness of Fee and Expenses

[1] Paragraph (a) requires that lawyers charge fees that are reasonable under the circumstances. The factors specified in (1) through (8) are not exclusive. Nor will each factor be relevant in each instance. Paragraph (a) also requires that expenses for which the client will be charged must be reasonable. A lawyer may seek reimbursement for the cost of services performed in-house, such as copying, or for other expenses incurred in-house, such as telephone charges, either by charging a reasonable amount to which the client has agreed in advance or by charging an amount that reasonably reflects the cost incurred by the lawyer.

Basis or Rate of Fee

[2] When the lawyer has regularly represented a client, they ordinarily will have evolved an understanding concerning the basis or rate of the fee and the expenses for which the client will be responsible. In a new client-lawyer relationship, however, an understanding as to fees and expenses must be promptly established. Generally, it is desirable to furnish the client with at least a simple memorandum or copy of the lawyer's customary fee arrangements that states the general nature of the legal services to be provided, the basis, rate or total amount of the fee and whether and to what extent the client will be responsible for any costs, expenses or disbursements in the course of the representation. A written statement concerning the terms of the engagement reduces the possibility of misunderstanding.

[3] Contingent fees, like any other fees, are subject to the reasonableness standard of paragraph (a) of this Rule. In determining whether a particular contingent fee is reasonable, or whether it is reasonable to charge any form of contingent fee, a lawyer must consider the factors that are relevant under the circumstances. Applicable law may impose limitations on contingent fees, such as a ceiling on the percentage allowable, or

may require a lawyer to offer clients an alternative basis for the fee. Applicable law also may apply to situations other than a contingent fee, for example, government regulations regarding fees in certain tax matters.

Terms of Payment

[4] A lawyer may require advance payment of a fee, but is obliged to return any unearned portion. See Rule 1.16(d). A lawyer may accept property in payment for services, such as an ownership interest in an enterprise, providing this does not involve acquisition of a proprietary interest in the cause of action or subject matter of the litigation contrary to Rule 1.8 (i). However, a fee paid in property instead of money may be subject to the requirements of Rule 1.8(a) because such fees often have the essential qualities of a business transaction with the client.

[5] An agreement may not be made whose terms might induce the lawyer improperly to curtail services for the client or perform them in a way contrary to the client's interest. For example, a lawyer should not enter into an agreement whereby services are to be provided only up to a stated amount when it is foreseeable that more extensive services probably will be required, unless the situation is adequately explained to the client. Otherwise, the client might have to bargain for further assistance in the midst of a proceeding or transaction. However, it is proper to define the extent of services in light of the client's ability to pay. A lawyer should not exploit a fee arrangement based primarily on hourly charges by using wasteful procedures.

Prohibited Contingent Fees

[6] Paragraph (d) prohibits a lawyer from charging a contingent fee in a domestic relations matter when payment is contingent upon the securing of a divorce or upon the amount of alimony or support or property settlement to be obtained. This provision does not preclude a contract for a contingent fee for legal representation in connection with the recovery of post-judgment balances due under support, alimony or other financial orders because such contracts do not implicate the same policy concerns.

Division of Fee

[7] A division of fee is a single billing to a client covering the fee of two or more lawyers who are not in the same firm. A division of fee facilitates association of more than one lawyer in a matter in which neither alone could serve the client as well, and most often is used when the fee

is contingent and the division is between a referring lawyer and a trial specialist. Paragraph (e) permits the lawyers to divide a fee either on the basis of the proportion of services they render or if each lawyer assumes responsibility for the representation as a whole. In addition, the client must agree to the arrangement, including the share that each lawyer is to receive, and the agreement must be confirmed in writing. Contingent fee agreements must be in a writing signed by the client and must otherwise comply with paragraph (c) of this Rule. Joint responsibility for the representation entails financial and ethical responsibility for the representation as if the lawyers were associated in a partnership. A lawyer should only refer a matter to a lawyer whom the referring lawyer reasonably believes is competent to handle the matter. See Rule 1.1.

[8] Paragraph (e) does not prohibit or regulate division of fees to be received in the future for work done when lawyers were previously associated in a law firm.

Disputes over Fees

[9] If a procedure has been established for resolution of fee disputes, such as an arbitration or mediation procedure established by the bar, the lawyer must comply with the procedure when it is mandatory, and, even when it is voluntary, the lawyer should conscientiously consider submitting to it. Law may prescribe a procedure for determining a lawyer's fee, for example, in representation of an executor or administrator, a class or a person entitled to a reasonable fee as part of the measure of damages. The lawyer entitled to such a fee and a lawyer representing another party concerned with the fee should comply with the prescribed procedure.

Definitional Cross-References

"Confirmed in writing" *See* Rule 1.0(b)
"Firm" *See* Rule 1.0(c)
"Writing" and "Written" and "Signed" *See* Rule 1.0(n)

RULE 1.6: CONFIDENTIALITY OF INFORMATION

(a) A lawyer shall not reveal information relating to the representation of a client unless the client gives informed consent, the disclosure is impliedly authorized in order to carry out the representation or the disclosure is permitted by paragraph (b).

(b) A lawyer may reveal information relating to the

representation of a client to the extent the lawyer reasonably believes necessary:

(1) to prevent reasonably certain death or substantial bodily harm;

(2) to prevent the client from committing a crime or fraud that is reasonably certain to result in substantial injury to the financial interests or property of another and in furtherance of which the client has used or is using the lawyer's services;

(3) to prevent, mitigate or rectify substantial injury to the financial interests or property of another that is reasonably certain to result or has resulted from the client's commission of a crime or fraud in furtherance of which the client has used the lawyer's services;

(4) to secure legal advice about the lawyer's compliance with these Rules;

(5) to establish a claim or defense on behalf of the lawyer in a controversy between the lawyer and the client, to establish a defense to a criminal charge or civil claim against the lawyer based upon conduct in which the client was involved, or to respond to allegations in any proceeding concerning the lawyer's representation of the client;

(6) to comply with other law or a court order; or

(7) to detect and resolve conflicts of interest arising from the lawyer's change of employment or from changes in the composition or ownership of a firm, but only if the revealed information would not compromise the attorney-client privilege or otherwise prejudice the client.

(c) A lawyer shall make reasonable efforts to prevent the inadvertent or unauthorized disclosure of, or unauthorized access to, information relating to the representation of a client.

Comment

[1] This Rule governs the disclosure by a lawyer of information relating to the representation of a client during the lawyer's representation of the client. See Rule 1.18 for the lawyer's duties with respect to information provided to the lawyer by a prospective client, Rule 1.9(c)(2) for the lawyer's duty not to reveal information relating to the lawyer's prior representation of a former client and Rules 1.8(b) and 1.9(c)(1) for the lawyer's duties with respect to the use of such information to the disadvantage of clients and former clients.

[2] A fundamental principle in the client-lawyer relationship is that, in the absence of the client's informed consent, the lawyer must not reveal information relating to the representation. See Rule 1.0(e) for the definition of informed consent. This contributes to the trust that is the hallmark of the client-lawyer relationship. The client is thereby encouraged to seek legal assistance and to communicate fully and frankly with the lawyer even as to embarrassing or legally damaging subject matter. The lawyer needs this information to represent the client effectively and, if necessary, to advise the client to refrain from wrongful conduct. Almost without exception, clients come to lawyers in order to determine their rights and what is, in the complex of laws and regulations, deemed to be legal and correct. Based upon experience, lawyers know that almost all clients follow the advice given, and the law is upheld.

[3] The principle of client-lawyer confidentiality is given effect by related bodies of law: the attorney-client privilege, the work product doctrine and the rule of confidentiality established in professional ethics. The attorney-client privilege and work product doctrine apply in judicial and other proceedings in which a lawyer may be called as a witness or otherwise required to produce evidence concerning a client. The rule of client-lawyer confidentiality applies in situations other than those where evidence is sought from the lawyer through compulsion of law. The confidentiality rule, for example, applies not only to matters communicated in confidence by the client but also to all information relating to the representation, whatever its source. A lawyer may not disclose such information except as authorized or required by the Rules of Professional Conduct or other law. See also Scope.

[4] Paragraph (a) prohibits a lawyer from revealing information relating to the representation of a client. This prohibition also applies to disclosures by a lawyer that do not in themselves reveal protected information but could reasonably lead to the discovery of such information by a third person. A lawyer's use of a hypothetical to discuss issues relating to the representation is permissible so long as there is no reasonable likelihood that the listener will be able to ascertain the identity of the client or the situation involved.

Authorized Disclosure

[5] Except to the extent that the client's instructions or special circumstances limit that authority, a lawyer is impliedly authorized to make disclosures about a client when appropriate in carrying out the represen-

tation. In some situations, for example, a lawyer may be impliedly authorized to admit a fact that cannot properly be disputed or to make a disclosure that facilitates a satisfactory conclusion to a matter. Lawyers in a firm may, in the course of the firm's practice, disclose to each other information relating to a client of the firm, unless the client has instructed that particular information be confined to specified lawyers.

Disclosure Adverse to Client

[6] Although the public interest is usually best served by a strict rule requiring lawyers to preserve the confidentiality of information relating to the representation of their clients, the confidentiality rule is subject to limited exceptions. Paragraph (b)(1) recognizes the overriding value of life and physical integrity and permits disclosure reasonably necessary to prevent reasonably certain death or substantial bodily harm. Such harm is reasonably certain to occur if it will be suffered imminently or if there is a present and substantial threat that a person will suffer such harm at a later date if the lawyer fails to take action necessary to eliminate the threat. Thus, a lawyer who knows that a client has accidentally discharged toxic waste into a town's water supply may reveal this information to the authorities if there is a present and substantial risk that a person who drinks the water will contract a life-threatening or debilitating disease and the lawyer's disclosure is necessary to eliminate the threat or reduce the number of victims.

[7] Paragraph (b)(2) is a limited exception to the rule of confidentiality that permits the lawyer to reveal information to the extent necessary to enable affected persons or appropriate authorities to prevent the client from committing a crime or fraud, as defined in Rule 1.0(d), that is reasonably certain to result in substantial injury to the financial or property interests of another and in furtherance of which the client has used or is using the lawyer's services. Such a serious abuse of the client-lawyer relationship by the client forfeits the protection of this Rule. The client can, of course, prevent such disclosure by refraining from the wrongful conduct. Although paragraph (b)(2) does not require the lawyer to reveal the client's misconduct, the lawyer may not counsel or assist the client in conduct the lawyer knows is criminal or fraudulent. See Rule 1.2(d). See also Rule 1.16 with respect to the lawyer's obligation or right to withdraw from the representation of the client in such circumstances, and Rule 1.13(c), which permits the lawyer, where the client is an organization, to reveal information relating to the representation in limited circumstances.

[8] Paragraph (b)(3) addresses the situation in which the lawyer does not learn of the client's crime or fraud until after it has been consummated. Although the client no longer has the option of preventing disclosure by refraining from the wrongful conduct, there will be situations in which the loss suffered by the affected person can be prevented, rectified or mitigated. In such situations, the lawyer may disclose information relating to the representation to the extent necessary to enable the affected persons to prevent or mitigate reasonably certain losses or to attempt to recoup their losses. Paragraph (b)(3) does not apply when a person who has committed a crime or fraud thereafter employs a lawyer for representation concerning that offense.

[9] A lawyer's confidentiality obligations do not preclude a lawyer from securing confidential legal advice about the lawyer's personal responsibility to comply with these Rules. In most situations, disclosing information to secure such advice will be impliedly authorized for the lawyer to carry out the representation. Even when the disclosure is not impliedly authorized, paragraph (b)(4) permits such disclosure because of the importance of a lawyer's compliance with the Rules of Professional Conduct.

[10] Where a legal claim or disciplinary charge alleges complicity of the lawyer in a client's conduct or other misconduct of the lawyer involving representation of the client, the lawyer may respond to the extent the lawyer reasonably believes necessary to establish a defense. The same is true with respect to a claim involving the conduct or representation of a former client. Such a charge can arise in a civil, criminal, disciplinary or other proceeding and can be based on a wrong allegedly committed by the lawyer against the client or on a wrong alleged by a third person, for example, a person claiming to have been defrauded by the lawyer and client acting together. The lawyer's right to respond arises when an assertion of such complicity has been made. Paragraph (b)(5) does not require the lawyer to await the commencement of an action or proceeding that charges such complicity, so that the defense may be established by responding directly to a third party who has made such an assertion. The right to defend also applies, of course, where a proceeding has been commenced.

[11] A lawyer entitled to a fee is permitted by paragraph (b)(5) to prove the services rendered in an action to collect it. This aspect of the rule expresses the principle that the beneficiary of a fiduciary relationship may not exploit it to the detriment of the fiduciary.

[12] Other law may require that a lawyer disclose information about a client. Whether such a law supersedes Rule 1.6 is a question of law beyond the scope of these Rules. When disclosure of information relating to the representation appears to be required by other law, the lawyer must discuss the matter with the client to the extent required by Rule 1.4. If, however, the other law supersedes this Rule and requires disclosure, paragraph (b)(6) permits the lawyer to make such disclosures as are necessary to comply with the law.

Detection of Conflicts of Interest

[13] Paragraph (b)(7) recognizes that lawyers in different firms may need to disclose limited information to each other to detect and resolve conflicts of interest, such as when a lawyer is considering an association with another firm, two or more firms are considering a merger, or a lawyer is considering the purchase of a law practice. See Rule 1.17, Comment [7]. Under these circumstances, lawyers and law firms are permitted to disclose limited information, but only once substantive discussions regarding the new relationship have occurred. Any such disclosure should ordinarily include no more than the identity of the persons and entities involved in a matter, a brief summary of the general issues involved, and information about whether the matter has terminated. Even this limited information, however, should be disclosed only to the extent reasonably necessary to detect and resolve conflicts of interest that might arise from the possible new relationship. Moreover, the disclosure of any information is prohibited if it would compromise the attorney-client privilege or otherwise prejudice the client (e.g., the fact that a corporate client is seeking advice on a corporate takeover that has not been publicly announced; that a person has consulted a lawyer about the possibility of divorce before the person's intentions are known to the person's spouse; or that a person has consulted a lawyer about a criminal investigation that has not led to a public charge). Under those circumstances, paragraph (a) prohibits disclosure unless the client or former client gives informed consent. A lawyer's fiduciary duty to the lawyer's firm may also govern a lawyer's conduct when exploring an association with another firm and is beyond the scope of these Rules.

[14] Any information disclosed pursuant to paragraph (b)(7) may be used or further disclosed only to the extent necessary to detect and resolve conflicts of interest. Paragraph (b)(7) does not restrict the use of information acquired by means independent of any disclosure pursu-

ant to paragraph (b)(7). Paragraph (b)(7) also does not affect the disclosure of information within a law firm when the disclosure is otherwise authorized, see Comment [5], such as when a lawyer in a firm discloses information to another lawyer in the same firm to detect and resolve conflicts of interest that could arise in connection with undertaking a new representation.

[15] A lawyer may be ordered to reveal information relating to the representation of a client by a court or by another tribunal or governmental entity claiming authority pursuant to other law to compel the disclosure. Absent informed consent of the client to do otherwise, the lawyer should assert on behalf of the client all nonfrivolous claims that the order is not authorized by other law or that the information sought is protected against disclosure by the attorney-client privilege or other applicable law. In the event of an adverse ruling, the lawyer must consult with the client about the possibility of appeal to the extent required by Rule 1.4. Unless review is sought, however, paragraph (b)(6) permits the lawyer to comply with the court's order.

[16] Paragraph (b) permits disclosure only to the extent the lawyer reasonably believes the disclosure is necessary to accomplish one of the purposes specified. Where practicable, the lawyer should first seek to persuade the client to take suitable action to obviate the need for disclosure. In any case, a disclosure adverse to the client's interest should be no greater than the lawyer reasonably believes necessary to accomplish the purpose. If the disclosure will be made in connection with a judicial proceeding, the disclosure should be made in a manner that limits access to the information to the tribunal or other persons having a need to know it and appropriate protective orders or other arrangements should be sought by the lawyer to the fullest extent practicable.

[17] Paragraph (b) permits but does not require the disclosure of information relating to a client's representation to accomplish the purposes specified in paragraphs (b)(1) through (b)(6). In exercising the discretion conferred by this Rule, the lawyer may consider such factors as the nature of the lawyer's relationship with the client and with those who might be injured by the client, the lawyer's own involvement in the transaction and factors that may extenuate the conduct in question. A lawyer's decision not to disclose as permitted by paragraph (b) does not violate this Rule. Disclosure may be required, however, by other Rules. Some Rules require disclosure only if such disclosure would be permitted by paragraph (b). See Rules 1.2(d), 4.1(b), 8.1 and 8.3. Rule 3.3, on the other hand,

requires disclosure in some circumstances regardless of whether such disclosure is permitted by this Rule. See Rule 3.3(c).

Acting Competently to Preserve Confidentiality

[18] Paragraph (c) requires a lawyer to act competently to safeguard information relating to the representation of a client against unauthorized access by third parties and against inadvertent or unauthorized disclosure by the lawyer or other persons who are participating in the representation of the client or who are subject to the lawyer's supervision. See Rules 1.1, 5.1 and 5.3. The unauthorized access to, or the inadvertent or unauthorized disclosure of, information relating to the representation of a client does not constitute a violation of paragraph (c) if the lawyer has made reasonable efforts to prevent the access or disclosure. Factors to be considered in determining the reasonableness of the lawyer's efforts include, but are not limited to, the sensitivity of the information, the likelihood of disclosure if additional safeguards are not employed, the cost of employing additional safeguards, the difficulty of implementing the safeguards, and the extent to which the safeguards adversely affect the lawyer's ability to represent clients (e.g., by making a device or important piece of software excessively difficult to use). A client may require the lawyer to implement special security measures not required by this Rule or may give informed consent to forgo security measures that would otherwise be required by this Rule. Whether a lawyer may be required to take additional steps to safeguard a client's information in order to comply with other law, such as state and federal laws that govern data privacy or that impose notification requirements upon the loss of, or unauthorized access to, electronic information, is beyond the scope of these Rules. For a lawyer's duties when sharing information with nonlawyers outside the lawyer's own firm, see Rule 5.3, Comments [3]-[4].

[19] When transmitting a communication that includes information relating to the representation of a client, the lawyer must take reasonable precautions to prevent the information from coming into the hands of unintended recipients. This duty, however, does not require that the lawyer use special security measures if the method of communication affords a reasonable expectation of privacy. Special circumstances, however, may warrant special precautions. Factors to be considered in determining the reasonableness of the lawyer's expectation of confidentiality include the sensitivity of the information and the extent to which the privacy of the communication is protected by law or by a confidentiality agreement. A client may require the lawyer to implement special security measures

not required by this Rule or may give informed consent to the use of a means of communication that would otherwise be prohibited by this Rule. Whether a lawyer may be required to take additional steps in order to comply with other law, such as state and federal laws that govern data privacy, is beyond the scope of these Rules.

Former Client

[20] The duty of confidentiality continues after the client-lawyer relationship has terminated. See Rule 1.9(c)(2). See Rule 1.9(c)(1) for the prohibition against using such information to the disadvantage of the former client.

Definitional Cross-References

"Firm" *See* Rule 1.0(c)
"Fraud" *See* Rule 1.0(d)
"Informed consent" *See* Rule 1.0(e)
"Reasonable" and "Reasonably" *See* Rule 1.0(h)
"Reasonably believes" *See* Rule 1.0(i)
"Substantial" *See* Rule 1.0(l)

RULE 1.7: CONFLICT OF INTEREST: CURRENT CLIENTS

(a) Except as provided in paragraph (b), a lawyer shall not represent a client if the representation involves a concurrent conflict of interest. A concurrent conflict of interest exists if:

(1) the representation of one client will be directly adverse to another client; or

(2) there is a significant risk that the representation of one or more clients will be materially limited by the lawyer's responsibilities to another client, a former client or a third person or by a personal interest of the lawyer.

(b) Notwithstanding the existence of a concurrent conflict of interest under paragraph (a), a lawyer may represent a client if:

(1) the lawyer reasonably believes that the lawyer will be able to provide competent and diligent representation to each affected client;

(2) the representation is not prohibited by law;

(3) the representation does not involve the assertion of a claim by one client against another client represented by

the lawyer in the same litigation or other proceeding before a tribunal; and

   (4) each affected client gives informed consent, confirmed in writing.

Comment
General Principles

[1] Loyalty and independent judgment are essential elements in the lawyer's relationship to a client. Concurrent conflicts of interest can arise from the lawyer's responsibilities to another client, a former client or a third person or from the lawyer's own interests. For specific Rules regarding certain concurrent conflicts of interest, see Rule 1.8. For former client conflicts of interest, see Rule 1.9. For conflicts of interest involving prospective clients, see Rule 1.18. For definitions of "informed consent" and "confirmed in writing," see Rule 1.0(e) and (b).

[2] Resolution of a conflict of interest problem under this Rule requires the lawyer to: 1) clearly identify the client or clients; 2) determine whether a conflict of interest exists; 3) decide whether the representation may be undertaken despite the existence of a conflict, i.e., whether the conflict is consentable; and 4) if so, consult with the clients affected under paragraph (a) and obtain their informed consent, confirmed in writing. The clients affected under paragraph (a) include both of the clients referred to in paragraph (a)(1) and the one or more clients whose representation might be materially limited under paragraph (a)(2).

[3] A conflict of interest may exist before representation is undertaken, in which event the representation must be declined, unless the lawyer obtains the informed consent of each client under the conditions of paragraph (b). To determine whether a conflict of interest exists, a lawyer should adopt reasonable procedures, appropriate for the size and type of firm and practice, to determine in both litigation and non-litigation matters the persons and issues involved. See also Comment to Rule 5.1. Ignorance caused by a failure to institute such procedures will not excuse a lawyer's violation of this Rule. As to whether a client-lawyer relationship exists or, having once been established, is continuing, see Comment to Rule 1.3 and Scope.

[4] If a conflict arises after representation has been undertaken, the lawyer ordinarily must withdraw from the representation, unless the lawyer has obtained the informed consent of the client under the conditions of paragraph (b). See Rule 1.16. Where more than one client is in-

volved, whether the lawyer may continue to represent any of the clients is determined both by the lawyer's ability to comply with duties owed to the former client and by the lawyer's ability to represent adequately the remaining client or clients, given the lawyer's duties to the former client. See Rule 1.9. See also Comments [5] and [29].

[5] Unforeseeable developments, such as changes in corporate and other organizational affiliations or the addition or realignment of parties in litigation, might create conflicts in the midst of a representation, as when a company sued by the lawyer on behalf of one client is bought by another client represented by the lawyer in an unrelated matter. Depending on the circumstances, the lawyer may have the option to withdraw from one of the representations in order to avoid the conflict. The lawyer must seek court approval where necessary and take steps to minimize harm to the clients. See Rule 1.16. The lawyer must continue to protect the confidences of the client from whose representation the lawyer has withdrawn. See Rule 1.9(c).

Identifying Conflicts of Interest: Directly Adverse

[6] Loyalty to a current client prohibits undertaking representation directly adverse to that client without that client's informed consent. Thus, absent consent, a lawyer may not act as an advocate in one matter against a person the lawyer represents in some other matter, even when the matters are wholly unrelated. The client as to whom the representation is directly adverse is likely to feel betrayed, and the resulting damage to the client-lawyer relationship is likely to impair the lawyer's ability to represent the client effectively. In addition, the client on whose behalf the adverse representation is undertaken reasonably may fear that the lawyer will pursue that client's case less effectively out of deference to the other client, i.e., that the representation may be materially limited by the lawyer's interest in retaining the current client. Similarly, a directly adverse conflict may arise when a lawyer is required to cross-examine a client who appears as a witness in a lawsuit involving another client, as when the testimony will be damaging to the client who is represented in the lawsuit. On the other hand, simultaneous representation in unrelated matters of clients whose interests are only economically adverse, such as representation of competing economic enterprises in unrelated litigation, does not ordinarily constitute a conflict of interest and thus may not require consent of the respective clients.

[7] Directly adverse conflicts can also arise in transactional matters. For example, if a lawyer is asked to represent the seller of a business in negotiations with a buyer represented by the lawyer, not in the same transaction but in another, unrelated matter, the lawyer could not undertake the representation without the informed consent of each client.

Identifying Conflicts of Interest: Material Limitation

[8] Even where there is no direct adverseness, a conflict of interest exists if there is a significant risk that a lawyer's ability to consider, recommend or carry out an appropriate course of action for the client will be materially limited as a result of the lawyer's other responsibilities or interests. For example, a lawyer asked to represent several individuals seeking to form a joint venture is likely to be materially limited in the lawyer's ability to recommend or advocate all possible positions that each might take because of the lawyer's duty of loyalty to the others. The conflict in effect forecloses alternatives that would otherwise be available to the client. The mere possibility of subsequent harm does not itself require disclosure and consent. The critical questions are the likelihood that a difference in interests will eventuate and, if it does, whether it will materially interfere with the lawyer's independent professional judgment in considering alternatives or foreclose courses of action that reasonably should be pursued on behalf of the client.

Lawyer's Responsibilities to Former Clients and Other Third Persons

[9] In addition to conflicts with other current clients, a lawyer's duties of loyalty and independence may be materially limited by responsibilities to former clients under Rule 1.9 or by the lawyer's responsibilities to other persons, such as fiduciary duties arising from a lawyer's service as a trustee, executor or corporate director.

Personal Interest Conflicts

[10] The lawyer's own interests should not be permitted to have an adverse effect on representation of a client. For example, if the probity of a lawyer's own conduct in a transaction is in serious question, it may be difficult or impossible for the lawyer to give a client detached advice. Similarly, when a lawyer has discussions concerning possible employment with an opponent of the lawyer's client, or with a law firm repre-

senting the opponent, such discussions could materially limit the lawyer's representation of the client. In addition, a lawyer may not allow related business interests to affect representation, for example, by referring clients to an enterprise in which the lawyer has an undisclosed financial interest. See Rule 1.8 for specific Rules pertaining to a number of personal interest conflicts, including business transactions with clients. See also Rule 1.10 (personal interest conflicts under Rule 1.7 ordinarily are not imputed to other lawyers in a law firm).

[11] When lawyers representing different clients in the same matter or in substantially related matters are closely related by blood or marriage, there may be a significant risk that client confidences will be revealed and that the lawyer's family relationship will interfere with both loyalty and independent professional judgment. As a result, each client is entitled to know of the existence and implications of the relationship between the lawyers before the lawyer agrees to undertake the representation. Thus, a lawyer related to another lawyer, e.g., as parent, child, sibling or spouse, ordinarily may not represent a client in a matter where that lawyer is representing another party, unless each client gives informed consent. The disqualification arising from a close family relationship is personal and ordinarily is not imputed to members of firms with whom the lawyers are associated. See Rule 1.10.

[12] A lawyer is prohibited from engaging in sexual relationships with a client unless the sexual relationship predates the formation of the client-lawyer relationship. See Rule 1.8(j).

Interest of Person Paying for a Lawyer's Service

[13] A lawyer may be paid from a source other than the client, including a co-client, if the client is informed of that fact and consents and the arrangement does not compromise the lawyer's duty of loyalty or independent judgment to the client. See Rule 1.8(f). If acceptance of the payment from any other source presents a significant risk that the lawyer's representation of the client will be materially limited by the lawyer's own interest in accommodating the person paying the lawyer's fee or by the lawyer's responsibilities to a payer who is also a co-client, then the lawyer must comply with the requirements of paragraph (b) before accepting the representation, including determining whether the conflict is consentable and, if so, that the client has adequate information about the material risks of the representation.

Prohibited Representations

[14] Ordinarily, clients may consent to representation notwithstanding a conflict. However, as indicated in paragraph (b), some conflicts are nonconsentable, meaning that the lawyer involved cannot properly ask for such agreement or provide representation on the basis of the client's consent. When the lawyer is representing more than one client, the question of consentability must be resolved as to each client.

[15] Consentability is typically determined by considering whether the interests of the clients will be adequately protected if the clients are permitted to give their informed consent to representation burdened by a conflict of interest. Thus, under paragraph (b)(1), representation is prohibited if in the circumstances the lawyer cannot reasonably conclude that the lawyer will be able to provide competent and diligent representation. See Rule 1.1 (competence) and Rule 1.3 (diligence).

[16] Paragraph (b)(2) describes conflicts that are nonconsentable because the representation is prohibited by applicable law. For example, in some states substantive law provides that the same lawyer may not represent more than one defendant in a capital case, even with the consent of the clients, and under federal criminal statutes certain representations by a former government lawyer are prohibited, despite the informed consent of the former client. In addition, decisional law in some states limits the ability of a governmental client, such as a municipality, to consent to a conflict of interest.

[17] Paragraph (b)(3) describes conflicts that are nonconsentable because of the institutional interest in vigorous development of each client's position when the clients are aligned directly against each other in the same litigation or other proceeding before a tribunal. Whether clients are aligned directly against each other within the meaning of this paragraph requires examination of the context of the proceeding. Although this paragraph does not preclude a lawyer's multiple representation of adverse parties to a mediation (because mediation is not a proceeding before a "tribunal" under Rule 1.0(m)), such representation may be precluded by paragraph (b)(1).

Informed Consent

[18] Informed consent requires that each affected client be aware of the relevant circumstances and of the material and reasonably foreseeable ways that the conflict could have adverse effects on the interests of that client. See Rule 1.0(e) (informed consent). The information required

depends on the nature of the conflict and the nature of the risks involved. When representation of multiple clients in a single matter is undertaken, the information must include the implications of the common representation, including possible effects on loyalty, confidentiality and the attorney-client privilege and the advantages and risks involved. See Comments [30] and [31] (effect of common representation on confidentiality).

[19] Under some circumstances it may be impossible to make the disclosure necessary to obtain consent. For example, when the lawyer represents different clients in related matters and one of the clients refuses to consent to the disclosure necessary to permit the other client to make an informed decision, the lawyer cannot properly ask the latter to consent. In some cases the alternative to common representation can be that each party may have to obtain separate representation with the possibility of incurring additional costs. These costs, along with the benefits of securing separate representation, are factors that may be considered by the affected client in determining whether common representation is in the client's interests.

Consent Confirmed in Writing

[20] Paragraph (b) requires the lawyer to obtain the informed consent of the client, confirmed in writing. Such a writing may consist of a document executed by the client or one that the lawyer promptly records and transmits to the client following an oral consent. See Rule 1.0(b). See also Rule 1.0(n) (writing includes electronic transmission). If it is not feasible to obtain or transmit the writing at the time the client gives informed consent, then the lawyer must obtain or transmit it within a reasonable time thereafter. See Rule 1.0(b). The requirement of a writing does not supplant the need in most cases for the lawyer to talk with the client, to explain the risks and advantages, if any, of representation burdened with a conflict of interest, as well as reasonably available alternatives, and to afford the client a reasonable opportunity to consider the risks and alternatives and to raise questions and concerns. Rather, the writing is required in order to impress upon clients the seriousness of the decision the client is being asked to make and to avoid disputes or ambiguities that might later occur in the absence of a writing.

Revoking Consent

[21] A client who has given consent to a conflict may revoke the consent and, like any other client, may terminate the lawyer's representation

at any time. Whether revoking consent to the client's own representation precludes the lawyer from continuing to represent other clients depends on the circumstances, including the nature of the conflict, whether the client revoked consent because of a material change in circumstances, the reasonable expectations of the other clients and whether material detriment to the other clients or the lawyer would result.

Consent to Future Conflict

[22] Whether a lawyer may properly request a client to waive conflicts that might arise in the future is subject to the test of paragraph (b). The effectiveness of such waivers is generally determined by the extent to which the client reasonably understands the material risks that the waiver entails. The more comprehensive the explanation of the types of future representations that might arise and the actual and reasonably foreseeable adverse consequences of those representations, the greater the likelihood that the client will have the requisite understanding. Thus, if the client agrees to consent to a particular type of conflict with which the client is already familiar, then the consent ordinarily will be effective with regard to that type of conflict. If the consent is general and open-ended, then the consent ordinarily will be ineffective, because it is not reasonably likely that the client will have understood the material risks involved. On the other hand, if the client is an experienced user of the legal services involved and is reasonably informed regarding the risk that a conflict may arise, such consent is more likely to be effective, particularly if, e.g., the client is independently represented by other counsel in giving consent and the consent is limited to future conflicts unrelated to the subject of the representation. In any case, advance consent cannot be effective if the circumstances that materialize in the future are such as would make the conflict nonconsentable under paragraph (b).

Conflicts in Litigation

[23] Paragraph (b)(3) prohibits representation of opposing parties in the same litigation, regardless of the clients' consent. On the other hand, simultaneous representation of parties whose interests in litigation may conflict, such as coplaintiffs or codefendants, is governed by paragraph (a)(2). A conflict may exist by reason of substantial discrepancy in the parties' testimony, incompatibility in positions in relation to an opposing party or the fact that there are substantially different possibilities of settlement of the claims or liabilities in question. Such conflicts can arise in

criminal cases as well as civil. The potential for conflict of interest in representing multiple defendants in a criminal case is so grave that ordinarily a lawyer should decline to represent more than one codefendant. On the other hand, common representation of persons having similar interests in civil litigation is proper if the requirements of paragraph (b) are met.

[24] Ordinarily a lawyer may take inconsistent legal positions in different tribunals at different times on behalf of different clients. The mere fact that advocating a legal position on behalf of one client might create precedent adverse to the interests of a client represented by the lawyer in an unrelated matter does not create a conflict of interest. A conflict of interest exists, however, if there is a significant risk that a lawyer's action on behalf of one client will materially limit the lawyer's effectiveness in representing another client in a different case; for example, when a decision favoring one client will create a precedent likely to seriously weaken the position taken on behalf of the other client. Factors relevant in determining whether the clients need to be advised of the risk include: where the cases are pending, whether the issue is substantive or procedural, the temporal relationship between the matters, the significance of the issue to the immediate and long-term interests of the clients involved and the clients' reasonable expectations in retaining the lawyer. If there is significant risk of material limitation, then absent informed consent of the affected clients, the lawyer must refuse one of the representations or withdraw from one or both matters.

[25] When a lawyer represents or seeks to represent a class of plaintiffs or defendants in a class-action lawsuit, unnamed members of the class are ordinarily not considered to be clients of the lawyer for purposes of applying paragraph (a)(1) of this Rule. Thus, the lawyer does not typically need to get the consent of such a person before representing a client suing the person in an unrelated matter. Similarly, a lawyer seeking to represent an opponent in a class action does not typically need the consent of an unnamed member of the class whom the lawyer represents in an unrelated matter.

Nonlitigation Conflicts

[26] Conflicts of interest under paragraphs (a)(1) and (a)(2) arise in contexts other than litigation. For a discussion of directly adverse conflicts in transactional matters, see Comment [7]. Relevant factors in determining whether there is significant potential for material limitation include the duration and intimacy of the lawyer's relationship with the

client or clients involved, the functions being performed by the lawyer, the likelihood that disagreements will arise and the likely prejudice to the client from the conflict. The question is often one of proximity and degree. See Comment [8].

[27] For example, conflict questions may arise in estate planning and estate administration. A lawyer may be called upon to prepare wills for several family members, such as husband and wife, and, depending upon the circumstances, a conflict of interest may be present. In estate administration the identity of the client may be unclear under the law of a particular jurisdiction. Under one view, the client is the fiduciary; under another view the client is the estate or trust, including its beneficiaries. In order to comply with conflict of interest rules, the lawyer should make clear the lawyer's relationship to the parties involved.

[28] Whether a conflict is consentable depends on the circumstances. For example, a lawyer may not represent multiple parties to a negotiation whose interests are fundamentally antagonistic to each other, but common representation is permissible where the clients are generally aligned in interest even though there is some difference in interest among them. Thus, a lawyer may seek to establish or adjust a relationship between clients on an amicable and mutually advantageous basis; for example, in helping to organize a business in which two or more clients are entrepreneurs, working out the financial reorganization of an enterprise in which two or more clients have an interest or arranging a property distribution in settlement of an estate. The lawyer seeks to resolve potentially adverse interests by developing the parties' mutual interests. Otherwise, each party might have to obtain separate representation, with the possibility of incurring additional cost, complication or even litigation. Given these and other relevant factors, the clients may prefer that the lawyer act for all of them.

Special Considerations in Common Representation

[29] In considering whether to represent multiple clients in the same matter, a lawyer should be mindful that if the common representation fails because the potentially adverse interests cannot be reconciled, the result can be additional cost, embarrassment and recrimination. Ordinarily, the lawyer will be forced to withdraw from representing all of the clients if the common representation fails. In some situations, the risk of failure is so great that multiple representation is plainly impossible. For example, a lawyer cannot undertake common representation of clients where

contentious litigation or negotiations between them are imminent or contemplated. Moreover, because the lawyer is required to be impartial between commonly represented clients, representation of multiple clients is improper when it is unlikely that impartiality can be maintained. Generally, if the relationship between the parties has already assumed antagonism, the possibility that the clients' interests can be adequately served by common representation is not very good. Other relevant factors are whether the lawyer subsequently will represent both parties on a continuing basis and whether the situation involves creating or terminating a relationship between the parties.

[30] A particularly important factor in determining the appropriateness of common representation is the effect on client-lawyer confidentiality and the attorney-client privilege. With regard to the attorney-client privilege, the prevailing rule is that, as between commonly represented clients, the privilege does not attach. Hence, it must be assumed that if litigation eventuates between the clients, the privilege will not protect any such communications, and the clients should be so advised.

[31] As to the duty of confidentiality, continued common representation will almost certainly be inadequate if one client asks the lawyer not to disclose to the other client information relevant to the common representation. This is so because the lawyer has an equal duty of loyalty to each client, and each client has the right to be informed of anything bearing on the representation that might affect that client's interests and the right to expect that the lawyer will use that information to that client's benefit. See Rule 1.4. The lawyer should, at the outset of the common representation and as part of the process of obtaining each client's informed consent, advise each client that information will be shared and that the lawyer will have to withdraw if one client decides that some matter material to the representation should be kept from the other. In limited circumstances, it may be appropriate for the lawyer to proceed with the representation when the clients have agreed, after being properly informed, that the lawyer will keep certain information confidential. For example, the lawyer may reasonably conclude that failure to disclose one client's trade secrets to another client will not adversely affect representation involving a joint venture between the clients and agree to keep that information confidential with the informed consent of both clients.

[32] When seeking to establish or adjust a relationship between clients, the lawyer should make clear that the lawyer's role is not that of partisanship normally expected in other circumstances and, thus, that

the clients may be required to assume greater responsibility for decisions than when each client is separately represented. Any limitations on the scope of the representation made necessary as a result of the common representation should be fully explained to the clients at the outset of the representation. See Rule 1.2(c).

[33] Subject to the above limitations, each client in the common representation has the right to loyal and diligent representation and the protection of Rule 1.9 concerning the obligations to a former client. The client also has the right to discharge the lawyer as stated in Rule 1.16.

Organizational Clients

[34] A lawyer who represents a corporation or other organization does not, by virtue of that representation, necessarily represent any constituent or affiliated organization, such as a parent or subsidiary. See Rule 1.13(a). Thus, the lawyer for an organization is not barred from accepting representation adverse to an affiliate in an unrelated matter, unless the circumstances are such that the affiliate should also be considered a client of the lawyer, there is an understanding between the lawyer and the organizational client that the lawyer will avoid representation adverse to the client's affiliates, or the lawyer's obligations to either the organizational client or the new client are likely to limit materially the lawyer's representation of the other client.

[35] A lawyer for a corporation or other organization who is also a member of its board of directors should determine whether the responsibilities of the two roles may conflict. The lawyer may be called on to advise the corporation in matters involving actions of the directors. Consideration should be given to the frequency with which such situations may arise, the potential intensity of the conflict, the effect of the lawyer's resignation from the board and the possibility of the corporation's obtaining legal advice from another lawyer in such situations. If there is material risk that the dual role will compromise the lawyer's independence of professional judgment, the lawyer should not serve as a director or should cease to act as the corporation's lawyer when conflicts of interest arise. The lawyer should advise the other members of the board that in some circumstances matters discussed at board meetings while the lawyer is present in the capacity of director might not be protected by the attorney-client privilege and that conflict of interest considerations might require the lawyer's recusal as a director or might require the lawyer and the lawyer's firm to decline representation of the corporation in a matter.

Definitional Cross-References

"Confirmed in writing" *See* Rule 1.0(b)
"Informed consent" *See* Rule 1.0(e)
"Reasonably believes" *See* Rule 1.0(i)
"Tribunal" *See* Rule 1.0(m)

RULE 1.8: CONFLICT OF INTEREST: CURRENT CLIENTS: SPECIFIC RULES

(a) A lawyer shall not enter into a business transaction with a client or knowingly acquire an ownership, possessory, security or other pecuniary interest adverse to a client unless:

(1) the transaction and terms on which the lawyer acquires the interest are fair and reasonable to the client and are fully disclosed and transmitted in writing in a manner that can be reasonably understood by the client;

(2) the client is advised in writing of the desirability of seeking and is given a reasonable opportunity to seek the advice of independent legal counsel on the transaction; and

(3) the client gives informed consent, in a writing signed by the client, to the essential terms of the transaction and the lawyer's role in the transaction, including whether the lawyer is representing the client in the transaction.

(b) A lawyer shall not use information relating to representation of a client to the disadvantage of the client unless the client gives informed consent, except as permitted or required by these Rules.

(c) A lawyer shall not solicit any substantial gift from a client, including a testamentary gift, or prepare on behalf of a client an instrument giving the lawyer or a person related to the lawyer any substantial gift unless the lawyer or other recipient of the gift is related to the client. For purposes of this paragraph, related persons include a spouse, child, grandchild, parent, grandparent or other relative or individual with whom the lawyer or the client maintains a close, familial relationship.

(d) Prior to the conclusion of representation of a client, a lawyer shall not make or negotiate an agreement giving the lawyer literary or media rights to a portrayal or account based in substantial part on information relating to the representation.

(e) A lawyer shall not provide financial assistance to a client in connection with pending or contemplated litigation, except that:

(1) a lawyer may advance court costs and expenses of litigation, the repayment of which may be contingent on the outcome of the matter; and

(2) a lawyer representing an indigent client may pay court costs and expenses of litigation on behalf of the client; and

(3) a lawyer representing an indigent client pro bono, a lawyer representing an indigent client pro bono through a nonprofit legal services or public interest organization and a lawyer representing an indigent client pro bono through a law school clinical or pro bono program may provide modest gifts to the client for food, rent, transportation, medicine and other basic living expenses. The lawyer:

(i) may not promise, assure or imply the availability of such gifts prior to retention or as an inducement to continue the client-lawyer relationship after retention;

(ii) may not seek or accept reimbursement from the client, a relative of the client or anyone affiliated with the client; and

(iii) may not publicize or advertise a willingness to provide such gifts to prospective clients.

Financial assistance under this Rule may be provided even if the representation is eligible for fees under a fee-shifting statute.

(f) A lawyer shall not accept compensation for representing a client from one other than the client unless:

(1) the client gives informed consent;

(2) there is no interference with the lawyer's independence of professional judgment or with the client-lawyer relationship; and

(3) information relating to representation of a client is protected as required by Rule 1.6..

(g) A lawyer who represents two or more clients shall not participate in making an aggregate settlement of the claims of or against the clients, or in a criminal case an aggregated agreement as to guilty or nolo contendere pleas, unless each client gives informed consent, in a writing signed by the client. The lawyer's disclosure shall include the existence and nature of all the claims or pleas involved and of the participation of each person in the settlement.

(h) A lawyer shall not:

(1) make an agreement prospectively limiting the lawyer's liability to a client for malpractice unless the client is independently represented in making the agreement; or

(2) settle a claim or potential claim for such liability with an unrepresented client or former client unless that person is advised in writing of the desirability of seeking and is given a reasonable opportunity to seek the advice of independent legal counsel in connection therewith.

(i) A lawyer shall not acquire a proprietary interest in the cause of action or subject matter of litigation the lawyer is conducting for a client, except that the lawyer may:

(1) acquire a lien authorized by law to secure the lawyer's fee or expenses; and

(2) contract with a client for a reasonable contingent fee in a civil case.

(j) A lawyer shall not have sexual relations with a client unless a consensual sexual relationship existed between them when the client-lawyer relationship commenced.

(k) While lawyers are associated in a firm, a prohibition in the foregoing paragraphs (a) through (i) that applies to any one of them shall apply to all of them.

Comment
Business Transactions between Client and Lawyer

[1] A lawyer's legal skill and training, together with the relationship of trust and confidence between lawyer and client, create the possibility of overreaching when the lawyer participates in a business, property or financial transaction with a client, for example, a loan or sales transaction or a lawyer investment on behalf of a client. The requirements of paragraph (a) must be met even when the transaction is not closely related to the subject matter of the representation, as when a lawyer drafting a will for a client learns that the client needs money for unrelated expenses and offers to make a loan to the client. The Rule applies to lawyers engaged in the sale of goods or services related to the practice of law, for example, the sale of title insurance or investment services to existing clients of the lawyer's legal practice. See Rule 5.7. It also applies to lawyers purchasing property from estates they represent. It does not apply to ordinary fee arrangements between client and lawyer, which are governed by Rule 1.5, although its requirements must be met when the lawyer accepts an in-

terest in the client's business or other nonmonetary property as payment of all or part of a fee. In addition, the Rule does not apply to standard commercial transactions between the lawyer and the client for products or services that the client generally markets to others, for example, banking or brokerage services, medical services, products manufactured or distributed by the client, and utilities' services. In such transactions, the lawyer has no advantage in dealing with the client, and the restrictions in paragraph (a) are unnecessary and impracticable.

[2] Paragraph (a)(1) requires that the transaction itself be fair to the client and that its essential terms be communicated to the client, in writing, in a manner that can be reasonably understood. Paragraph (a)(2) requires that the client also be advised, in writing, of the desirability of seeking the advice of independent legal counsel. It also requires that the client be given a reasonable opportunity to obtain such advice. Paragraph (a)(3) requires that the lawyer obtain the client's informed consent, in a writing signed by the client, both to the essential terms of the transaction and to the lawyer's role. When necessary, the lawyer should discuss both the material risks of the proposed transaction, including any risk presented by the lawyer's involvement, and the existence of reasonably available alternatives and should explain why the advice of independent legal counsel is desirable. See Rule 1.0(e) (definition of informed consent).

[3] The risk to a client is greatest when the client expects the lawyer to represent the client in the transaction itself or when the lawyer's financial interest otherwise poses a significant risk that the lawyer's representation of the client will be materially limited by the lawyer's financial interest in the transaction. Here the lawyer's role requires that the lawyer must comply, not only with the requirements of paragraph (a), but also with the requirements of Rule 1.7. Under that Rule, the lawyer must disclose the risks associated with the lawyer's dual role as both legal adviser and participant in the transaction, such as the risk that the lawyer will structure the transaction or give legal advice in a way that favors the lawyer's interests at the expense of the client. Moreover, the lawyer must obtain the client's informed consent. In some cases, the lawyer's interest may be such that Rule 1.7 will preclude the lawyer from seeking the client's consent to the transaction.

[4] If the client is independently represented in the transaction, paragraph (a)(2) of this Rule is inapplicable, and the paragraph (a)(1) requirement for full disclosure is satisfied either by a written disclosure by the lawyer involved in the transaction or by the client's independent counsel. The fact that the client was independently represented in the transaction

is relevant in determining whether the agreement was fair and reasonable to the client as paragraph (a)(1) further requires.

Use of Information Related to Representation

[5] Use of information relating to the representation to the disadvantage of the client violates the lawyer's duty of loyalty. Paragraph (b) applies when the information is used to benefit either the lawyer or a third person, such as another client or business associate of the lawyer. For example, if a lawyer learns that a client intends to purchase and develop several parcels of land, the lawyer may not use that information to purchase one of the parcels in competition with the client or to recommend that another client make such a purchase. The Rule does not prohibit uses that do not disadvantage the client. For example, a lawyer who learns a government agency's interpretation of trade legislation during the representation of one client may properly use that information to benefit other clients. Paragraph (b) prohibits disadvantageous use of client information unless the client gives informed consent, except as permitted or required by these Rules. See Rules 1.2(d), 1.6, 1.9(c), 3.3, 4.1(b), 8.1 and 8.3.

Gifts to Lawyers

[6] A lawyer may accept a gift from a client, if the transaction meets general standards of fairness. For example, a simple gift such as a present given at a holiday or as a token of appreciation is permitted. If a client offers the lawyer a more substantial gift, paragraph (c) does not prohibit the lawyer from accepting it, although such a gift may be voidable by the client under the doctrine of undue influence, which treats client gifts as presumptively fraudulent. In any event, due to concerns about overreaching and imposition on clients, a lawyer may not suggest that a substantial gift be made to the lawyer or for the lawyer's benefit, except where the lawyer is related to the client as set forth in paragraph (c).

[7] If effectuation of a substantial gift requires preparing a legal instrument such as a will or conveyance, the client should have the detached advice that another lawyer can provide. The sole exception to this Rule is where the client is a relative of the donee.

[8] This Rule does not prohibit a lawyer from seeking to have the lawyer or a partner or associate of the lawyer named as executor of the client's estate or to another potentially lucrative fiduciary position. Nevertheless, such appointments will be subject to the general conflict of interest provision in Rule 1.7 when there is a significant risk that the lawyer's interest in obtaining the appointment will materially limit the lawyer's independent

professional judgment in advising the client concerning the choice of an executor or other fiduciary. In obtaining the client's informed consent to the conflict, the lawyer should advise the client concerning the nature and extent of the lawyer's financial interest in the appointment, as well as the availability of alternative candidates for the position.

Literary Rights

[9] An agreement by which a lawyer acquires literary or media rights concerning the conduct of the representation creates a conflict between the interests of the client and the personal interests of the lawyer. Measures suitable in the representation of the client may detract from the publication value of an account of the representation. Paragraph (d) does not prohibit a lawyer representing a client in a transaction concerning literary property from agreeing that the lawyer's fee shall consist of a share in ownership in the property, if the arrangement conforms to Rule 1.5 and paragraphs (a) and (i).

Financial Assistance

[10] Lawyers may not subsidize lawsuits or administrative proceedings brought on behalf of their clients, including making or guaranteeing loans to their clients for living expenses, because to do so would encourage clients to pursue lawsuits that might not otherwise be brought and because such assistance gives lawyers too great a financial stake in the litigation. These dangers do not warrant a prohibition on a lawyer lending a client court costs and litigation expenses, including the expenses of medical examination and the costs of obtaining and presenting evidence, because these advances are virtually indistinguishable from contingent fees and help ensure access to the courts. Similarly, an exception allowing lawyers representing indigent clients to pay court costs and litigation expenses regardless of whether these funds will be repaid is warranted.

[11] Paragraph (e)(3) provides another exception. A lawyer representing an indigent client without fee, a lawyer representing an indigent client pro bono through a nonprofit legal services or public interest organization and a lawyer representing an indigent client pro bono through a law school clinical or pro bono program may give the client modest gifts. Gifts permitted under paragraph (e)(3) include modest contributions for food, rent, transportation, medicine and similar basic necessities of life. If the gift may have consequences for the client, including, e.g., for receipt of government benefits, social services, or tax liability, the lawyer should consult with the client about these. See Rule 1.4.

[12] The paragraph (e)(3) exception is narrow. Modest gifts are allowed in specific circumstances where it is unlikely to create conflicts of interest or invite abuse. Paragraph (e)(3) prohibits the lawyer from (i) promising, assuring or implying the availability of financial assistance prior to retention or as an inducement to continue the client-lawyer relationship after retention; (ii) seeking or accepting reimbursement from the client, a relative of the client or anyone affiliated with the client; and (iii) publicizing or advertising a willingness to provide gifts to prospective to clients beyond court costs and expenses of litigation in connection with contemplated or pending litigation or administrative proceedings.

[13] Financial assistance, including modest gifts pursuant to paragraph (e)(3), may be provided even if the representation is eligible for fees under a fee-shifting statute. However, paragraph (e)(3) does not permit lawyers to provide assistance in other contemplated or pending litigation in which the lawyer may eventually recover a fee, such as contingent-fee personal injury cases or cases in which fees may be available under a contractual fee-shifting provision, even if the lawyer does not eventually receive a fee.

Person Paying for a Lawyer's Services

[14] Lawyers are frequently asked to represent a client under circumstances in which a third person will compensate the lawyer, in whole or in part. The third person might be a relative or friend, an indemnitor (such as a liability insurance company) or a co-client (such as a corporation sued along with one or more of its employees). Because third-party payers frequently have interests that differ from those of the client, including interests in minimizing the amount spent on the representation and in learning how the representation is progressing, lawyers are prohibited from accepting or continuing such representations unless the lawyer determines that there will be no interference with the lawyer's independent professional judgment and there is informed consent from the client. See also Rule 5.4(c) (prohibiting interference with a lawyer's professional judgment by one who recommends, employs or pays the lawyer to render legal services for another).

[15] Sometimes, it will be sufficient for the lawyer to obtain the client's informed consent regarding the fact of the payment and the identity of the third-party payer. If, however, the fee arrangement creates a conflict of interest for the lawyer, then the lawyer must comply with Rule 1.7. The lawyer must also conform to the requirements of Rule 1.6 concerning confidentiality. Under Rule 1.7(a), a conflict of interest exists if there

is significant risk that the lawyer's representation of the client will be materially limited by the lawyer's own interest in the fee arrangement or by the lawyer's responsibilities to the third-party payer (for example, when the third-party payer is a co-client). Under Rule 1.7(b), the lawyer may accept or continue the representation with the informed consent of each affected client, unless the conflict is nonconsentable under that paragraph. Under Rule 1.7(b), the informed consent must be confirmed in writing..

Aggregate Settlements

[16] Differences in willingness to make or accept an offer of settlement are among the risks of common representation of multiple clients by a single lawyer. Under Rule 1.7, this is one of the risks that should be discussed before undertaking the representation, as part of the process of obtaining the clients' informed consent. In addition, Rule 1.2(a) protects each client's right to have the final say in deciding whether to accept or reject an offer of settlement and in deciding whether to enter a guilty or nolo contendere plea in a criminal case. The rule stated in this paragraph is a corollary of both these Rules and provides that, before any settlement offer or plea bargain is made or accepted on behalf of multiple clients, the lawyer must inform each of them about all the material terms of the settlement, including what the other clients will receive or pay if the settlement or plea offer is accepted. See also Rule 1.0(e) (definition of informed consent). Lawyers representing a class of plaintiffs or defendants, or those proceeding derivatively, may not have a full client-lawyer relationship with each member of the class; nevertheless, such lawyers must comply with applicable rules regulating notification of class members and other procedural requirements designed to ensure adequate protection of the entire class.

Limiting Liability and Settling Malpractice Claims

[17] Agreements prospectively limiting a lawyer's liability for malpractice are prohibited unless the client is independently represented in making the agreement because they are likely to undermine competent and diligent representation. Also, many clients are unable to evaluate the desirability of making such an agreement before a dispute has arisen, particularly if they are then represented by the lawyer seeking the agreement. This paragraph does not, however, prohibit a lawyer from entering into an agreement with the client to arbitrate legal malpractice claims, provided such agreements are enforceable and the client is fully informed of the scope and effect of the agreement. Nor does this paragraph limit

the ability of lawyers to practice in the form of a limited-liability entity, where permitted by law, provided that each lawyer remains personally liable to the client for his or her own conduct and the firm complies with any conditions required by law, such as provisions requiring client notification or maintenance of adequate liability insurance. Nor does it prohibit an agreement in accordance with Rule 1.2 that defines the scope of the representation, although a definition of scope that makes the obligations of representation illusory will amount to an attempt to limit liability.

[18] Agreements settling a claim or a potential claim for malpractice are not prohibited by this Rule. Nevertheless, in view of the danger that a lawyer will take unfair advantage of an unrepresented client or former client, the lawyer must first advise such a person in writing of the appropriateness of independent representation in connection with such a settlement. In addition, the lawyer must give the client or former client a reasonable opportunity to find and consult independent counsel.

Acquiring Proprietary Interest in Litigation

[19] Paragraph (i) states the traditional general rule that lawyers are prohibited from acquiring a proprietary interest in litigation. Like paragraph (e), the general rule has its basis in common law champerty and maintenance and is designed to avoid giving the lawyer too great an interest in the representation. In addition, when the lawyer acquires an ownership interest in the subject of the representation, it will be more difficult for a client to discharge the lawyer if the client so desires. The Rule is subject to specific exceptions developed in decisional law and continued in these Rules. The exception for certain advances of the costs of litigation is set forth in paragraph (e). In addition, paragraph (i) sets forth exceptions for liens authorized by law to secure the lawyer's fees or expenses and contracts for reasonable contingent fees. The law of each jurisdiction determines which liens are authorized by law. These may include liens granted by statute, liens originating in common law and liens acquired by contract with the client. When a lawyer acquires by contract a security interest in property other than that recovered through the lawyer's efforts in the litigation, such an acquisition is a business or financial transaction with a client and is governed by the requirements of paragraph (a). Contracts for contingent fees in civil cases are governed by Rule 1.5.

Client-Lawyer Sexual Relationships

[20] The relationship between lawyer and client is a fiduciary one in which the lawyer occupies the highest position of trust and confidence.

The relationship is almost always unequal; thus, a sexual relationship between lawyer and client can involve unfair exploitation of the lawyer's fiduciary role, in violation of the lawyer's basic ethical obligation not to use the trust of the client to the client's disadvantage. In addition, such a relationship presents a significant danger that, because of the lawyer's emotional involvement, the lawyer will be unable to represent the client without impairment of the exercise of independent professional judgment. Moreover, a blurred line between the professional and personal relationships may make it difficult to predict to what extent client confidences will be protected by the attorney-client evidentiary privilege, since client confidences are protected by privilege only when they are imparted in the context of the client-lawyer relationship. Because of the significant danger of harm to client interests and because the client's own emotional involvement renders it unlikely that the client could give adequate informed consent, this Rule prohibits the lawyer from having sexual relations with a client regardless of whether the relationship is consensual and regardless of the absence of prejudice to the client.

[21] Sexual relationships that predate the client-lawyer relationship are not prohibited. Issues relating to the exploitation of the fiduciary relationship and client dependency are diminished when the sexual relationship existed prior to the commencement of the client-lawyer relationship. However, before proceeding with the representation in these circumstances, the lawyer should consider whether the lawyer's ability to represent the client will be materially limited by the relationship. See Rule 1.7(a)(2).

[22] When the client is an organization, paragraph (j) of this Rule prohibits a lawyer for the organization (whether inside counsel or outside counsel) from having a sexual relationship with a constituent of the organization who supervises, directs or regularly consults with that lawyer concerning the organization's legal matters.

Imputation of Prohibitions

[23] Under paragraph (k), a prohibition on conduct by an individual lawyer in paragraphs (a) through (i) also applies to all lawyers associated in a firm with the personally prohibited lawyer. For example, one lawyer in a firm may not enter into a business transaction with a client of another member of the firm without complying with paragraph (a), even if the first lawyer is not personally involved in the representation of the client. The prohibition set forth in paragraph (j) is personal and is not applied to associated lawyers.

Definitional Cross-References

"Firm" *See* Rule 1.0(c)
"Informed consent" *See* Rule 1.0(e)
"Knowingly" *See* Rule 1.0(f)
"Substantial" *See* Rule 1.0(l)
"Writing" and "Signed" *See* Rule 1.0(n)

RULE 1.9: DUTIES TO FORMER CLIENTS

(a) A lawyer who has formerly represented a client in a matter shall not thereafter represent another person in the same or a substantially related matter in which that person's interests are materially adverse to the interests of the former client unless the former client gives informed consent, confirmed in writing.

(b) A lawyer shall not knowingly represent a person in the same or a substantially related matter in which a firm with which the lawyer formerly was associated had previously represented a client

(1) whose interests are materially adverse to that person; and

(2) about whom the lawyer had acquired information protected by Rules 1.6 and 1.9(c) that is material to the matter; unless the former client gives informed consent, confirmed in writing.

(c) A lawyer who has formerly represented a client in a matter or whose present or former firm has formerly represented a client in a matter shall not thereafter:

(1) use information relating to the representation to the disadvantage of the former client except as these Rules would permit or require with respect to a client, or when the information has become generally known; or

(2) reveal information relating to the representation except as these Rules would permit or require with respect to a client.

Comment

[1] After termination of a client-lawyer relationship, a lawyer has certain continuing duties with respect to confidentiality and conflicts of interest and thus may not represent another client except in conformity with this Rule. Under this Rule, for example, a lawyer could not properly

seek to rescind on behalf of a new client a contract drafted on behalf of the former client. So also a lawyer who has prosecuted an accused person could not properly represent the accused in a subsequent civil action against the government concerning the same transaction. Nor could a lawyer who has represented multiple clients in a matter represent one of the clients against the others in the same or a substantially related matter after a dispute arose among the clients in that matter, unless all affected clients give informed consent. See Comment [9]. Current and former government lawyers must comply with this Rule to the extent required by Rule 1.11.

[2] The scope of a "matter" for purposes of this Rule depends on the facts of a particular situation or transaction. The lawyer's involvement in a matter can also be a question of degree. When a lawyer has been directly involved in a specific transaction, subsequent representation of other clients with materially adverse interests in that transaction clearly is prohibited. On the other hand, a lawyer who recurrently handled a type of problem for a former client is not precluded from later representing another client in a factually distinct problem of that type even though the subsequent representation involves a position adverse to the prior client. Similar considerations can apply to the reassignment of military lawyers between defense and prosecution functions within the same military jurisdictions. The underlying question is whether the lawyer was so involved in the matter that the subsequent representation can be justly regarded as a changing of sides in the matter in question.

[3] Matters are "substantially related" for purposes of this Rule if they involve the same transaction or legal dispute or if there otherwise is a substantial risk that confidential factual information as would normally have been obtained in the prior representation would materially advance the client's position in the subsequent matter. For example, a lawyer who has represented a businessperson and learned extensive private financial information about that person may not then represent that person's spouse in seeking a divorce. Similarly, a lawyer who has previously represented a client in securing environmental permits to build a shopping center would be precluded from representing neighbors seeking to oppose rezoning of the property on the basis of environmental considerations; however, the lawyer would not be precluded, on the grounds of substantial relationship, from defending a tenant of the completed shopping center in resisting eviction for nonpayment of rent. Information that has been disclosed to the public or to other parties adverse to the former

client ordinarily will not be disqualifying. Information acquired in a prior representation may have been rendered obsolete by the passage of time, a circumstance that may be relevant in determining whether two representations are substantially related. In the case of an organizational client, general knowledge of the client's policies and practices ordinarily will not preclude a subsequent representation; on the other hand, knowledge of specific facts gained in a prior representation that are relevant to the matter in question ordinarily will preclude such a representation. A former client is not required to reveal the confidential information learned by the lawyer in order to establish a substantial risk that the lawyer has confidential information to use in the subsequent matter. A conclusion about the possession of such information may be based on the nature of the services the lawyer provided the former client and information that would in ordinary practice be learned by a lawyer providing such services.

Lawyers Moving Between Firms

[4] When lawyers have been associated within a firm but then end their association, the question of whether a lawyer should undertake representation is more complicated. There are several competing considerations. First, the client previously represented by the former firm must be reasonably assured that the principle of loyalty to the client is not compromised. Second, the rule should not be so broadly cast as to preclude other persons from having reasonable choice of legal counsel. Third, the rule should not unreasonably hamper lawyers from forming new associations and taking on new clients after having left a previous association. In this connection, it should be recognized that today many lawyers practice in firms, that many lawyers to some degree limit their practice to one field or another, and that many move from one association to another several times in their careers. If the concept of imputation were applied with unqualified rigor, the result would be radical curtailment of the opportunity of lawyers to move from one practice setting to another and of the opportunity of clients to change counsel.

[5] Paragraph (b) operates to disqualify the lawyer only when the lawyer involved has actual knowledge of information protected by Rules 1.6 and 1.9(c). Thus, if a lawyer while with one firm acquired no knowledge or information relating to a particular client of the firm, and that lawyer later joined another firm, neither the lawyer individually nor the second firm is disqualified from representing another client in the same

or a related matter even though the interests of the two clients conflict. See Rule 1.10(b) for the restrictions on a firm once a lawyer has terminated association with the firm.

[6] Application of paragraph (b) depends on a situation's particular facts, aided by inferences, deductions or working presumptions that reasonably may be made about the way in which lawyers work together. A lawyer may have general access to files of all clients of a law firm and may regularly participate in discussions of their affairs; it should be inferred that such a lawyer in fact is privy to all information about all the firm's clients. In contrast, another lawyer may have access to the files of only a limited number of clients and participate in discussions of the affairs of no other clients; in the absence of information to the contrary, it should be inferred that such a lawyer in fact is privy to information about the clients actually served but not those of other clients. In such an inquiry, the burden of proof should rest upon the firm whose disqualification is sought.

[7] Independent of the question of disqualification of a firm, a lawyer changing professional association has a continuing duty to preserve confidentiality of information about a client formerly represented. See Rules 1.6 and 1.9(c).

[8] Paragraph (c) provides that information acquired by the lawyer in the course of representing a client may not subsequently be used or revealed by the lawyer to the disadvantage of the client. However, the fact that a lawyer has once served a client does not preclude the lawyer from using generally known information about that client when later representing another client.

[9] The provisions of this Rule are for the protection of former clients and can be waived if the client gives informed consent, which consent must be confirmed in writing under paragraphs (a) and (b). See Rule 1.0(e). With regard to the effectiveness of an advance waiver, see Comment [22] to Rule 1.7. With regard to disqualification of a firm with which a lawyer is or was formerly associated, see Rule 1.10.

Definitional Cross-References

"Confirmed in writing" *See* Rule 1.0(b)
"Firm" *See* Rule 1.0(c)
"Informed consent" *See* Rule 1.0(e)
"Knowingly" and "Known" *See* Rule 1.0(f)
"Writing" *See* Rule 1.0(n)

Rule 1.10: Imputation of Conflicts of Interest: General Rule

(a) While lawyers are associated in a firm, none of them shall knowingly represent a client when any one of them practicing alone would be prohibited from doing so by Rules 1.7 or 1.9, unless

(1) the prohibition is based on a personal interest of the disqualified lawyer and does not present a significant risk of materially limiting the representation of the client by the remaining lawyers in the firm; or

(2) the prohibition is based upon Rule 1.9(a) or (b), and arises out of the disqualified lawyer's association with a prior firm, and

  (i) the disqualified lawyer is timely screened from any participation in the matter and is apportioned no part of the fee therefrom;

  (ii) written notice is promptly given to any affected former client to enable the former client to ascertain compliance with the provisions of this Rule, which shall include a description of the screening procedures employed; a statement of the firm's and of the screened lawyer's compliance with these Rules; a statement that review may be available before a tribunal; and an agreement by the firm to respond promptly to any written inquiries or objections by the former client about the screening procedures; and

  (iii) certifications of compliance with these Rules and with the screening procedures are provided to the former client by the screened lawyer and by a partner of the firm, at reasonable intervals upon the former client's written request and upon termination of the screening procedures.

(b) When a lawyer has terminated an association with a firm, the firm is not prohibited from thereafter representing a person with interests materially adverse to those of a client represented by the formerly associated lawyer and not currently represented by the firm, unless:

(1) the matter is the same or substantially related to that in which the formerly associated lawyer represented the client; and

(2) any lawyer remaining in the firm has information protected by Rules 1.6 and 1.9(c) that is material to the matter.

(c) A disqualification prescribed by this Rule may be waived by the affected client under the conditions stated in Rule 1.7.

(d) The disqualification of lawyers associated in a firm with former or current government lawyers is governed by Rule 1.11.

Comment

Definition of "Firm"

[1] For purposes of the Rules of Professional Conduct, the term "firm" denotes lawyers in a law partnership, professional corporation, sole proprietorship or other association authorized to practice law; or lawyers employed in a legal services organization or the legal department of a corporation or other organization. See Rule 1.0(c). Whether two or more lawyers constitute a firm within this definition can depend on the specific facts. See Rule 1.0, Comments [2]–[4].

Principles of Imputed Disqualification

[2] The rule of imputed disqualification stated in paragraph (a) gives effect to the principle of loyalty to the client as it applies to lawyers who practice in a law firm. Such situations can be considered from the premise that a firm of lawyers is essentially one lawyer for purposes of the rules governing loyalty to the client, or from the premise that each lawyer is vicariously bound by the obligation of loyalty owed by each lawyer with whom the lawyer is associated. Paragraph (a)(1) operates only among the lawyers currently associated in a firm. When a lawyer moves from one firm to another, the situation is governed by Rules 1.9(b) and 1.10(a)(2) and 1.10(b).

[3] The rule in paragraph (a) does not prohibit representation where neither questions of client loyalty nor protection of confidential information are presented. Where one lawyer in a firm could not effectively represent a given client because of strong political beliefs, for example, but that lawyer will do no work on the case and the personal beliefs of the lawyer will not materially limit the representation by others in the firm, the firm should not be disqualified. On the other hand, if an opposing party in a case were owned by a lawyer in the law firm, and others in the firm would be materially limited in pursuing the matter because of loyalty to that lawyer, the personal disqualification of the lawyer would be imputed to all others in the firm.

[4] The rule in paragraph (a) also does not prohibit representation by others in the law firm where the person prohibited from involvement in a matter is a nonlawyer, such as a paralegal or legal secretary. Nor does

paragraph (a) prohibit representation if the lawyer is prohibited from acting because of events before the person became a lawyer, for example, work that the person did while a law student. Such persons, however, ordinarily must be screened from any personal participation in the matter to avoid communication to others in the firm of confidential information that both the nonlawyers and the firm have a legal duty to protect. See Rules 1.0(k) and 5.3.

[5] Rule 1.10(b) operates to permit a law firm, under certain circumstances, to represent a person with interests directly adverse to those of a client represented by a lawyer who formerly was associated with the firm. The Rule applies regardless of when the formerly associated lawyer represented the client. However, the law firm may not represent a person with interests adverse to those of a present client of the firm, which would violate Rule 1.7. Moreover, the firm may not represent the person where the matter is the same or substantially related to that in which the formerly associated lawyer represented the client and any other lawyer currently in the firm has material information protected by Rules 1.6 and 1.9(c).

[6] Rule 1.10(c) removes imputation with the informed consent of the affected client or former client under the conditions stated in Rule 1.7. The conditions stated in Rule 1.7 require the lawyer to determine that the representation is not prohibited by Rule 1.7(b) and that each affected client or former client has given informed consent to the representation, confirmed in writing. In some cases, the risk may be so severe that the conflict may not be cured by client consent. For a discussion of the effectiveness of client waivers of conflicts that might arise in the future, see Rule 1.7, Comment [22]. For a definition of informed consent, see Rule 1.0(e).

[7] Rule 1.10(a)(2) similarly removes the imputation otherwise required by Rule 1.10(a), but unlike section (c), it does so without requiring that there be informed consent by the former client. Instead, it requires that the procedures laid out in sections (a)(2)(i)-(iii) be followed. A description of effective screening mechanisms appears in Rule 1.0(k). Lawyers should be aware, however, that, even where screening mechanisms have been adopted, tribunals may consider additional factors in ruling upon motions to disqualify a lawyer from pending litigation.

[8] Paragraph (a)(2)(i) does not prohibit the screened lawyer from receiving a salary or partnership share established by prior independent agreement, but that lawyer may not receive compensation directly related to the matter in which the lawyer is disqualified.

[9] The notice required by paragraph (a)(2)(ii) generally should include a description of the screened lawyer's prior representation and be

given as soon as practicable after the need for screening becomes apparent. It also should include a statement by the screened lawyer and the firm that the client's material confidential information has not been disclosed or used in violation of the Rules. The notice is intended to enable the former client to evaluate and comment upon the effectiveness of the screening procedures.

[10] The certifications required by paragraph (a)(2)(iii) give the former client assurance that the client's material confidential information has not been disclosed or used inappropriately, either prior to timely implementation of a screen or thereafter. If compliance cannot be certified, the certificate must describe the failure to comply.

[11] Where a lawyer has joined a private firm after having represented the government, imputation is governed by Rule 1.11(b) and (c), not this Rule. Under Rule 1.11(d), where a lawyer represents the government after having served clients in private practice, nongovernmental employment or in another government agency, former-client conflicts are not imputed to government lawyers associated with the individually disqualified lawyer.

[12] Where a lawyer is prohibited from engaging in certain transactions under Rule 1.8, paragraph (k) of that Rule, and not this Rule, determines whether that prohibition also applies to other lawyers associated in a firm with the personally prohibited lawyer.

Definitional Cross-References

"Firm" *See* Rule 1.0(c)
"Knowingly" *See* Rule 1.0(f)
"Partner" *See* Rule 1.0(g)
"Screened" *See* Rule 1.0(k)
"Tribunal" *See* Rule 1.0(m)
"Written" *See* Rule 1.0(n)

RULE 1.11: SPECIAL CONFLICTS OF INTEREST FOR FORMER AND CURRENT GOVERNMENT OFFICERS AND EMPLOYEES

(a) Except as law may otherwise expressly permit, a lawyer who has formerly served as a public officer or employee of the government:

(1) is subject to Rule 1.9(c); and

(2) shall not otherwise represent a client in connection with a matter in which the lawyer participated personally and substantially as a public officer or employee, unless the appropriate government agency gives its informed consent, confirmed in writing, to the representation.

(b) When a lawyer is disqualified from representation under paragraph (a), no lawyer in a firm with which that lawyer is associated may knowingly undertake or continue representation in such a matter unless:

(1) the disqualified lawyer is timely screened from any participation in the matter and is apportioned no part of the fee therefrom; and

(2) written notice is promptly given to the appropriate government agency to enable it to ascertain compliance with the provisions of this Rule.

(c) Except as law may otherwise expressly permit, a lawyer having information that the lawyer knows is confidential government information about a person acquired when the lawyer was a public officer or employee, may not represent a private client whose interests are adverse to that person in a matter in which the information could be used to the material disadvantage of that person. As used in this Rule, the term "confidential government information" means information that has been obtained under governmental authority and which, at the time this Rule is applied, the government is prohibited by law from disclosing to the public or has a legal privilege not to disclose and which is not otherwise available to the public. A firm with which that lawyer is associated may undertake or continue representation in the matter only if the disqualified lawyer is timely screened from any participation in the matter and is apportioned no part of the fee therefrom.

(d) Except as law may otherwise expressly permit, a lawyer currently serving as a public officer or employee:

(1) is subject to Rules 1.7 and 1.9; and

(2) shall not:

(i) participate in a matter in which the lawyer participated personally and substantially while in private practice or nongovernmental employment, unless the appropriate government agency gives its informed consent, confirmed in writing; or

(ii) negotiate for private employment with any person who is involved as a party or as lawyer for a party in a matter in which the lawyer is participating personally and substantially, except that a lawyer serving as a law clerk to a judge, other adjudicative officer or arbitrator may negotiate for private employment as permitted by Rule 1.12(b) and subject to the conditions stated in Rule 1.12(b).

(e) As used in this Rule, the term "matter" includes:

(1) any judicial or other proceeding, application, request for a ruling or other determination, contract, claim, controversy, investigation, charge, accusation, arrest or other particular matter involving a specific party or parties, and

(2) any other matter covered by the conflict of interest rules of the appropriate government agency.

Comment

[1] A lawyer who has served or is currently serving as a public officer or employee is personally subject to the Rules of Professional Conduct, including the prohibition against concurrent conflicts of interest stated in Rule 1.7. In addition, such a lawyer may be subject to statutes and government regulations regarding conflict of interest. Such statutes and regulations may circumscribe the extent to which the government agency may give consent under this Rule. See Rule 1.0(e) for the definition of informed consent.

[2] Paragraphs (a)(1), (a)(2) and (d)(1) restate the obligations of an individual lawyer who has served or is currently serving as an officer or employee of the government toward a former government or private client. Rule 1.10 is not applicable to the conflicts of interest addressed by this Rule. Rather, paragraph (b) sets forth a special imputation rule for former government lawyers that provides for screening and notice. Because of the special problems raised by imputation within a government agency, paragraph (d) does not impute the conflicts of a lawyer currently serving as an officer or employee of the government to other associated government officers or employees, although ordinarily it will be prudent to screen such lawyers.

[3] Paragraphs (a)(2) and (d)(2) apply regardless of whether a lawyer is adverse to a former client and are thus designed not only to protect the former client, but also to prevent a lawyer from exploiting public office for the advantage of another client. For example, a lawyer who has pur-

sued a claim on behalf of the government may not pursue the same claim on behalf of a later private client after the lawyer has left government service, except when authorized to do so by the government agency under paragraph (a). Similarly, a lawyer who has pursued a claim on behalf of a private client may not pursue the claim on behalf of the government, except when authorized to do so by paragraph (d). As with paragraphs (a)(1) and (d)(1), Rule 1.10 is not applicable to the conflicts of interest addressed by these paragraphs.

[4] This Rule represents a balancing of interests. On the one hand, where the successive clients are a government agency and another client, public or private, the risk exists that power or discretion vested in that agency might be used for the special benefit of the other client. A lawyer should not be in a position where benefit to the other client might affect performance of the lawyer's professional functions on behalf of the government. Also, unfair advantage could accrue to the other client by reason of access to confidential government information about the client's adversary obtainable only through the lawyer's government service. On the other hand, the rules governing lawyers presently or formerly employed by a government agency should not be so restrictive as to inhibit transfer of employment to and from the government. The government has a legitimate need to attract qualified lawyers as well as to maintain high ethical standards. Thus a former government lawyer is disqualified only from particular matters in which the lawyer participated personally and substantially. The provisions for screening and waiver in paragraph (b) are necessary to prevent the disqualification rule from imposing too severe a deterrent against entering public service. The limitation of disqualification in paragraphs (a)(2) and (d)(2) to matters involving a specific party or parties, rather than extending disqualification to all substantive issues on which the lawyer worked, serves a similar function.

[5] When a lawyer has been employed by one government agency and then moves to a second government agency, it may be appropriate to treat that second agency as another client for purposes of this Rule, as when a lawyer is employed by a city and subsequently is employed by a federal agency. However, because the conflict of interest is governed by paragraph (d), the latter agency is not required to screen the lawyer as paragraph (b) requires a law firm to do. The question of whether two government agencies should be regarded as the same or different clients for conflict of interest purposes is beyond the scope of these Rules. See Rule 1.13 Comment [9].

[6] Paragraphs (b) and (c) contemplate a screening arrangement. See Rule 1.0(k) (requirements for screening procedures). These paragraphs do not prohibit a lawyer from receiving a salary or partnership share established by prior independent agreement, but that lawyer may not receive compensation directly relating the lawyer's compensation to the fee in the matter in which the lawyer is disqualified.

[7] Notice, including a description of the screened lawyer's prior representation and of the screening procedures employed, generally should be given as soon as practicable after the need for screening becomes apparent.

[8] Paragraph (c) operates only when the lawyer in question has knowledge of the information, which means actual knowledge; it does not operate with respect to information that merely could be imputed to the lawyer.

[9] Paragraphs (a) and (d) do not prohibit a lawyer from jointly representing a private party and a government agency when doing so is permitted by Rule 1.7 and is not otherwise prohibited by law.

[10] For purposes of paragraph (e) of this Rule, a "matter" may continue in another form. In determining whether two particular matters are the same, the lawyer should consider the extent to which the matters involve the same basic facts, the same or related parties, and the time elapsed.

Definitional Cross-References

"Confirmed in writing" *See* Rule 1.0(b)
"Firm" *See* Rule 1.0(c)
"Informed consent" *See* Rule 1.0(e)
"Knowingly" and "Knows" *See* Rule 1.0(f)
"Screened" *See* Rule 1.0(k)
"Written" *See* Rule 1.0(n)

RULE 1.12: FORMER JUDGE, ARBITRATOR, MEDIATOR OR OTHER THIRD-PARTY NEUTRAL

(a) Except as stated in paragraph (d), a lawyer shall not represent anyone in connection with a matter in which the lawyer participated personally and substantially as a judge or other adjudicative officer or law clerk to such a person or as an arbitrator, mediator or other third-party neutral, unless all parties to the proceeding give informed consent, confirmed in writing.

(b) A lawyer shall not negotiate for employment with any person who is involved as a party or as lawyer for a party in a matter in which the lawyer is participating personally and substantially as a judge or other adjudicative officer or as an arbitrator, mediator or other third-party neutral. A lawyer serving as a law clerk to a judge or other adjudicative officer may negotiate for employment with a party or lawyer involved in a matter in which the clerk is participating personally and substantially, but only after the lawyer has notified the judge or other adjudicative officer.

(c) If a lawyer is disqualified by paragraph (a), no lawyer in a firm with which that lawyer is associated may knowingly undertake or continue representation in the matter unless:

(1) the disqualified lawyer is timely screened from any participation in the matter and is apportioned no part of the fee therefrom; and

(2) written notice is promptly given to the parties and any appropriate tribunal to enable them to ascertain compliance with the provisions of this Rule.

(d) An arbitrator selected as a partisan of a party in a multimember arbitration panel is not prohibited from subsequently representing that party.

Comment

[1] This Rule generally parallels Rule 1.11. The term "personally and substantially" signifies that a judge who was a member of a multimember court, and thereafter left judicial office to practice law, is not prohibited from representing a client in a matter pending in the court, but in which the former judge did not participate. So also the fact that a former judge exercised administrative responsibility in a court does not prevent the former judge from acting as a lawyer in a matter where the judge had previously exercised remote or incidental administrative responsibility that did not affect the merits. Compare the Comment to Rule 1.11. The term "adjudicative officer" includes such officials as judges pro tempore, referees, special masters, hearing officers and other parajudicial officers, and also lawyers who serve as part-time judges. Paragraphs C(2), D(2) and E(2) of the Application Section of the Model Code of Judicial Con-

duct provide that a part-time judge, judge pro tempore or retired judge recalled to active service, shall not "act as a lawyer in a proceeding in which the judge has served as a judge or in any other proceeding related thereto." Although phrased differently from this Rule, those Rules correspond in meaning.

[2] Like former judges, lawyers who have served as arbitrators, mediators or other third-party neutrals may be asked to represent a client in a matter in which the lawyer participated personally and substantially. This Rule forbids such representation unless all of the parties to the proceedings give their informed consent, confirmed in writing. See Rule 1.0(e) and (b). Other law or codes of ethics governing third-party neutrals may impose more stringent standards of personal or imputed disqualification. See Rule 2.4.

[3] Although lawyers who serve as third-party neutrals do not have information concerning the parties that is protected under Rule 1.6, they typically owe the parties an obligation of confidentiality under law or codes of ethics governing third-party neutrals. Thus, paragraph (c) provides that conflicts of the personally disqualified lawyer will be imputed to other lawyers in a law firm unless the conditions of this paragraph are met.

[4] Requirements for screening procedures are stated in Rule 1.0(k). Paragraph (c)(1) does not prohibit the screened lawyer from receiving a salary or partnership share established by prior independent agreement, but that lawyer may not receive compensation directly related to the matter in which the lawyer is disqualified.

[5] Notice, including a description of the screened lawyer's prior representation and of the screening procedures employed, generally should be given as soon as practicable after the need for screening becomes apparent.

Definitional Cross-References

"Confirmed in writing" *See* Rule 1.0(b)
"Firm" *See* Rule 1.0(c)
"Informed consent" *See* Rule 1.0(e)
"Knowingly" *See* Rule 1.0(f)
"Screened" *See* Rule 1.0(k)
"Tribunal" *See* Rule 1.0(m)
"Writing" and "Written" *See* Rule 1.0(n)

RULE 1.13: ORGANIZATION AS CLIENT

(a) A lawyer employed or retained by an organization represents the organization acting through its duly authorized constituents.

(b) If a lawyer for an organization knows that an officer, employee or other person associated with the organization is engaged in action, intends to act or refuses to act in a matter related to the representation that is a violation of a legal obligation to the organization, or a violation of law that reasonably might be imputed to the organization, and that is likely to result in substantial injury to the organization, then the lawyer shall proceed as is reasonably necessary in the best interest of the organization. Unless the lawyer reasonably believes that it is not necessary in the best interest of the organization to do so, the lawyer shall refer the matter to higher authority in the organization, including, if warranted by the circumstances, to the highest authority that can act on behalf of the organization as determined by applicable law.

(c) Except as provided in paragraph (d), if

(1) despite the lawyer's efforts in accordance with paragraph (b) the highest authority that can act on behalf of the organization insists upon or fails to address in a timely and appropriate manner an action or a refusal to act, that is clearly a violation of law; and

(2) the lawyer reasonably believes that the violation is reasonably certain to result in substantial injury to the organization,

then the lawyer may reveal information relating to the representation whether or not Rule 1.6 permits such disclosure, but only if and to the extent the lawyer reasonably believes necessary to prevent substantial injury to the organization.

(d) Paragraph (c) shall not apply with respect to information relating to a lawyer's representation of an organization to investigate an alleged violation of law, or to defend the organization or an officer, employee or other constituent associated with the organization against a claim arising out of an alleged violation of law.

(e) A lawyer who reasonably believes that he or she has been discharged because of the lawyer's actions taken pursuant to paragraphs (b) or (c), or who withdraws under circumstances that require or permit the lawyer to take action under either of those paragraphs, shall proceed as the lawyer reasonably believes necessary to assure that the organization's highest authority is informed of the lawyer's discharge or withdrawal.

(f) In dealing with an organization's directors, officers, employees, members, shareholders or other constituents, a lawyer shall explain the identity of the client when the lawyer knows or reasonably should know that the organization's interests are adverse to those of the constituents with whom the lawyer is dealing.

(g) A lawyer representing an organization may also represent any of its directors, officers, employees, members, shareholders or other constituents, subject to the provisions of Rule 1.7. If the organization's consent to the dual representation is required by Rule 1.7, the consent shall be given by an appropriate official of the organization other than the individual who is to be represented, or by the shareholders.

Comment
The Entity as the Client

[1] An organizational client is a legal entity, but it cannot act except through its officers, directors, employees, shareholders and other constituents. Officers, directors, employees and shareholders are the constituents of the corporate organizational client. The duties defined in this Comment apply equally to unincorporated associations. "Other constituents" as used in this Comment means the positions equivalent to officers, directors, employees and shareholders held by persons acting for organizational clients that are not corporations.

[2] When one of the constituents of an organizational client communicates with the organization's lawyer in that person's organizational capacity, the communication is protected by Rule 1.6. Thus, by way of example, if an organizational client requests its lawyer to investigate allegations of wrongdoing, interviews made in the course of that investigation between the lawyer and the client's employees or other constituents are covered by Rule 1.6. This does not mean, however, that constituents of an organizational client are the clients of the lawyer. The lawyer may not disclose to such constituents information relating to the representation except for disclosures explicitly or impliedly authorized by the organizational client in order to carry out the representation or as otherwise permitted by Rule 1.6.

[3] When constituents of the organization make decisions for it, the decisions ordinarily must be accepted by the lawyer even if their utility or prudence is doubtful. Decisions concerning policy and operations, including ones entailing serious risk, are not as such in the lawyer's province. Paragraph (b) makes clear, however, that when the lawyer knows that the organization is likely to be substantially injured by action of an officer or other constituent that violates a legal obligation to the organization or is in violation of law that might be imputed to the organization, the lawyer must proceed as is reasonably necessary in the best interest of the organization. As defined in Rule 1.0(f), knowledge can be inferred from circumstances, and a lawyer cannot ignore the obvious.

[4] In determining how to proceed under paragraph (b), the lawyer should give due consideration to the seriousness of the violation and its consequences, the responsibility in the organization and the apparent motivation of the person involved, the policies of the organization concerning such matters, and any other relevant considerations. Ordinarily, referral to a higher authority would be necessary. In some circumstances, however, it may be appropriate for the lawyer to ask the constituent to reconsider the matter; for example, if the circumstances involve a constituent's innocent misunderstanding of law and subsequent acceptance of the lawyer's advice, the lawyer may reasonably conclude that the best interest of the organization does not require that the matter be referred to higher authority. If a constituent persists in conduct contrary to the lawyer's advice, it will be necessary for the lawyer to take steps to have the matter reviewed by a higher authority in the organization. If the matter is of sufficient seriousness and importance or urgency to the organization, referral to higher authority in the organization may be necessary even if the lawyer has not communicated with the constituent. Any measures taken should, to the extent practicable, minimize the risk of revealing information relating to the representation to persons outside the organization. Even in circumstances where a lawyer is not obligated by Rule 1.13 to proceed, a lawyer may bring to the attention of an organizational client, including its highest authority, matters that the lawyer reasonably believes to be of sufficient importance to warrant doing so in the best interest of the organization.

[5] Paragraph (b) also makes clear that when it is reasonably necessary to enable the organization to address the matter in a timely and appropriate manner, the lawyer must refer the matter to higher authority, including, if warranted by the circumstances, the highest authority that

can act on behalf of the organization under applicable law. The organization's highest authority to whom a matter may be referred ordinarily will be the board of directors or similar governing body. However, applicable law may prescribe that under certain conditions the highest authority reposes elsewhere, for example, in the independent directors of a corporation.

Relation to Other Rules

[6] The authority and responsibility provided in this Rule are concurrent with the authority and responsibility provided in other Rules. In particular, this Rule does not limit or expand the lawyer's responsibility under Rules 1.8, 1.16, 3.3 or 4.1. Paragraph (c) of this Rule supplements Rule 1.6(b) by providing an additional basis upon which the lawyer may reveal information relating to the representation, but does not modify, restrict, or limit the provisions of Rule 1.6(b)(1) – (6). Under paragraph (c) the lawyer may reveal such information only when the organization's highest authority insists upon or fails to address threatened or ongoing action that is clearly a violation of law, and then only to the extent the lawyer reasonably believes necessary to prevent reasonably certain substantial injury to the organization. It is not necessary that the lawyer's services be used in furtherance of the violation, but it is required that the matter be related to the lawyer's representation of the organization. If the lawyer's services are being used by an organization to further a crime or fraud by the organization, Rules 1.6(b)(2) and 1.6(b)(3) may permit the lawyer to disclose confidential information. In such circumstances Rule 1.2(d) may also be applicable, in which event, withdrawal from the representation under Rule 1.16(a)(1) may be required.

[7] Paragraph (d) makes clear that the authority of a lawyer to disclose information relating to a representation in circumstances described in paragraph (c) does not apply with respect to information relating to a lawyer's engagement by an organization to investigate an alleged violation of law or to defend the organization or an officer, employee or other person associated with the organization against a claim arising out of an alleged violation of law. This is necessary in order to enable organizational clients to enjoy the full benefits of legal counsel in conducting an investigation or defending against a claim.

[8] A lawyer who reasonably believes that he or she has been discharged because of the lawyer's actions taken pursuant to paragraph (b) or (c), or who withdraws in circumstances that require or permit the

lawyer to take action under either of these paragraphs, must proceed as the lawyer reasonably believes necessary to assure that the organization's highest authority is informed of the lawyer's discharge or withdrawal.

Government Agency

[9] The duty defined in this Rule applies to governmental organizations. Defining precisely the identity of the client and prescribing the resulting obligations of such lawyers may be more difficult in the government context and is a matter beyond the scope of these Rules. See Scope [18]. Although in some circumstances the client may be a specific agency, it may also be a branch of government, such as the executive branch, or the government as a whole. For example, if the action or failure to act involves the head of a bureau, either the department of which the bureau is a part or the relevant branch of government may be the client for purposes of this Rule. Moreover, in a matter involving the conduct of government officials, a government lawyer may have authority under applicable law to question such conduct more extensively than that of a lawyer for a private organization in similar circumstances. Thus, when the client is a governmental organization, a different balance may be appropriate between maintaining confidentiality and assuring that the wrongful act is prevented or rectified, for public business is involved. In addition, duties of lawyers employed by the government or lawyers in military service may be defined by statutes and regulation. This Rule does not limit that authority. See Scope.

Clarifying the Lawyer's Role

[10] There are times when the organization's interest may be or become adverse to those of one or more of its constituents. In such circumstances the lawyer should advise any constituent, whose interest the lawyer finds adverse to that of the organization of the conflict or potential conflict of interest, that the lawyer cannot represent such constituent, and that such person may wish to obtain independent representation. Care must be taken to assure that the individual understands that, when there is such adversity of interest, the lawyer for the organization cannot provide legal representation for that constituent individual, and that discussions between the lawyer for the organization and the individual may not be privileged.

[11] Whether such a warning should be given by the lawyer for the organization to any constituent individual may turn on the facts of each case.

Dual Representation

[12] Paragraph (g) recognizes that a lawyer for an organization may also represent a principal officer or major shareholder.

Derivative Actions

[13] Under generally prevailing law, the shareholders or members of a corporation may bring suit to compel the directors to perform their legal obligations in the supervision of the organization. Members of unincorporated associations have essentially the same right. Such an action may be brought nominally by the organization, but usually is, in fact, a legal controversy over management of the organization.

[14] The question can arise whether counsel for the organization may defend such an action. The proposition that the organization is the lawyer's client does not alone resolve the issue. Most derivative actions are a normal incident of an organization's affairs, to be defended by the organization's lawyer like any other suit. However, if the claim involves serious charges of wrongdoing by those in control of the organization, a conflict may arise between the lawyer's duty to the organization and the lawyer's relationship with the board. In those circumstances, Rule 1.7 governs who should represent the directors and the organization.

Definitional Cross-References

"Knows" *See* Rule 1.0(f)
"Reasonably" *See* Rule 1.0(h)
"Reasonably believes" *See* Rule 1.0(i)
"Reasonably should know" *See* Rule 1.0(j)
"Substantial" *See* Rule 1.0(l)

RULE 1.14: CLIENT WITH DIMINISHED CAPACITY

(a) When a client's capacity to make adequately considered decisions in connection with a representation is diminished, whether because of minority, mental impairment or for some other reason, the lawyer shall, as far as reasonably possible, maintain a normal client-lawyer relationship with the client.

(b) When the lawyer reasonably believes that the client has diminished capacity, is at risk of substantial physical, financial or other harm unless action is taken and cannot adequately act in the client's own interest, the lawyer may take reasonably necessary protective action, including consulting with individuals or entities that have the ability to take action to protect the client and, in appropriate cases, seeking the appointment of a guardian ad litem, conservator or guardian.

(c) Information relating to the representation of a client with diminished capacity is protected by Rule 1.6. When taking protective action pursuant to paragraph (b), the lawyer is impliedly authorized under Rule 1.6(a) to reveal information about the client, but only to the extent reasonably necessary to protect the client's interests.

Comment

[1] The normal client-lawyer relationship is based on the assumption that the client, when properly advised and assisted, is capable of making decisions about important matters. When the client is a minor or suffers from a diminished mental capacity, however, maintaining the ordinary client-lawyer relationship may not be possible in all respects. In particular, a severely incapacitated person may have no power to make legally binding decisions. Nevertheless, a client with diminished capacity often has the ability to understand, deliberate upon, and reach conclusions about matters affecting the client's own well-being. For example, children as young as five or six years of age, and certainly those of ten or twelve, are regarded as having opinions that are entitled to weight in legal proceedings concerning their custody. So also, it is recognized that some persons of advanced age can be quite capable of handling routine financial matters while needing special legal protection concerning major transactions.

[2] The fact that a client suffers a disability does not diminish the lawyer's obligation to treat the client with attention and respect. Even if the person has a legal representative, the lawyer should as far as possible accord the represented person the status of client, particularly in maintaining communication.

[3] The client may wish to have family members or other persons participate in discussions with the lawyer. When necessary to assist in the representation, the presence of such persons generally does not affect the applicability of the attorney-client evidentiary privilege. Nevertheless, the lawyer must keep the client's interests foremost and, except for protective action authorized under paragraph (b), must look to the client, and not family members, to make decisions on the client's behalf.

[4] If a legal representative has already been appointed for the client, the lawyer should ordinarily look to the representative for decisions

on behalf of the client. In matters involving a minor, whether the lawyer should look to the parents as natural guardians may depend on the type of proceeding or matter in which the lawyer is representing the minor. If the lawyer represents the guardian as distinct from the ward, and is aware that the guardian is acting adversely to the ward's interest, the lawyer may have an obligation to prevent or rectify the guardian's misconduct. See Rule 1.2(d).

Taking Protective Action

[5] If a lawyer reasonably believes that a client is at risk of substantial physical, financial or other harm unless action is taken, and that a normal client-lawyer relationship cannot be maintained as provided in paragraph (a) because the client lacks sufficient capacity to communicate or to make adequately considered decisions in connection with the representation, then paragraph (b) permits the lawyer to take protective measures deemed necessary. Such measures could include: consulting with family members, using a reconsideration period to permit clarification or improvement of circumstances, using voluntary surrogate decisionmaking tools such as durable powers of attorney or consulting with support groups, professional services, adult-protective agencies or other individuals or entities that have the ability to protect the client. In taking any protective action, the lawyer should be guided by such factors as the wishes and values of the client to the extent known, the client's best interests and the goals of intruding into the client's decisionmaking autonomy to the least extent feasible, maximizing client capacities and respecting the client's family and social connections.

[6] In determining the extent of the client's diminished capacity, the lawyer should consider and balance such factors as: the client's ability to articulate reasoning leading to a decision, variability of state of mind and ability to appreciate consequences of a decision; the substantive fairness of a decision; and the consistency of a decision with the known long-term commitments and values of the client. In appropriate circumstances, the lawyer may seek guidance from an appropriate diagnostician.

[7] If a legal representative has not been appointed, the lawyer should consider whether appointment of a guardian ad litem, conservator or guardian is necessary to protect the client's interests. Thus, if a client with diminished capacity has substantial property that should be sold for the client's benefit, effective completion of the transaction may require appointment of a legal representative. In addition, rules of pro-

cedure in litigation sometimes provide that minors or persons with diminished capacity must be represented by a guardian or next friend if they do not have a general guardian. In many circumstances, however, appointment of a legal representative may be more expensive or traumatic for the client than circumstances in fact require. Evaluation of such circumstances is a matter entrusted to the professional judgment of the lawyer. In considering alternatives, however, the lawyer should be aware of any law that requires the lawyer to advocate the least restrictive action on behalf of the client.

Disclosure of the Client's Condition

[8] Disclosure of the client's diminished capacity could adversely affect the client's interests. For example, raising the question of diminished capacity could, in some circumstances, lead to proceedings for involuntary commitment. Information relating to the representation is protected by Rule 1.6. Therefore, unless authorized to do so, the lawyer may not disclose such information. When taking protective action pursuant to paragraph (b), the lawyer is impliedly authorized to make the necessary disclosures, even when the client directs the lawyer to the contrary. Nevertheless, given the risks of disclosure, paragraph (c) limits what the lawyer may disclose in consulting with other individuals or entities or seeking the appointment of a legal representative. At the very least, the lawyer should determine whether it is likely that the person or entity consulted with will act adversely to the client's interests before discussing matters related to the client. The lawyer's position in such cases is an unavoidably difficult one.

Emergency Legal Assistance

[9] In an emergency where the health, safety or a financial interest of a person with seriously diminished capacity is threatened with imminent and irreparable harm, a lawyer may take legal action on behalf of such a person even though the person is unable to establish a client-lawyer relationship or to make or express considered judgments about the matter, when the person or another acting in good faith on that person's behalf has consulted with the lawyer. Even in such an emergency, however, the lawyer should not act unless the lawyer reasonably believes that the person has no other lawyer, agent or other representative available. The lawyer should take legal action on behalf of the person only to the extent reasonably necessary to maintain the status quo or otherwise avoid im-

minent and irreparable harm. A lawyer who undertakes to represent a person in such an exigent situation has the same duties under these Rules as the lawyer would with respect to a client.

[10] A lawyer who acts on behalf of a person with seriously diminished capacity in an emergency should keep the confidences of the person as if dealing with a client, disclosing them only to the extent necessary to accomplish the intended protective action. The lawyer should disclose to any tribunal involved and to any other counsel involved the nature of his or her relationship with the person. The lawyer should take steps to regularize the relationship or implement other protective solutions as soon as possible. Normally, a lawyer would not seek compensation for such emergency actions taken.

Definitional Cross-References
"Reasonably" *See* Rule 1.0(h)
"Reasonably believes" *See* Rule 1.0(i)
"Substantial" *See* Rule 1.0(l)

RULE 1.15: SAFEKEEPING PROPERTY

(a) A lawyer shall hold property of clients or third persons that is in a lawyer's possession in connection with a representation separate from the lawyer's own property. Funds shall be kept in a separate account maintained in the state where the lawyer's office is situated, or elsewhere with the consent of the client or third person. Other property shall be identified as such and appropriately safeguarded. Complete records of such account funds and other property shall be kept by the lawyer and shall be preserved for a period of [five years] after termination of the representation.

(b) A lawyer may deposit the lawyer's own funds in a client trust account for the sole purpose of paying bank service charges on that account, but only in an amount necessary for that purpose.

(c) A lawyer shall deposit into a client trust account legal fees and expenses that have been paid in advance, to be withdrawn by the lawyer only as fees are earned or expenses incurred.

(d) Upon receiving funds or other property in which a client or third person has an interest, a lawyer shall promptly notify the client or third person. Except as stated in this Rule or otherwise permitted by law or by agreement with the client, a lawyer shall promptly deliver to the client or third person any funds or other property that the client or third person is entitled to receive and, upon request by the client or third person, shall promptly render a full accounting regarding such property.

(e) When in the course of representation a lawyer is in possession of property in which two or more persons (one of whom may be the lawyer) claim interests, the property shall be kept separate by the lawyer until the dispute is resolved. The lawyer shall promptly distribute all portions of the property as to which the interests are not in dispute.

Comment

[1] A lawyer should hold property of others with the care required of a professional fiduciary. Securities should be kept in a safe deposit box, except when some other form of safekeeping is warranted by special circumstances. All property that is the property of clients or third persons, including prospective clients, must be kept separate from the lawyer's business and personal property and, if monies, in one or more trust accounts. Separate trust accounts may be warranted when administering estate monies or acting in similar fiduciary capacities. A lawyer should maintain on a current basis books and records in accordance with generally accepted accounting practice and comply with any recordkeeping rules established by law or court order. See, e.g., ABA Model Rules for Client Trust Account Records.

[2] While normally it is impermissible to commingle the lawyer's own funds with client funds, paragraph (b) provides that it is permissible when necessary to pay bank service charges on that account. Accurate records must be kept regarding which part of the funds are the lawyer's.

[3] Lawyers often receive funds from which the lawyer's fee will be paid. The lawyer is not required to remit to the client funds that the lawyer reasonably believes represent fees owed. However, a lawyer may not hold funds to coerce a client into accepting the lawyer's contention. The disputed portion of the funds must be kept in a trust account and the lawyer should suggest means for prompt resolution of the dispute, such as arbitration. The undisputed portion of the funds shall be promptly distributed.

[4] Paragraph (e) also recognizes that third parties may have lawful claims against specific funds or other property in a lawyer's custody, such as a client's creditor who has a lien on funds recovered in a personal injury action. A lawyer may have a duty under applicable law to protect such third-party claims against wrongful interference by the client. In

such cases, when the third-party claim is not frivolous under applicable law, the lawyer must refuse to surrender the property to the client until the claims are resolved. A lawyer should not unilaterally assume to arbitrate a dispute between the client and the third party, but, when there are substantial grounds for dispute as to the person entitled to the funds, the lawyer may file an action to have a court resolve the dispute.

[5] The obligations of a lawyer under this Rule are independent of those arising from activity other than rendering legal services. For example, a lawyer who serves only as an escrow agent is governed by the applicable law relating to fiduciaries even though the lawyer does not render legal services in the transaction and is not governed by this Rule.

[6] A lawyers' fund for client protection provides a means through the collective efforts of the bar to reimburse persons who have lost money or property as a result of dishonest conduct of a lawyer. Where such a fund has been established, a lawyer must participate where it is mandatory, and, even when it is voluntary, the lawyer should participate.

RULE 1.16: DECLINING OR TERMINATING REPRESENTATION

(a) A lawyer shall inquire into and assess the facts and circumstances of each representation to determine whether the lawyer may accept or continue the representation. Except as stated in paragraph (c), a lawyer shall not represent a client or, where representation has commenced, shall withdraw from the representation of a client if:

(1) the representation will result in violation of the Rules of Professional Conduct or other law;

(2) the lawyer's physical or mental condition materially impairs the lawyer's ability to represent the client;

(3) the lawyer is discharged; or

(4) the client or prospective client seeks to use or persists in using the lawyer's services to commit or further a crime or fraud, despite the lawyer's discussion pursuant to Rules 1.2(d) and 1.4(a)(5) regarding the limitations on the lawyer assisting with the proposed conduct.

(b) Except as stated in paragraph (c), a lawyer may withdraw from representing a client if:

(1) withdrawal can be accomplished without material adverse effect on the interests of the client;

(2) the client persists in a course of action involving the lawyer's services that the lawyer reasonably believes is criminal or fraudulent;

(3) the client has used the lawyer's services to perpetrate a crime or fraud;

(4) the client insists upon taking action that the lawyer considers repugnant or with which the lawyer has a fundamental disagreement;

(5) the client fails substantially to fulfill an obligation to the lawyer regarding the lawyer's services and has been given reasonable warning that the lawyer will withdraw unless the obligation is fulfilled;

(6) the representation will result in an unreasonable financial burden on the lawyer or has been rendered unreasonably difficult by the client; or

(7) other good cause for withdrawal exists.

(c) A lawyer must comply with applicable law requiring notice to or permission of a tribunal when terminating a representation. When ordered to do so by a tribunal, a lawyer shall continue representation notwithstanding good cause for terminating the representation.

(d) Upon termination of representation, a lawyer shall take steps to the extent reasonably practicable to protect a client's interests, such as giving reasonable notice to the client, allowing time for employment of other counsel, surrendering papers and property to which the client is entitled and refunding any advance payment of fee or expense that has not been earned or incurred. The lawyer may retain papers relating to the client to the extent permitted by other law.

Comment

[1] Paragraph (a) imposes an obligation on a lawyer to inquire into and assess the facts and circumstances of the representation before accepting it. The obligation imposed by Paragraph (a) continues throughout the representation. A change in the facts and circumstances relating to the representation may trigger a lawyer's need to make further inquiry and assessment. For example, a client traditionally uses a lawyer to acquire local real estate through the use of domestic limited liability companies, with financing from a local bank. The same client then asks the lawyer to create a multi-tier corporate structure, formed in another state

to acquire property in a third jurisdiction, and requests to route the transaction's funding through the lawyer's trust account. Another example is when, during the course of a representation, a new party is named or a new entity becomes involved. A lawyer should not accept representation in a matter unless it can be performed competently, promptly, without improper conflict of interest and to completion. Ordinarily, a representation in a matter is completed when the agreed-upon assistance has been concluded. See Rules 1.1, 1.2(c) and 6.5. See also Rule 1.3, Comment [4].

Mandatory Withdrawal

[2] A lawyer ordinarily must decline or withdraw from representation if the client demands that the lawyer engage in conduct that is illegal or violates the Rules of Professional Conduct or other law. The lawyer is not obliged to decline or withdraw simply because the client suggests such a course of conduct; a client may make such a suggestion in the hope that a lawyer will not be constrained by a professional obligation. Under paragraph (a)(4), the lawyer's inquiry into and assessment of the facts and circumstances will be informed by the risk that the client or prospective client seeks to use or persists in using the lawyer's services to commit or further a crime or fraud. This analysis means that the required level of a lawyer's inquiry and assessment will vary for each client or prospective client, depending on the nature of the risk posed by each situation. Factors to be considered in determining the level of risk may include: (i) the identity of the client, such as whether the client is a natural person or an entity and, if an entity, the beneficial owners of that entity, (ii) the lawyer's experience and familiarity with the client, (iii) the nature of the requested legal services, (iv) the relevant jurisdictions involved in the representation (for example, whether a jurisdiction is considered at high risk for money laundering or terrorist financing), and (v) the identities of those depositing into or receiving funds from the lawyer's client trust account, or any other accounts in which client funds are held. For further guidance assessing risk, see, e.g., as amended or updated, Financial Action Task Force Guidance for a Risk-Based Approach for Legal Professionals, the ABA Voluntary Good Practices Guidance for Lawyers to Detect and Combat Money Laundering and Terrorist Financing, A Lawyer's Guide to Detecting and Preventing Money Laundering (a collaborative publication of the International Bar Association, the American Bar Association and the Council of Bars and Law Societies of Europe), the Organization for Economic Cooperation and Development (OECD) Due Diligence Guidance for Responsible Business Conduct, and the U.S.

Department of Treasury Specially Designated Nationals and Blocked Persons List.

[3] When a lawyer has been appointed to represent a client, withdrawal ordinarily requires approval of the appointing authority. See also Rule 6.2. Similarly, court approval or notice to the court is often required by applicable law before a lawyer withdraws from pending litigation. Difficulty may be encountered if withdrawal is based on the client's demand that the lawyer engage in unprofessional conduct. The court may request an explanation for the withdrawal, while the lawyer may be bound to keep confidential the facts that would constitute such an explanation. The lawyer's statement that professional considerations require termination of the representation ordinarily should be accepted as sufficient. Lawyers should be mindful of their obligations to both clients and the court under Rules 1.6 and 3.3.

Discharge

[4] A client has a right to discharge a lawyer at any time, with or without cause, subject to liability for payment for the lawyer's services. Where future dispute about the withdrawal may be anticipated, it may be advisable to prepare a written statement reciting the circumstances.

[5] Whether a client can discharge appointed counsel may depend on applicable law. A client seeking to do so should be given a full explanation of the consequences. These consequences may include a decision by the appointing authority that appointment of successor counsel is unjustified, thus requiring self-representation by the client.

[6] If the client has severely diminished capacity, the client may lack the legal capacity to discharge the lawyer, and in any event the discharge may be seriously adverse to the client's interests. The lawyer should make special effort to help the client consider the consequences and may take reasonably necessary protective action as provided in Rule 1.14.

Optional Withdrawal

[7] A lawyer may withdraw from representation in some circumstances. The lawyer has the option to withdraw if it can be accomplished without material adverse effect on the client's interests. Withdrawal is also justified if the client persists in a course of action that the lawyer reasonably believes is criminal or fraudulent, for a lawyer is not required to be associated with such conduct even if the lawyer does not further it. Withdrawal is also permitted if the lawyer's services were misused in the past even if that would materially prejudice the client. The law-

yer may also withdraw where the client insists on taking action that the lawyer considers repugnant or with which the lawyer has a fundamental disagreement.

[8] A lawyer may withdraw if the client refuses to abide by the terms of an agreement relating to the representation, such as an agreement concerning fees or court costs or an agreement limiting the objectives of the representation.

Assisting the Client upon Withdrawal

[9] Even if the lawyer has been unfairly discharged by the client, a lawyer must take all reasonable steps to mitigate the consequences to the client. The lawyer may retain papers as security for a fee only to the extent permitted by law. See Rule 1.15.

Definitional Cross-References

"Fraud" and "Fraudulent" *See* Rule 1.0(d)
"Reasonable" *See* Rule 1.0(h)
"Reasonably believes" *See* Rule 1.0(i)
"Tribunal" *See* Rule 1.0(m)

RULE 1.17: SALE OF LAW PRACTICE

A lawyer or a law firm may sell or purchase a law practice, or an area of law practice, including good will, if the following conditions are satisfied:

(a) The seller ceases to engage in the private practice of law, or in the area of practice that has been sold, [in the geographic area] [in the jurisdiction] (a jurisdiction may elect either version) in which the practice has been conducted;

(b) The entire practice, or the entire area of practice, is sold to one or more lawyers or law firms;

(c) The seller gives written notice to each of the seller's clients regarding:

(1) the proposed sale;

(2) the client's right to retain other counsel or to take possession of the file; and

(3) the fact that the client's consent to the transfer of the client's files will be presumed if the client does not take any

action or does not otherwise object within ninety (90) days of receipt of the notice.

If a client cannot be given notice, the representation of that client may be transferred to the purchaser only upon entry of an order so authorizing by a court having jurisdiction. The seller may disclose to the court in camera information relating to the representation only to the extent necessary to obtain an order authorizing the transfer of a file.

(d) The fees charged clients shall not be increased by reason of the sale.

Comment

[1] The practice of law is a profession, not merely a business. Clients are not commodities that can be purchased and sold at will. Pursuant to this Rule, when a lawyer or an entire firm ceases to practice, or ceases to practice in an area of law, and other lawyers or firms take over the representation, the selling lawyer or firm may obtain compensation for the reasonable value of the practice as may withdrawing partners of law firms. See Rules 5.4 and 5.6.

Termination of Practice by the Seller

[2] The requirement that all of the private practice, or all of an area of practice, be sold is satisfied if the seller in good faith makes the entire practice, or the area of practice, available for sale to the purchasers. The fact that a number of the seller's clients decide not to be represented by the purchasers but take their matters elsewhere, therefore, does not result in a violation. Return to private practice as a result of an unanticipated change in circumstances does not necessarily result in a violation. For example, a lawyer who has sold the practice to accept an appointment to judicial office does not violate the requirement that the sale be attendant to cessation of practice if the lawyer later resumes private practice upon being defeated in a contested or a retention election for the office or resigns from a judiciary position.

[3] The requirement that the seller cease to engage in the private practice of law does not prohibit employment as a lawyer on the staff of a public agency or a legal services entity that provides legal services to the poor, or as in-house counsel to a business.

[4] The Rule permits a sale of an entire practice attendant upon retirement from the private practice of law within the jurisdiction. Its pro-

visions, therefore, accommodate the lawyer who sells the practice on the occasion of moving to another state. Some states are so large that a move from one locale therein to another is tantamount to leaving the jurisdiction in which the lawyer has engaged in the practice of law. To also accommodate lawyers so situated, states may permit the sale of the practice when the lawyer leaves the geographical area rather than the jurisdiction. The alternative desired should be indicated by selecting one of the two provided for in Rule 1.17(a).

[5] This Rule also permits a lawyer or law firm to sell an area of practice. If an area of practice is sold and the lawyer remains in the active practice of law, the lawyer must cease accepting any matters in the area of practice that has been sold, either as counsel or co-counsel or by assuming joint responsibility for a matter in connection with the division of a fee with another lawyer as would otherwise be permitted by Rule 1.5(e). For example, a lawyer with a substantial number of estate planning matters and a substantial number of probate administration cases may sell the estate planning portion of the practice but remain in the practice of law by concentrating on probate administration; however, that practitioner may not thereafter accept any estate planning matters. Although a lawyer who leaves a jurisdiction or geographical area typically would sell the entire practice, this Rule permits the lawyer to limit the sale to one or more areas of the practice, thereby preserving the lawyer's right to continue practice in the areas of the practice that were not sold.

Sale of Entire Practice or Entire Area of Practice

[6] The Rule requires that the seller's entire practice, or an entire area of practice, be sold. The prohibition against sale of less than an entire practice area protects those clients whose matters are less lucrative and who might find it difficult to secure other counsel if a sale could be limited to substantial fee-generating matters. The purchasers are required to undertake all client matters in the practice or practice area, subject to client consent. This requirement is satisfied, however, even if a purchaser is unable to undertake a particular client matter because of a conflict of interest.

Client Confidences, Consent and Notice

[7] Negotiations between seller and prospective purchaser prior to disclosure of information relating to a specific representation of an identifiable client no more violate the confidentiality provisions of Model

Rule 1.6 than do preliminary discussions concerning the possible association of another lawyer or mergers between firms, with respect to which client consent is not required. See Rule 1.6(b)(7). Providing the purchaser access to detailed information relating to the representation, such as the client's file, however, requires client consent. The Rule provides that before such information can be disclosed by the seller to the purchaser the client must be given actual written notice of the contemplated sale, including the identity of the purchaser, and must be told that the decision to consent or make other arrangements must be made within 90 days. If nothing is heard from the client within that time, consent to the sale is presumed.

[8] A lawyer or law firm ceasing to practice cannot be required to remain in practice because some clients cannot be given actual notice of the proposed purchase. Since these clients cannot themselves consent to the purchase or direct any other disposition of their files, the Rule requires an order from a court having jurisdiction authorizing their transfer or other disposition. The court can be expected to determine whether reasonable efforts to locate the client have been exhausted, and whether the absent client's legitimate interests will be served by authorizing the transfer of the file so that the purchaser may continue the representation. Preservation of client confidences requires that the petition for a court order be considered in camera. (A procedure by which such an order can be obtained needs to be established in jurisdictions in which it presently does not exist).

[9] All elements of client autonomy, including the client's absolute right to discharge a lawyer and transfer the representation to another, survive the sale of the practice or area of practice.

Fee Arrangements Between Client and Purchaser

[10] The sale may not be financed by increases in fees charged the clients of the practice. Existing arrangements between the seller and the client as to fees and the scope of the work must be honored by the purchaser.

Other Applicable Ethical Standards

[11] Lawyers participating in the sale of a law practice or a practice area are subject to the ethical standards applicable to involving another lawyer in the representation of a client. These include, for example, the seller's obligation to exercise competence in identifying a purchaser qualified to assume the practice and the purchaser's obligation to undertake the representation competently (see Rule 1.1); the obligation to avoid dis-

qualifying conflicts, and to secure the client's informed consent for those conflicts that can be agreed to (see Rule 1.7 regarding conflicts and Rule 1.0(e) for the definition of informed consent); and the obligation to protect information relating to the representation (see Rules 1.6 and 1.9).

[12] If approval of the substitution of the purchasing lawyer for the selling lawyer is required by the rules of any tribunal in which a matter is pending, such approval must be obtained before the matter can be included in the sale (see Rule 1.16).

Applicability of the Rule

[13] This Rule applies to the sale of a law practice of a deceased, disabled or disappeared lawyer. Thus, the seller may be represented by a non-lawyer representative not subject to these Rules. Since, however, no lawyer may participate in a sale of a law practice which does not conform to the requirements of this Rule, the representatives of the seller as well as the purchasing lawyer can be expected to see to it that they are met.

[14] Admission to or retirement from a law partnership or professional association, retirement plans and similar arrangements, and a sale of tangible assets of a law practice, do not constitute a sale or purchase governed by this Rule.

[15] This Rule does not apply to the transfers of legal representation between lawyers when such transfers are unrelated to the sale of a practice or an area of practice.

Definitional Cross-References

"Law firm" *See* Rule 1.0(c)
"Written" *See* Rule 1.0(n)

RULE 1.18: DUTIES TO PROSPECTIVE CLIENT

(a) A person who consults with a lawyer about the possibility of forming a client-lawyer relationship with respect to a matter is a prospective client.

(b) Even when no client-lawyer relationship ensues, a lawyer who has learned information from a prospective client shall not use or reveal that information, except as Rule 1.9 would permit with respect to information of a former client.

(c) A lawyer subject to paragraph (b) shall not represent a client with interests materially adverse to those of a prospective client in the same or a substantially related matter if the lawyer received information from the prospective client that could be significantly harmful to that person in the matter, except as provided in paragraph (d). If a lawyer is disqualified from representation under this paragraph, no lawyer in a firm with which that lawyer is associated may knowingly undertake or continue representation in such a matter, except as provided in paragraph (d).

(d) When the lawyer has received disqualifying information as defined in paragraph (c), representation is permissible if:

(1) both the affected client and the prospective client have given informed consent, confirmed in writing; or:

(2) the lawyer who received the information took reasonable measures to avoid exposure to more disqualifying information than was reasonably necessary to determine whether to represent the prospective client; and

(i) the disqualified lawyer is timely screened from any participation in the matter and is apportioned no part of the fee therefrom; and

(ii) written notice is promptly given to the prospective client.

Comment

[1] Prospective clients, like clients, may disclose information to a lawyer, place documents or other property in the lawyer's custody, or rely on the lawyer's advice. A lawyer's consultations with a prospective client usually are limited in time and depth and leave both the prospective client and the lawyer free (and sometimes required) to proceed no further. Hence, prospective clients should receive some but not all of the protection afforded clients.

[2] A person becomes a prospective client by consulting with a lawyer about the possibility of forming a client-lawyer relationship with respect to a matter. Whether communications, including written, oral, or electronic communications, constitute a consultation depends on the circumstances. For example, a consultation is likely to have occurred if a lawyer, either in person or through the lawyer's advertising in any medium, specifically requests or invites the submission of information about a potential representation without clear and reasonably understandable warnings and cautionary statements that limit the lawyer's obligations, and a person provides information in response. See also Comment [4]. In contrast, a consultation does not occur if a person provides information to a lawyer in response to advertising that merely describes the lawyer's education, experience, areas of practice, and contact information, or pro-

vides legal information of general interest. Such a person communicates information unilaterally to a lawyer, without any reasonable expectation that the lawyer is willing to discuss the possibility of forming a client-lawyer relationship, and is thus not a "prospective client." Moreover, a person who communicates with a lawyer for the purpose of disqualifying the lawyer is not a "prospective client."

[3] It is often necessary for a prospective client to reveal information to the lawyer during an initial consultation prior to the decision about formation of a client-lawyer relationship. The lawyer often must learn such information to determine whether there is a conflict of interest with an existing client and whether the matter is one that the lawyer is willing to undertake. Paragraph (b) prohibits the lawyer from using or revealing that information, except as permitted by Rule 1.9, even if the client or lawyer decides not to proceed with the representation. The duty exists regardless of how brief the initial conference may be.

[4] In order to avoid acquiring disqualifying information from a prospective client, a lawyer considering whether or not to undertake a new matter should limit the initial consultation to only such information as reasonably appears necessary for that purpose. Where the information indicates that a conflict of interest or other reason for non-representation exists, the lawyer should so inform the prospective client or decline the representation. If the prospective client wishes to retain the lawyer, and if consent is possible under Rule 1.7, then consent from all affected present or former clients must be obtained before accepting the representation.

[5] A lawyer may condition a consultation with a prospective client on the person's informed consent that no information disclosed during the consultation will prohibit the lawyer from representing a different client in the matter. See Rule 1.0(e) for the definition of informed consent. If the agreement expressly so provides, the prospective client may also consent to the lawyer's subsequent use of information received from the prospective client.

[6] Even in the absence of an agreement, under paragraph (c), the lawyer is not prohibited from representing a client with interests adverse to those of the prospective client in the same or a substantially related matter unless the lawyer has received from the prospective client information that could be significantly harmful if used in the matter.

[7] Under paragraph (c), the prohibition in this Rule is imputed to other lawyers as provided in Rule 1.10, but, under paragraph (d)(1), imputation may be avoided if the lawyer obtains the informed consent, confirmed in writing, of both the prospective and affected clients. In the

alternative, imputation may be avoided if the conditions of paragraph (d)(2) are met and all disqualified lawyers are timely screened and written notice is promptly given to the prospective client. See Rule 1.0(k) (requirements for screening procedures). Paragraph (d)(2)(i) does not prohibit the screened lawyer from receiving a salary or partnership share established by prior independent agreement, but that lawyer may not receive compensation directly related to the matter in which the lawyer is disqualified.

[8] Notice, including a general description of the subject matter about which the lawyer was consulted, and of the screening procedures employed, generally should be given as soon as practicable after the need for screening becomes apparent.

[9] For the duty of competence of a lawyer who gives assistance on the merits of a matter to a prospective client, see Rule 1.1. For a lawyer's duties when a prospective client entrusts valuables or papers to the lawyer's care, see Rule 1.15.

Definitional Cross-References

"Confirmed in writing" *See* Rule 1.0(b)
"Firm" *See* Rule 1.0(c)
"Informed consent" *See* Rule 1.0(e)
"Knowingly" *See* Rule 1.0(f)
"Reasonable" and "Reasonably" *See* Rule 1.0(h)
"Screened" *See* Rule 1.0(k)
"Written" *See* Rule 1.0(n)

COUNSELOR

RULE 2.1: ADVISOR

In representing a client, a lawyer shall exercise independent professional judgment and render candid advice. In rendering advice, a lawyer may refer not only to law but to other considerations such as moral, economic, social and political factors, that may be relevant to the client's situation.

Comment

Scope of Advice

[1] A client is entitled to straightforward advice expressing the lawyer's honest assessment. Legal advice often involves unpleasant facts

and alternatives that a client may be disinclined to confront. In presenting advice, a lawyer endeavors to sustain the client's morale and may put advice in as acceptable a form as honesty permits. However, a lawyer should not be deterred from giving candid advice by the prospect that the advice will be unpalatable to the client.

[2] Advice couched in narrow legal terms may be of little value to a client, especially where practical considerations, such as cost or effects on other people, are predominant. Purely technical legal advice, therefore, can sometimes be inadequate. It is proper for a lawyer to refer to relevant moral and ethical considerations in giving advice. Although a lawyer is not a moral advisor as such, moral and ethical considerations impinge upon most legal questions and may decisively influence how the law will be applied.

[3] A client may expressly or impliedly ask the lawyer for purely technical advice. When such a request is made by a client experienced in legal matters, the lawyer may accept it at face value. When such a request is made by a client inexperienced in legal matters, however, the lawyer's responsibility as advisor may include indicating that more may be involved than strictly legal considerations.

[4] Matters that go beyond strictly legal questions may also be in the domain of another profession. Family matters can involve problems within the professional competence of psychiatry, clinical psychology or social work; business matters can involve problems within the competence of the accounting profession or of financial specialists. Where consultation with a professional in another field is itself something a competent lawyer would recommend, the lawyer should make such a recommendation. At the same time, a lawyer's advice at its best often consists of recommending a course of action in the face of conflicting recommendations of experts.

Offering Advice

[5] In general, a lawyer is not expected to give advice until asked by the client. However, when a lawyer knows that a client proposes a course of action that is likely to result in substantial adverse legal consequences to the client, the lawyer's duty to the client under Rule 1.4 may require that the lawyer offer advice if the client's course of action is related to the representation. Similarly, when a matter is likely to involve litigation, it may be necessary under Rule 1.4 to inform the client of forms of dispute resolution that might constitute reasonable alternatives to litigation. A

lawyer ordinarily has no duty to initiate investigation of a client's affairs or to give advice that the client has indicated is unwanted, but a lawyer may initiate advice to a client when doing so appears to be in the client's interest.

RULE 2.2 (DELETED 2002)

RULE 2.3: EVALUATION FOR USE BY THIRD PERSONS

(a) A lawyer may provide an evaluation of a matter affecting a client for the use of someone other than the client if the lawyer reasonably believes that making the evaluation is compatible with other aspects of the lawyer's relationship with the client.

(b) When the lawyer knows or reasonably should know that the evaluation is likely to affect the client's interests materially and adversely, the lawyer shall not provide the evaluation unless the client gives informed consent.

(c) Except as disclosure is authorized in connection with a report of an evaluation, information relating to the evaluation is otherwise protected by Rule 1.6.

Comment

Definition

[1] An evaluation may be performed at the client's direction or when impliedly authorized in order to carry out the representation. See Rule 1.2. Such an evaluation may be for the primary purpose of establishing information for the benefit of third parties; for example, an opinion concerning the title of property rendered at the behest of a vendor for the information of a prospective purchaser, or at the behest of a borrower for the information of a prospective lender. In some situations, the evaluation may be required by a government agency; for example, an opinion concerning the legality of the securities registered for sale under the securities laws. In other instances, the evaluation may be required by a third person, such as a purchaser of a business.

[2] A legal evaluation should be distinguished from an investigation of a person with whom the lawyer does not have a client-lawyer relationship. For example, a lawyer retained by a purchaser to analyze a

vendor's title to property does not have a client-lawyer relationship with the vendor. So also, an investigation into a person's affairs by a government lawyer or by special counsel employed by the government, is not an evaluation as that term is used in this Rule. The question is whether the lawyer is retained by the person whose affairs are being examined. When the lawyer is retained by that person, the general rules concerning loyalty to client and preservation of confidences apply, which is not the case if the lawyer is retained by someone else. For this reason, it is essential to identify the person by whom the lawyer is retained. This should be made clear not only to the person under examination, but also to others to whom the results are to be made available.

Duties Owed to Third Person and Client

[3] When the evaluation is intended for the information or use of a third person, a legal duty to that person may or may not arise. That legal question is beyond the scope of this Rule. However, since such an evaluation involves a departure from the normal client-lawyer relationship, careful analysis of the situation is required. The lawyer must be satisfied as a matter of professional judgment that making the evaluation is compatible with other functions undertaken in behalf of the client. For example, if the lawyer is acting as advocate in defending the client against charges of fraud, it would normally be incompatible with that responsibility for the lawyer to perform an evaluation for others concerning the same or a related transaction. Assuming no such impediment is apparent, however, the lawyer should advise the client of the implications of the evaluation, particularly the lawyer's responsibilities to third persons and the duty to disseminate the findings.

Access to and Disclosure of Information

[4] The quality of an evaluation depends on the freedom and extent of the investigation upon which it is based. Ordinarily a lawyer should have whatever latitude of investigation seems necessary as a matter of professional judgment. Under some circumstances, however, the terms of the evaluation may be limited. For example, certain issues or sources may be categorically excluded, or the scope of search may be limited by time constraints or the noncooperation of persons having relevant information. Any such limitations that are material to the evaluation should be described in the report. If after a lawyer has commenced an evaluation, the client refuses to comply with the terms upon which it was un-

derstood the evaluation was to have been made, the lawyer's obligations are determined by law, having reference to the terms of the client's agreement and the surrounding circumstances. In no circumstances is the lawyer permitted to knowingly make a false statement of material fact or law in providing an evaluation under this Rule. See Rule 4.1.

Obtaining Client's Informed Consent

[5] Information relating to an evaluation is protected by Rule 1.6. In many situations, providing an evaluation to a third party poses no significant risk to the client; thus, the lawyer may be impliedly authorized to disclose information to carry out the representation. See Rule 1.6(a). Where, however, it is reasonably likely that providing the evaluation will affect the client's interests materially and adversely, the lawyer must first obtain the client's consent after the client has been adequately informed concerning the important possible effects on the client's interests. See Rules 1.6(a) and 1.0(e).

Financial Auditors' Requests for Information

[6] When a question concerning the legal situation of a client arises at the instance of the client's financial auditor and the question is referred to the lawyer, the lawyer's response may be made in accordance with procedures recognized in the legal profession. Such a procedure is set forth in the American Bar Association Statement of Policy Regarding Lawyers' Responses to Auditors' Requests for Information, adopted in 1975.

Definitional Cross-References
"Informed consent" *See* Rule 1.0(e)
"Knows" *See* Rule 1.0(f)
"Reasonably believes" *See* Rule 1.0(i)
"Reasonably should know" *See* Rule 1.0(j)

RULE 2.4: LAWYER SERVING AS THIRD-PARTY NEUTRAL

(a) A lawyer serves as a third-party neutral when the lawyer assists two or more persons who are not clients of the lawyer to reach a resolution of a dispute or other matter that has arisen between them. Service as a third-party neutral may include service as an arbitrator, a mediator or in such other capacity as will enable the lawyer to assist the parties to resolve the matter.

(b) A lawyer serving as a third-party neutral shall inform unrepresented parties that the lawyer is not representing them. When the lawyer knows or reasonably should know that a party does not understand the lawyer's role in the matter, the lawyer shall explain the difference between the lawyer's role as a third-party neutral and a lawyer's role as one who represents a client.

Comment

[1] Alternative dispute resolution has become a substantial part of the civil justice system. Aside from representing clients in dispute-resolution processes, lawyers often serve as third-party neutrals. A third-party neutral is a person, such as a mediator, arbitrator, conciliator or evaluator, who assists the parties, represented or unrepresented, in the resolution of a dispute or in the arrangement of a transaction. Whether a third-party neutral serves primarily as a facilitator, evaluator or decisionmaker depends on the particular process that is either selected by the parties or mandated by a court.

[2] The role of a third-party neutral is not unique to lawyers, although, in some court-connected contexts, only lawyers are allowed to serve in this role or to handle certain types of cases. In performing this role, the lawyer may be subject to court rules or other law that apply either to third-party neutrals generally or to lawyers serving as third-party neutrals. Lawyer-neutrals may also be subject to various codes of ethics, such as the Code of Ethics for Arbitrators in Commercial Disputes prepared by a joint committee of the American Bar Association and the American Arbitration Association or the Model Standards of Conduct for Mediators jointly prepared by the American Bar Association, the American Arbitration Association and the Society of Professionals in Dispute Resolution.

[3] Unlike nonlawyers who serve as third-party neutrals, lawyers serving in this role may experience unique problems as a result of differences between the role of a third-party neutral and a lawyer's service as a client representative. The potential for confusion is significant when the parties are unrepresented in the process. Thus, paragraph (b) requires a lawyer-neutral to inform unrepresented parties that the lawyer is not representing them. For some parties, particularly parties who frequently use dispute-resolution processes, this information will be sufficient. For others, particularly those who are using the process for the first time, more information will be required. Where appropriate, the lawyer should inform unrepresented parties of the important differences between the

lawyer's role as third-party neutral and a lawyer's role as a client representative, including the inapplicability of the attorney-client evidentiary privilege. The extent of disclosure required under this paragraph will depend on the particular parties involved and the subject matter of the proceeding, as well as the particular features of the dispute-resolution process selected.

[4] A lawyer who serves as a third-party neutral subsequently may be asked to serve as a lawyer representing a client in the same matter. The conflicts of interest that arise for both the individual lawyer and the lawyer's law firm are addressed in Rule 1.12.

[5] Lawyers who represent clients in alternative dispute-resolution processes are governed by the Rules of Professional Conduct. When the dispute-resolution process takes place before a tribunal, as in binding arbitration (see Rule 1.0(m)), the lawyer's duty of candor is governed by Rule 3.3. Otherwise, the lawyer's duty of candor toward both the third-party neutral and other parties is governed by Rule 4.1.

Definitional Cross-References

"Knows" *See* Rule 1.0(f)
"Reasonably should know" *See* Rule 1.0(j)

ADVOCATE

RULE 3.1: MERITORIOUS CLAIMS AND CONTENTIONS

A lawyer shall not bring or defend a proceeding, or assert or controvert an issue therein, unless there is a basis in law and fact for doing so that is not frivolous, which includes a good faith argument for an extension, modification or reversal of existing law. A lawyer for the defendant in a criminal proceeding, or the respondent in a proceeding that could result in incarceration, may nevertheless so defend the proceeding as to require that every element of the case be established.

Comment

[1] The advocate has a duty to use legal procedure for the fullest benefit of the client's cause, but also a duty not to abuse legal procedure. The law, both procedural and substantive, establishes the limits within which an advocate may proceed. However, the law is not always clear and

never is static. Accordingly, in determining the proper scope of advocacy, account must be taken of the law's ambiguities and potential for change.

[2] The filing of an action or defense or similar action taken for a client is not frivolous merely because the facts have not first been fully substantiated or because the lawyer expects to develop vital evidence only by discovery. What is required of lawyers, however, is that they inform themselves about the facts of their clients' cases and the applicable law and determine that they can make good faith arguments in support of their clients' positions. Such action is not frivolous even though the lawyer believes that the client's position ultimately will not prevail. The action is frivolous, however, if the lawyer is unable either to make a good faith argument on the merits of the action taken or to support the action taken by a good faith argument for an extension, modification or reversal of existing law.

[3] The lawyer's obligations under this Rule are subordinate to federal or state constitutional law that entitles a defendant in a criminal matter to the assistance of counsel in presenting a claim or contention that otherwise would be prohibited by this Rule.

RULE 3.2: EXPEDITING LITIGATION

A lawyer shall make reasonable efforts to expedite litigation consistent with the interests of the client.

Comment

[1] Dilatory practices bring the administration of justice into disrepute. Although there will be occasions when a lawyer may properly seek a postponement for personal reasons, it is not proper for a lawyer to routinely fail to expedite litigation solely for the convenience of the advocates. Nor will a failure to expedite be reasonable if done for the purpose of frustrating an opposing party's attempt to obtain rightful redress or repose. It is not a justification that similar conduct is often tolerated by the bench and bar. The question is whether a competent lawyer acting in good faith would regard the course of action as having some substantial purpose other than delay. Realizing financial or other benefit from otherwise improper delay in litigation is not a legitimate interest of the client.

Definitional Cross-References

"Reasonable" *See* Rule 1.0(h)

Rule 3.3: Candor Toward the Tribunal

(a) A lawyer shall not knowingly:

(1) make a false statement of fact or law to a tribunal or fail to correct a false statement of material fact or law previously made to the tribunal by the lawyer;

(2) fail to disclose to the tribunal legal authority in the controlling jurisdiction known to the lawyer to be directly adverse to the position of the client and not disclosed by opposing counsel; or

(3) offer evidence that the lawyer knows to be false. If a lawyer, the lawyer's client, or a witness called by the lawyer, has offered material evidence and the lawyer comes to know of its falsity, the lawyer shall take reasonable remedial measures, including, if necessary, disclosure to the tribunal. A lawyer may refuse to offer evidence, other than the testimony of a defendant in a criminal matter, that the lawyer reasonably believes is false.

(b) A lawyer who represents a client in an adjudicative proceeding and who knows that a person intends to engage, is engaging or has engaged in criminal or fraudulent conduct related to the proceeding shall take reasonable remedial measures, including, if necessary, disclosure to the tribunal.

(c) The duties stated in paragraphs (a) and (b) continue to the conclusion of the proceeding, and apply even if compliance requires disclosure of information otherwise protected by Rule 1.6.

(d) In an ex parte proceeding, a lawyer shall inform the tribunal of all material facts known to the lawyer that will enable the tribunal to make an informed decision, whether or not the facts are adverse.

Comment

[1] This Rule governs the conduct of a lawyer who is representing a client in the proceedings of a tribunal. See Rule 1.0(m) for the definition of "tribunal." It also applies when the lawyer is representing a client in an ancillary proceeding conducted pursuant to the tribunal's adjudicative authority, such as a deposition. Thus, for example, paragraph (a)(3) requires a lawyer to take reasonable remedial measures if the lawyer comes to know that a client who is testifying in a deposition has offered evidence that is false.

[2] This Rule sets forth the special duties of lawyers as officers of the court to avoid conduct that undermines the integrity of the adjudicative process. A lawyer acting as an advocate in an adjudicative proceeding has an obligation to present the client's case with persuasive force. Performance of that duty while maintaining confidences of the client, however, is qualified by the advocate's duty of candor to the tribunal. Consequently, although a lawyer in an adversary proceeding is not required to present an impartial exposition of the law or to vouch for the evidence submitted in a cause, the lawyer must not allow the tribunal to be misled by false statements of law or fact or evidence that the lawyer knows to be false.

Representations by a Lawyer

[3] An advocate is responsible for pleadings and other documents prepared for litigation, but is usually not required to have personal knowledge of matters asserted therein, for litigation documents ordinarily present assertions by the client, or by someone on the client's behalf, and not assertions by the lawyer. Compare Rule 3.1. However, an assertion purporting to be on the lawyer's own knowledge, as in an affidavit by the lawyer or in a statement in open court, may properly be made only when the lawyer knows the assertion is true or believes it to be true on the basis of a reasonably diligent inquiry. There are circumstances where failure to make a disclosure is the equivalent of an affirmative misrepresentation. The obligation prescribed in Rule 1.2(d) not to counsel a client to commit or assist the client in committing a fraud applies in litigation. Regarding compliance with Rule 1.2(d), see the Comment to that Rule. See also the Comment to Rule 8.4(b).

Legal Argument

[4] Legal argument based on a knowingly false representation of law constitutes dishonesty toward the tribunal. A lawyer is not required to make a disinterested exposition of the law, but must recognize the existence of pertinent legal authorities. Furthermore, as stated in paragraph (a)(2), an advocate has a duty to disclose directly adverse authority in the controlling jurisdiction that has not been disclosed by the opposing party. The underlying concept is that legal argument is a discussion seeking to determine the legal premises properly applicable to the case.

Offering Evidence

[5] Paragraph (a)(3) requires that the lawyer refuse to offer evidence that the lawyer knows to be false, regardless of the client's wishes. This duty is premised on the lawyer's obligation as an officer of the court to prevent the trier of fact from being misled by false evidence. A lawyer does not violate this Rule if the lawyer offers the evidence for the purpose of establishing its falsity.

[6] If a lawyer knows that the client intends to testify falsely or wants the lawyer to introduce false evidence, the lawyer should seek to persuade the client that the evidence should not be offered. If the persuasion is ineffective and the lawyer continues to represent the client, the lawyer must refuse to offer the false evidence. If only a portion of a witness's testimony will be false, the lawyer may call the witness to testify but may not elicit or otherwise permit the witness to present the testimony that the lawyer knows is false.

[7] The duties stated in paragraphs (a) and (b) apply to all lawyers, including defense counsel in criminal cases. In some jurisdictions, however, courts have required counsel to present the accused as a witness or to give a narrative statement if the accused so desires, even if counsel knows that the testimony or statement will be false. The obligation of the advocate under the Rules of Professional Conduct is subordinate to such requirements. See also Comment [9].

[8] The prohibition against offering false evidence only applies if the lawyer knows that the evidence is false. A lawyer's reasonable belief that evidence is false does not preclude its presentation to the trier of fact. A lawyer's knowledge that evidence is false, however, can be inferred from the circumstances. See Rule 1.0(f). Thus, although a lawyer should resolve doubts about the veracity of testimony or other evidence in favor of the client, the lawyer cannot ignore an obvious falsehood.

[9] Although paragraph (a)(3) only prohibits a lawyer from offering evidence the lawyer knows to be false, it permits the lawyer to refuse to offer testimony or other proof that the lawyer reasonably believes is false. Offering such proof may reflect adversely on the lawyer's ability to discriminate in the quality of evidence and thus impair the lawyer's effectiveness as an advocate. Because of the special protections historically provided criminal defendants, however, this Rule does not permit a lawyer to refuse to offer the testimony of such a client where the lawyer reasonably believes but does not know that the testimony will be false. Un-

less the lawyer knows the testimony will be false, the lawyer must honor the client's decision to testify. See also Comment [7].

Remedial Measures

[10] Having offered material evidence in the belief that it was true, a lawyer may subsequently come to know that the evidence is false. Or, a lawyer may be surprised when the lawyer's client, or another witness called by the lawyer, offers testimony the lawyer knows to be false, either during the lawyer's direct examination or in response to cross-examination by the opposing lawyer. In such situations or if the lawyer knows of the falsity of testimony elicited from the client during a deposition, the lawyer must take reasonable remedial measures. In such situations, the advocate's proper course is to remonstrate with the client confidentially, advise the client of the lawyer's duty of candor to the tribunal and seek the client's cooperation with respect to the withdrawal or correction of the false statements or evidence. If that fails, the advocate must take further remedial action. If withdrawal from the representation is not permitted or will not undo the effect of the false evidence, the advocate must make such disclosure to the tribunal as is reasonably necessary to remedy the situation, even if doing so requires the lawyer to reveal information that otherwise would be protected by Rule 1.6. It is for the tribunal then to determine what should be done—making a statement about the matter to the trier of fact, ordering a mistrial or perhaps nothing.

[11] The disclosure of a client's false testimony can result in grave consequences to the client, including not only a sense of betrayal but also loss of the case and perhaps a prosecution for perjury. But the alternative is that the lawyer cooperate in deceiving the court, thereby subverting the truth-finding process which the adversary system is designed to implement. See Rule 1.2(d). Furthermore, unless it is clearly understood that the lawyer will act upon the duty to disclose the existence of false evidence, the client can simply reject the lawyer's advice to reveal the false evidence and insist that the lawyer keep silent. Thus the client could in effect coerce the lawyer into being a party to fraud on the court.

Preserving Integrity of Adjudicative Process

[12] Lawyers have a special obligation to protect a tribunal against criminal or fraudulent conduct that undermines the integrity of the adjudicative process, such as bribing, intimidating or otherwise unlawfully communicating with a witness, juror, court official or other participant in

the proceeding, unlawfully destroying or concealing documents or other evidence or failing to disclose information to the tribunal when required by law to do so. Thus, paragraph (b) requires a lawyer to take reasonable remedial measures, including disclosure if necessary, whenever the lawyer knows that a person, including the lawyer's client, intends to engage, is engaging or has engaged in criminal or fraudulent conduct related to the proceeding.

Duration of Obligation

[13] A practical time limit on the obligation to rectify false evidence or false statements of law and fact has to be established. The conclusion of the proceeding is a reasonably definite point for the termination of the obligation. A proceeding has concluded within the meaning of this Rule when a final judgment in the proceeding has been affirmed on appeal or the time for review has passed.

Ex Parte Proceedings

[14] Ordinarily, an advocate has the limited responsibility of presenting one side of the matters that a tribunal should consider in reaching a decision; the conflicting position is expected to be presented by the opposing party. However, in any ex parte proceeding, such as an application for a temporary restraining order, there is no balance of presentation by opposing advocates. The object of an ex parte proceeding is nevertheless to yield a substantially just result. The judge has an affirmative responsibility to accord the absent party just consideration. The lawyer for the represented party has the correlative duty to make disclosures of material facts known to the lawyer and that the lawyer reasonably believes are necessary to an informed decision.

Withdrawal

[15] Normally, a lawyer's compliance with the duty of candor imposed by this Rule does not require that the lawyer withdraw from the representation of a client whose interests will be or have been adversely affected by the lawyer's disclosure. The lawyer may, however, be required by Rule 1.16(a) to seek permission of the tribunal to withdraw if the lawyer's compliance with this Rule's duty of candor results in such an extreme deterioration of the client-lawyer relationship that the lawyer can no longer competently represent the client. Also see Rule 1.16(b) for the circumstances in which a lawyer will be permitted to seek a tribu-

nal's permission to withdraw. In connection with a request for permission to withdraw that is premised on a client's misconduct, a lawyer may reveal information relating to the representation only to the extent reasonably necessary to comply with this Rule or as otherwise permitted by Rule 1.6.

Definitional Cross-References

"Fraudulent" *See* Rule 1.0(d)
"Knowingly" and "Known" and "Knows" *See* Rule 1.0(f)
"Reasonable" *See* Rule 1.0(h)
"Reasonably believes" *See* Rule 1.0(i)
"Tribunal" *See* Rule 1.0(m)

RULE 3.4: FAIRNESS TO OPPOSING PARTY AND COUNSEL

A lawyer shall not:

(a) unlawfully obstruct another party's access to evidence or unlawfully alter, destroy or conceal a document or other material having potential evidentiary value. A lawyer shall not counsel or assist another person to do any such act;

(b) falsify evidence, counsel or assist a witness to testify falsely, or offer an inducement to a witness that is prohibited by law;

(c) knowingly disobey an obligation under the rules of a tribunal, except for an open refusal based on an assertion that no valid obligation exists;

(d) in pretrial procedure, make a frivolous discovery request or fail to make reasonably diligent effort to comply with a legally proper discovery request by an opposing party;

(e) in trial, allude to any matter that the lawyer does not reasonably believe is relevant or that will not be supported by admissible evidence, assert personal knowledge of facts in issue except when testifying as a witness, or state a personal opinion as to the justness of a cause, the credibility of a witness, the culpability of a civil litigant or the guilt or innocence of an accused; or

(f) request a person other than a client to refrain from voluntarily giving relevant information to another party unless:

(1) the person is a relative or an employee or other agent of a client; and

(2) the lawyer reasonably believes that the person's interests will not be adversely affected by refraining from giving such information.

Comment

[1] The procedure of the adversary system contemplates that the evidence in a case is to be marshalled competitively by the contending parties. Fair competition in the adversary system is secured by prohibitions against destruction or concealment of evidence, improperly influencing witnesses, obstructive tactics in discovery procedure, and the like.

[2] Documents and other items of evidence are often essential to establish a claim or defense. Subject to evidentiary privileges, the right of an opposing party, including the government, to obtain evidence through discovery or subpoena is an important procedural right. The exercise of that right can be frustrated if relevant material is altered, concealed or destroyed. Applicable law in many jurisdictions makes it an offense to destroy material for purpose of impairing its availability in a pending proceeding or one whose commencement can be foreseen. Falsifying evidence is also generally a criminal offense. Paragraph (a) applies to evidentiary material generally, including computerized information. Applicable law may permit a lawyer to take temporary possession of physical evidence of client crimes for the purpose of conducting a limited examination that will not alter or destroy material characteristics of the evidence. In such a case, applicable law may require the lawyer to turn the evidence over to the police or other prosecuting authority, depending on the circumstances.

[3] With regard to paragraph (b), it is not improper to pay a witness's expenses or to compensate an expert witness on terms permitted by law. The common law rule in most jurisdictions is that it is improper to pay an occurrence witness any fee for testifying and that it is improper to pay an expert witness a contingent fee.

[4] Paragraph (f) permits a lawyer to advise employees of a client to refrain from giving information to another party, for the employees may identify their interests with those of the client. See also Rule 4.2.

Definitional Cross-References

"Knowingly" *See* Rule 1.0(f)
"Reasonably" *See* Rule 1.0(h)
"Reasonably believes" *See* Rule 1.0(i)
"Tribunal" *See* Rule 1.0(m)

RULE 3.5: IMPARTIALITY AND DECORUM OF THE TRIBUNAL

A lawyer shall not:

(a) seek to influence a judge, juror, prospective juror or other official by means prohibited by law;

(b) communicate ex parte with such a person during the proceeding unless authorized to do so by law or court order;

(c) communicate with a juror or prospective juror after discharge of the jury if:

(1) the communication is prohibited by law or court order;

(2) the juror has made known to the lawyer a desire not to communicate; or

(3) the communication involves misrepresentation, coercion, duress or harassment; or

(d) engage in conduct intended to disrupt a tribunal.

Comment

[1] Many forms of improper influence upon a tribunal are proscribed by criminal law. Others are specified in the ABA Model Code of Judicial Conduct, with which an advocate should be familiar. A lawyer is required to avoid contributing to a violation of such provisions.

[2] During a proceeding a lawyer may not communicate ex parte with persons serving in an official capacity in the proceeding, such as judges, masters or jurors, unless authorized to do so by law or court order.

[3] A lawyer may on occasion want to communicate with a juror or prospective juror after the jury has been discharged. The lawyer may do so unless the communication is prohibited by law or a court order but must respect the desire of the juror not to talk with the lawyer. The lawyer may not engage in improper conduct during the communication.

[4] The advocate's function is to present evidence and argument so that the cause may be decided according to law. Refraining from abusive or obstreperous conduct is a corollary of the advocate's right to speak on behalf of litigants. A lawyer may stand firm against abuse by a judge but should avoid reciprocation; the judge's default is no justification for similar dereliction by an advocate. An advocate can present the cause, protect the record for subsequent review and preserve professional integrity by patient firmness no less effectively than by belligerence or theatrics.

[5] The duty to refrain from disruptive conduct applies to any proceeding of a tribunal, including a deposition. See Rule 1.0(m).

Definitional Cross-References
"Known" *See* Rule 1.0(f)
"Tribunal" *See* Rule 1.0(m)

RULE 3.6: TRIAL PUBLICITY

(a) A lawyer who is participating or has participated in the investigation or litigation of a matter shall not make an extrajudicial statement that the lawyer knows or reasonably should know will be disseminated by means of public communication and will have a substantial likelihood of materially prejudicing an adjudicative proceeding in the matter.

(b) Notwithstanding paragraph (a), a lawyer may state:

(1) the claim, offense or defense involved and, except when prohibited by law, the identity of the persons involved;

(2) information contained in a public record;

(3) that an investigation of a matter is in progress;

(4) the scheduling or result of any step in litigation;

(5) a request for assistance in obtaining evidence and information necessary thereto;

(6) a warning of danger concerning the behavior of a person involved, when there is reason to believe that there exists the likelihood of substantial harm to an individual or to the public interest; and

(7) in a criminal case, in addition to subparagraphs (1) through (6):

(i) the identity, residence, occupation and family status of the accused;

(ii) if the accused has not been apprehended, information necessary to aid in apprehension of that person;

(iii) the fact, time and place of arrest; and

(iv) the identity of investigating and arresting officers or agencies and the length of the investigation.

(c) Notwithstanding paragraph (a), a lawyer may make a statement that a reasonable lawyer would believe is required to protect a client from the substantial undue prejudicial effect of recent publicity not initiated by the lawyer or the lawyer's client. A statement made pursuant to this paragraph shall be limited to such information as is necessary to mitigate the recent adverse publicity.

(d) No lawyer associated in a firm or government agency with a lawyer subject to paragraph (a) shall make a statement prohibited by paragraph (a).

Comment

[1] It is difficult to strike a balance between protecting the right to a fair trial and safeguarding the right of free expression. Preserving the right to a fair trial necessarily entails some curtailment of the information that may be disseminated about a party prior to trial, particularly where trial by jury is involved. If there were no such limits, the result would be the practical nullification of the protective effect of the rules of forensic decorum and the exclusionary rules of evidence. On the other hand, there are vital social interests served by the free dissemination of information about events having legal consequences and about legal proceedings themselves. The public has a right to know about threats to its safety and measures aimed at assuring its security. It also has a legitimate interest in the conduct of judicial proceedings, particularly in matters of general public concern. Furthermore, the subject matter of legal proceedings is often of direct significance in debate and deliberation over questions of public policy.

[2] Special rules of confidentiality may validly govern proceedings in juvenile, domestic relations and mental disability proceedings, and perhaps other types of litigation. Rule 3.4(c) requires compliance with such rules.

[3] The Rule sets forth a basic general prohibition against a lawyer's making statements that the lawyer knows or should know will have a substantial likelihood of materially prejudicing an adjudicative proceeding. Recognizing that the public value of informed commentary is great and the likelihood of prejudice to a proceeding by the commentary of a lawyer who is not involved in the proceeding is small, the Rule applies only to lawyers who are, or who have been involved in the investigation or litigation of a case, and their associates.

[4] Paragraph (b) identifies specific matters about which a lawyer's statements would not ordinarily be considered to present a substantial likelihood of material prejudice, and should not in any event be considered prohibited by the general prohibition of paragraph (a). Paragraph (b) is not intended to be an exhaustive listing of the subjects upon which a lawyer may make a statement, but statements on other matters may be subject to paragraph (a).

[5] There are, on the other hand, certain subjects that are more likely than not to have a material prejudicial effect on a proceeding, particularly

when they refer to a civil matter triable to a jury, a criminal matter, or any other proceeding that could result in incarceration. These subjects relate to:

(1) the character, credibility, reputation or criminal record of a party, suspect in a criminal investigation or witness, or the identity of a witness, or the expected testimony of a party or witness;

(2) in a criminal case or proceeding that could result in incarceration, the possibility of a plea of guilty to the offense or the existence or contents of any confession, admission, or statement given by a defendant or suspect or that person's refusal or failure to make a statement;

(3) the performance or results of any examination or test or the refusal or failure of a person to submit to an examination or test, or the identity or nature of physical evidence expected to be presented;

(4) any opinion as to the guilt or innocence of a defendant or suspect in a criminal case or proceeding that could result in incarceration;

(5) information that the lawyer knows or reasonably should know is likely to be inadmissible as evidence in a trial and that would, if disclosed, create a substantial risk of prejudicing an impartial trial; or

(6) the fact that a defendant has been charged with a crime, unless there is included therein a statement explaining that the charge is merely an accusation and that the defendant is presumed innocent until and unless proven guilty.

[6] Another relevant factor in determining prejudice is the nature of the proceeding involved. Criminal jury trials will be most sensitive to extrajudicial speech. Civil trials may be less sensitive. Non-jury hearings and arbitration proceedings may be even less affected. The Rule will still place limitations on prejudicial comments in these cases, but the likelihood of prejudice may be different depending on the type of proceeding.

[7] Finally, extrajudicial statements that might otherwise raise a question under this Rule may be permissible when they are made in response to statements made publicly by another party, another party's lawyer, or third persons, where a reasonable lawyer would believe a public response is required in order to avoid prejudice to the lawyer's client. When prejudicial statements have been publicly made by others, responsive statements may have the salutary effect of lessening any resulting adverse impact on the adjudicative proceeding. Such responsive statements should be limited to contain only such information as is necessary to mitigate undue prejudice created by the statements made by others.

[8] See Rule 3.8(f) for additional duties of prosecutors in connection with extrajudicial statements about criminal proceedings.

Definitional Cross-References

"Firm" *See* Rule 1.0(c)
"Knows" *See* Rule 1.0(f)
"Reasonable" *See* Rule 1.0(h)
"Reasonably should know" *See* Rule 1.0(j)
"Substantial" *See* Rule 1.0(l)

RULE 3.7: LAWYER AS WITNESS

(a) A lawyer shall not act as advocate at a trial in which the lawyer is likely to be a necessary witness unless:

(1) the testimony relates to an uncontested issue;

(2) the testimony relates to the nature and value of legal services rendered in the case; or

(3) disqualification of the lawyer would work substantial hardship on the client.

(b) A lawyer may act as advocate in a trial in which another lawyer in the lawyer's firm is likely to be called as a witness unless precluded from doing so by Rule 1.7 or Rule 1.9.

Comment

[1] Combining the roles of advocate and witness can prejudice the tribunal and the opposing party and can also involve a conflict of interest between the lawyer and client.

Advocate-Witness Rule

[2] The tribunal has proper objection when the trier of fact may be confused or misled by a lawyer serving as both advocate and witness. The opposing party has proper objection where the combination of roles may prejudice that party's rights in the litigation. A witness is required to testify on the basis of personal knowledge, while an advocate is expected to explain and comment on evidence given by others. It may not be clear whether a statement by an advocate-witness should be taken as proof or as an analysis of the proof.

[3] To protect the tribunal, paragraph (a) prohibits a lawyer from simultaneously serving as advocate and necessary witness except in those circumstances specified in paragraphs (a)(1) through (a)(3). Paragraph (a)(1) recognizes that if the testimony will be uncontested, the ambiguities in the dual role are purely theoretical. Paragraph (a)(2) recognizes

that where the testimony concerns the extent and value of legal services rendered in the action in which the testimony is offered, permitting the lawyers to testify avoids the need for a second trial with new counsel to resolve that issue. Moreover, in such a situation the judge has firsthand knowledge of the matter in issue; hence, there is less dependence on the adversary process to test the credibility of the testimony.

[4] Apart from these two exceptions, paragraph (a)(3) recognizes that a balancing is required between the interests of the client and those of the tribunal and the opposing party. Whether the tribunal is likely to be misled or the opposing party is likely to suffer prejudice depends on the nature of the case, the importance and probable tenor of the lawyer's testimony, and the probability that the lawyer's testimony will conflict with that of other witnesses. Even if there is risk of such prejudice, in determining whether the lawyer should be disqualified, due regard must be given to the effect of disqualification on the lawyer's client. It is relevant that one or both parties could reasonably foresee that the lawyer would probably be a witness. The conflict of interest principles stated in Rules 1.7, 1.9 and 1.10 have no application to this aspect of the problem.

[5] Because the tribunal is not likely to be misled when a lawyer acts as advocate in a trial in which another lawyer in the lawyer's firm will testify as a necessary witness, paragraph (b) permits the lawyer to do so except in situations involving a conflict of interest.

Conflict of Interest

[6] In determining if it is permissible to act as advocate in a trial in which the lawyer will be a necessary witness, the lawyer must also consider that the dual role may give rise to a conflict of interest that will require compliance with Rules 1.7 or 1.9. For example, if there is likely to be substantial conflict between the testimony of the client and that of the lawyer the representation involves a conflict of interest that requires compliance with Rule 1.7. This would be true even though the lawyer might not be prohibited by paragraph (a) from simultaneously serving as advocate and witness because the lawyer's disqualification would work a substantial hardship on the client. Similarly, a lawyer who might be permitted to simultaneously serve as an advocate and a witness by paragraph (a)(3) might be precluded from doing so by Rule 1.9. The problem can arise whether the lawyer is called as a witness on behalf of the client or is called by the opposing party. Determining whether or not such a conflict exists is primarily the responsibility of the lawyer involved. If there is a conflict of

interest, the lawyer must secure the client's informed consent, confirmed in writing. In some cases, the lawyer will be precluded from seeking the client's consent. See Rule 1.7. See Rule 1.0(b) for the definition of "confirmed in writing" and Rule 1.0(e) for the definition of "informed consent."

[7] Paragraph (b) provides that a lawyer is not disqualified from serving as an advocate because a lawyer with whom the lawyer is associated in a firm is precluded from doing so by paragraph (a). If, however, the testifying lawyer would also be disqualified by Rule 1.7 or Rule 1.9 from representing the client in the matter, other lawyers in the firm will be precluded from representing the client by Rule 1.10 unless the client gives informed consent under the conditions stated in Rule 1.7.

Definitional Cross-References

"Firm" *See* Rule 1.0(c)
"Substantial" *See* Rule 1.0(l)

RULE 3.8: SPECIAL RESPONSIBILITIES OF A PROSECUTOR

The prosecutor in a criminal case shall:

(a) refrain from prosecuting a charge that the prosecutor knows is not supported by probable cause;

(b) make reasonable efforts to assure that the accused has been advised of the right to, and the procedure for obtaining, counsel and has been given reasonable opportunity to obtain counsel;

(c) not seek to obtain from an unrepresented accused a waiver of important pretrial rights, such as the right to a preliminary hearing;

(d) make timely disclosure to the defense of all evidence or information known to the prosecutor that tends to negate the guilt of the accused or mitigates the offense, and, in connection with sentencing, disclose to the defense and to the tribunal all unprivileged mitigating information known to the prosecutor, except when the prosecutor is relieved of this responsibility by a protective order of the tribunal;

(e) not subpoena a lawyer in a grand jury or other criminal proceeding to present evidence about a past or present client unless the prosecutor reasonably believes:

(1) the information sought is not protected from disclosure by any applicable privilege;

(2) the evidence sought is essential to the successful completion of an ongoing investigation or prosecution; and

(3) there is no other feasible alternative to obtain the information;

(f) except for statements that are necessary to inform the public of the nature and extent of the prosecutor's action and that serve a legitimate law enforcement purpose, refrain from making extrajudicial comments that have a substantial likelihood of heightening public condemnation of the accused and exercise reasonable care to prevent investigators, law enforcement personnel, employees or other persons assisting or associated with the prosecutor in a criminal case from making an extrajudicial statement that the prosecutor would be prohibited from making under Rule 3.6 or this Rule.

(g) When a prosecutor knows of new, credible and material evidence creating a reasonable likelihood that a convicted defendant did not commit an offense of which the defendant was convicted, the prosecutor shall:

(1) promptly disclose that evidence to an appropriate court or authority, and

(2) if the conviction was obtained in the prosecutor's jurisdiction,

(i) promptly disclose that evidence to the defendant unless a court authorizes delay, and

(ii) undertake further investigation, or make reasonable efforts to cause an investigation, to determine whether the defendant was convicted of an offense that the defendant did not commit.

(h) When a prosecutor knows of clear and convincing evidence establishing that a defendant in the prosecutor's jurisdiction was convicted of an offense that the defendant did not commit, the prosecutor shall seek to remedy the conviction.

Comment

[1] A prosecutor has the responsibility of a minister of justice and not simply that of an advocate. This responsibility carries with it specific obligations to see that the defendant is accorded procedural justice, that

guilt is decided upon the basis of sufficient evidence, and that special precautions are taken to prevent and to rectify the conviction of innocent persons. The extent of mandated remedial action is a matter of debate and varies in different jurisdictions. Many jurisdictions have adopted the ABA Standards for Criminal Justice Relating to the Prosecution Function, which are the product of prolonged and careful deliberation by lawyers experienced in both criminal prosecution and defense. Competent representation of the sovereignty may require a prosecutor to undertake some procedural and remedial measures as a matter of obligation. Applicable law may require other measures by the prosecutor and knowing disregard of those obligations or a systematic abuse of prosecutorial discretion could constitute a violation of Rule 8.4.

[2] In some jurisdictions, a defendant may waive a preliminary hearing and thereby lose a valuable opportunity to challenge probable cause. Accordingly, prosecutors should not seek to obtain waivers of preliminary hearings or other important pretrial rights from unrepresented accused persons. Paragraph (c) does not apply, however, to an accused appearing *pro se* with the approval of the tribunal. Nor does it forbid the lawful questioning of an uncharged suspect who has knowingly waived the rights to counsel and silence.

[3] The exception in paragraph (d) recognizes that a prosecutor may seek an appropriate protective order from the tribunal if disclosure of information to the defense could result in substantial harm to an individual or to the public interest.

[4] Paragraph (e) is intended to limit the issuance of lawyer subpoenas in grand jury and other criminal proceedings to those situations in which there is a genuine need to intrude into the client-lawyer relationship.

[5] Paragraph (f) supplements Rule 3.6, which prohibits extrajudicial statements that have a substantial likelihood of prejudicing an adjudicatory proceeding. In the context of a criminal prosecution, a prosecutor's extrajudicial statement can create the additional problem of increasing public condemnation of the accused. Although the announcement of an indictment, for example, will necessarily have severe consequences for the accused, a prosecutor can, and should, avoid comments which have no legitimate law enforcement purpose and have a substantial likelihood of increasing public opprobrium of the accused. Nothing in this Comment is intended to restrict the statements which a prosecutor may make which comply with Rule 3.6(b) or 3.6(c).

[6] Like other lawyers, prosecutors are subject to Rules 5.1 and 5.3, which relate to responsibilities regarding lawyers and nonlawyers who work for or are associated with the lawyer's office. Paragraph (f) reminds the prosecutor of the importance of these obligations in connection with the unique dangers of improper extrajudicial statements in a criminal case. In addition, paragraph (f) requires a prosecutor to exercise reasonable care to prevent persons assisting or associated with the prosecutor from making improper extrajudicial statements, even when such persons are not under the direct supervision of the prosecutor. Ordinarily, the reasonable care standard will be satisfied if the prosecutor issues the appropriate cautions to law enforcement personnel and other relevant individuals.

[7] When a prosecutor knows of new, credible and material evidence creating a reasonable likelihood that a person outside the prosecutor's jurisdiction was convicted of a crime that the person did not commit, paragraph (g) requires prompt disclosure to the court or other appropriate authority, such as the chief prosecutor of the jurisdiction where the conviction occurred. If the conviction was obtained in the prosecutor's jurisdiction, paragraph (g) requires the prosecutor to examine the evidence and undertake further investigation to determine whether the defendant is in fact innocent or make reasonable efforts to cause another appropriate authority to undertake the necessary investigation, and to promptly disclose the evidence to the court and, absent court-authorized delay, to the defendant. Consistent with the objectives of Rules 4.2 and 4.3, disclosure to a represented defendant must be made through the defendant's counsel, and, in the case of an unrepresented defendant, would ordinarily be accompanied by a request to a court for the appointment of counsel to assist the defendant in taking such legal measures as may be appropriate.

[8] Under paragraph (h), once the prosecutor knows of clear and convincing evidence that the defendant was convicted of an offense that the defendant did not commit, the prosecutor must seek to remedy the conviction. Necessary steps may include disclosure of the evidence to the defendant, requesting that the court appoint counsel for an unrepresented indigent defendant and, where appropriate, notifying the court that the prosecutor has knowledge that the defendant did not commit the offense of which the defendant was convicted.

[9] A prosecutor's independent judgment, made in good faith, that the new evidence is not of such nature as to trigger the obligations of sec-

tions (g) and (h), though subsequently determined to have been erroneous, does not constitute a violation of this Rule.

Definitional Cross-References
"Known" and "Knows" *See* Rule 1.0(f)
"Reasonable" *See* Rule 1.0(h)
"Reasonably believes" *See* Rule 1.0(i)
"Substantial" *See* Rule 1.0(l)
"Tribunal" *See* Rule 1.0(m)

RULE 3.9: ADVOCATE IN NONADJUDICATIVE PROCEEDINGS

A lawyer representing a client before a legislative body or administrative agency in a nonadjudicative proceeding shall disclose that the appearance is in a representative capacity and shall conform to the provisions of Rules 3.3(a) through (c), 3.4(a) through (c), and 3.5.

Comment

[1] In representation before bodies such as legislatures, municipal councils, and executive and administrative agencies acting in a rule-making or policy-making capacity, lawyers present facts, formulate issues and advance argument in the matters under consideration. The decision-making body, like a court, should be able to rely on the integrity of the submissions made to it. A lawyer appearing before such a body must deal with it honestly and in conformity with applicable rules of procedure. See Rules 3.3(a) through (c), 3.4(a) through (c) and 3.5.

[2] Lawyers have no exclusive right to appear before nonadjudicative bodies, as they do before a court. The requirements of this Rule therefore may subject lawyers to regulations inapplicable to advocates who are not lawyers. However, legislatures and administrative agencies have a right to expect lawyers to deal with them as they deal with courts.

[3] This Rule only applies when a lawyer represents a client in connection with an official hearing or meeting of a governmental agency or a legislative body to which the lawyer or the lawyer's client is presenting evidence or argument. It does not apply to representation of a client in a negotiation or other bilateral transaction with a governmental agency or in connection with an application for a license or other privilege or the client's compliance with generally applicable reporting requirements,

such as the filing of income-tax returns. Nor does it apply to the representation of a client in connection with an investigation or examination of the client's affairs conducted by government investigators or examiners. Representation in such matters is governed by Rules 4.1 through 4.4.

TRANSACTIONS WITH PERSONS OTHER THAN CLIENTS

RULE 4.1: TRUTHFULNESS IN STATEMENTS TO OTHERS

In the course of representing a client a lawyer shall not knowingly:

(a) make a false statement of material fact or law to a third person; or

(b) fail to disclose a material fact when disclosure is necessary to avoid assisting a criminal or fraudulent act by a client, unless disclosure is prohibited by Rule 1.6.

Comment

Misrepresentation

[1] A lawyer is required to be truthful when dealing with others on a client's behalf, but generally has no affirmative duty to inform an opposing party of relevant facts. A misrepresentation can occur if the lawyer incorporates or affirms a statement of another person that the lawyer knows is false. Misrepresentations can also occur by partially true but misleading statements or omissions that are the equivalent of affirmative false statements. For dishonest conduct that does not amount to a false statement or for misrepresentations by a lawyer other than in the course of representing a client, see Rule 8.4.

Statements of Fact

[2] This Rule refers to statements of fact. Whether a particular statement should be regarded as one of fact can depend on the circumstances. Under generally accepted conventions in negotiation, certain types of statements ordinarily are not taken as statements of material fact. Estimates of price or value placed on the subject of a transaction and a party's intentions as to an acceptable settlement of a claim are ordinarily in this category, and so is the existence of an undisclosed principal except where nondisclosure of the principal would constitute fraud. Lawyers should

be mindful of their obligations under applicable law to avoid criminal and tortious misrepresentation.

Crime or Fraud by Client

[3] Under Rule 1.2(d), a lawyer is prohibited from counseling or assisting a client in conduct that the lawyer knows is criminal or fraudulent. Paragraph (b) states a specific application of the principle set forth in Rule 1.2(d) and addresses the situation where a client's crime or fraud takes the form of a lie or misrepresentation. Ordinarily, a lawyer can avoid assisting a client's crime or fraud by withdrawing from the representation. Sometimes it may be necessary for the lawyer to give notice of the fact of withdrawal and to disaffirm an opinion, document, affirmation or the like. In extreme cases, substantive law may require a lawyer to disclose information relating to the representation to avoid being deemed to have assisted the client's crime or fraud. If the lawyer can avoid assisting a client's crime or fraud only by disclosing this information, then under paragraph (b) the lawyer is required to do so, unless the disclosure is prohibited by Rule 1.6.

Definitional Cross-References

"Fraudulent" *See* Rule 1.0(d)
"Knowingly" *See* Rule 1.0(f)

RULE 4.2: COMMUNICATION WITH PERSON REPRESENTED BY COUNSEL

In representing a client, a lawyer shall not communicate about the subject of the representation with a person the lawyer knows to be represented by another lawyer in the matter, unless the lawyer has the consent of the other lawyer or is authorized to do so by law or a court order.

Comment

[1] This Rule contributes to the proper functioning of the legal system by protecting a person who has chosen to be represented by a lawyer in a matter against possible overreaching by other lawyers who are participating in the matter, interference by those lawyers with the client-lawyer relationship and the uncounselled disclosure of information relating to the representation.

[2] This Rule applies to communications with any person who is represented by counsel concerning the matter to which the communication relates.

[3] The Rule applies even though the represented person initiates or consents to the communication. A lawyer must immediately terminate communication with a person if, after commencing communication, the lawyer learns that the person is one with whom communication is not permitted by this Rule.

[4] This Rule does not prohibit communication with a represented person, or an employee or agent of such a person, concerning matters outside the representation. For example, the existence of a controversy between a government agency and a private party, or between two organizations, does not prohibit a lawyer for either from communicating with nonlawyer representatives of the other regarding a separate matter. Nor does this Rule preclude communication with a represented person who is seeking advice from a lawyer who is not otherwise representing a client in the matter. A lawyer may not make a communication prohibited by this Rule through the acts of another. See Rule 8.4(a). Parties to a matter may communicate directly with each other, and a lawyer is not prohibited from advising a client concerning a communication that the client is legally entitled to make. Also, a lawyer having independent justification or legal authorization for communicating with a represented person is permitted to do so.

[5] Communications authorized by law may include communications by a lawyer on behalf of a client who is exercising a constitutional or other legal right to communicate with the government. Communications authorized by law may also include investigative activities of lawyers representing governmental entities, directly or through investigative agents, prior to the commencement of criminal or civil enforcement proceedings. When communicating with the accused in a criminal matter, a government lawyer must comply with this Rule in addition to honoring the constitutional rights of the accused. The fact that a communication does not violate a state or federal constitutional right is insufficient to establish that the communication is permissible under this Rule.

[6] A lawyer who is uncertain whether a communication with a represented person is permissible may seek a court order. A lawyer may also seek a court order in exceptional circumstances to authorize a communication that would otherwise be prohibited by this Rule, for example, where communication with a person represented by counsel is necessary to avoid reasonably certain injury.

[7] In the case of a represented organization, this Rule prohibits communications with a constituent of the organization who supervises, directs or regularly consults with the organization's lawyer concerning the matter or has authority to obligate the organization with respect to the matter or whose act or omission in connection with the matter may be imputed to the organization for purposes of civil or criminal liability. Consent of the organization's lawyer is not required for communication with a former constituent. If a constituent of the organization is represented in the matter by his or her own counsel, the consent by that counsel to a communication will be sufficient for purposes of this Rule. Compare Rule 3.4(f). In communicating with a current or former constituent of an organization, a lawyer must not use methods of obtaining evidence that violate the legal rights of the organization. See Rule 4.4.

[8] The prohibition on communications with a represented person only applies in circumstances where the lawyer knows that the person is in fact represented in the matter to be discussed. This means that the lawyer has actual knowledge of the fact of the representation; but such actual knowledge may be inferred from the circumstances. See Rule 1.0(f). Thus, the lawyer cannot evade the requirement of obtaining the consent of counsel by closing eyes to the obvious.

[9] In the event the person with whom the lawyer communicates is not known to be represented by counsel in the matter, the lawyer's communications are subject to Rule 4.3.

Definitional Cross-References

"Knows" *See* Rule 1.0(f)

RULE 4.3: DEALING WITH UNREPRESENTED PERSON

In dealing on behalf of a client with a person who is not represented by counsel, a lawyer shall not state or imply that the lawyer is disinterested. When the lawyer knows or reasonably should know that the unrepresented person misunderstands the lawyer's role in the matter, the lawyer shall make reasonable efforts to correct the misunderstanding. The lawyer shall not give legal advice to an unrepresented person, other than the advice to secure counsel, if the lawyer knows or reasonably should know that the interests of such a person are or have a reasonable possibility of being in conflict with the interests of the client.

Comment

[1] An unrepresented person, particularly one not experienced in dealing with legal matters, might assume that a lawyer is disinterested in loyalties or is a disinterested authority on the law even when the lawyer represents a client. In order to avoid a misunderstanding, a lawyer will typically need to identify the lawyer's client and, where necessary, explain that the client has interests opposed to those of the unrepresented person. For misunderstandings that sometimes arise when a lawyer for an organization deals with an unrepresented constituent, see Rule 1.13(f).

[2] The Rule distinguishes between situations involving unrepresented persons whose interests may be adverse to those of the lawyer's client and those in which the person's interests are not in conflict with the client's. In the former situation, the possibility that the lawyer will compromise the unrepresented person's interests is so great that the Rule prohibits the giving of any advice, apart from the advice to obtain counsel. Whether a lawyer is giving impermissible advice may depend on the experience and sophistication of the unrepresented person, as well as the setting in which the behavior and comments occur. This Rule does not prohibit a lawyer from negotiating the terms of a transaction or settling a dispute with an unrepresented person. So long as the lawyer has explained that the lawyer represents an adverse party and is not representing the person, the lawyer may inform the person of the terms on which the lawyer's client will enter into an agreement or settle a matter, prepare documents that require the person's signature and explain the lawyer's own view of the meaning of the document or the lawyer's view of the underlying legal obligations.

Definitional Cross-References

"Knows" *See* Rule 1.0(f)
"Reasonable" *See* Rule 1.0(h)
"Reasonably should know" *See* Rule 1.0(j)

RULE 4.4: RESPECT FOR RIGHTS OF THIRD PERSONS

(a) In representing a client, a lawyer shall not use means that have no substantial purpose other than to embarrass, delay, or burden a third person, or use methods of obtaining evidence that violate the legal rights of such a person.

(b) A lawyer who receives a document or electronically stored information relating to the representation of the lawyer's client and knows or reasonably should know that the document or electronically stored information was inadvertently sent shall promptly notify the sender.

Comment

[1] Responsibility to a client requires a lawyer to subordinate the interests of others to those of the client, but that responsibility does not imply that a lawyer may disregard the rights of third persons. It is impractical to catalogue all such rights, but they include legal restrictions on methods of obtaining evidence from third persons and unwarranted intrusions into privileged relationships, such as the client-lawyer relationship.

[2] Paragraph (b) recognizes that lawyers sometimes receive a document or electronically stored information that was mistakenly sent or produced by opposing parties or their lawyers. A document or electronically stored information is inadvertently sent when it is accidentally transmitted, such as when an email or letter is misaddressed or a document or electronically stored information is accidentally included with information that was intentionally transmitted. If a lawyer knows or reasonably should know that such a document or electronically stored information was sent inadvertently, then this Rule requires the lawyer to promptly notify the sender in order to permit that person to take protective measures. Whether the lawyer is required to take additional steps, such as returning the document or deleting electronically stored information, is a matter of law beyond the scope of these Rules, as is the question of whether the privileged status of a document or electronically stored information has been waived. Similarly, this Rule does not address the legal duties of a lawyer who receives a document or electronically stored information that the lawyer knows or reasonably should know may have been inappropriately obtained by the sending person. For purposes of this Rule, "document or electronically stored information" includes, in addition to paper documents, email and other forms of electronically stored information, including embedded data (commonly referred to as "metadata"), that is subject to being read or put into readable form. Metadata in electronic documents creates an obligation under this Rule only if the receiving lawyer knows or reasonably should know that the metadata was inadvertently sent to the receiving lawyer.

[3] Some lawyers may choose to return a document or delete electronically stored information unread, for example, when the lawyer learns

before receiving it that it was inadvertently sent. Where a lawyer is not required by applicable law to do so, the decision to voluntarily return such a document or delete electronically stored information is a matter of professional judgment ordinarily reserved to the lawyer. See Rules 1.2 and 1.4.

Definitional Cross-References
"Knows" *See* Rule 1.0(f)
"Reasonably should know" *See* Rule 1.0(j)
"Substantial" *See* Rule 1.0(l)

LAW FIRMS AND ASSOCIATIONS

RULE 5.1: RESPONSIBILITIES OF PARTNERS, MANAGERS, AND SUPERVISORY LAWYERS

(a) A partner in a law firm, and a lawyer who individually or together with other lawyers possesses comparable managerial authority in a law firm, shall make reasonable efforts to ensure that the firm has in effect measures giving reasonable assurance that all lawyers in the firm conform to the Rules of Professional Conduct.

(b) A lawyer having direct supervisory authority over another lawyer shall make reasonable efforts to ensure that the other lawyer conforms to the Rules of Professional Conduct.

(c) A lawyer shall be responsible for another lawyer's violation of the Rules of Professional Conduct if:

(1) the lawyer orders or, with knowledge of the specific conduct, ratifies the conduct involved; or

(2) the lawyer is a partner or has comparable managerial authority in the law firm in which the other lawyer practices, or has direct supervisory authority over the other lawyer, and knows of the conduct at a time when its consequences can be avoided or mitigated but fails to take reasonable remedial action.

Comment

[1] Paragraph (a) applies to lawyers who have managerial authority over the professional work of a firm. See Rule 1.0(c). This includes members of a partnership, the shareholders in a law firm organized as a professional corporation, and members of other associations authorized to practice law; lawyers having comparable managerial authority in a legal

services organization or a law department of an enterprise or government agency; and lawyers who have intermediate managerial responsibilities in a firm. Paragraph (b) applies to lawyers who have supervisory authority over the work of other lawyers in a firm.

[2] Paragraph (a) requires lawyers with managerial authority within a firm to make reasonable efforts to establish internal policies and procedures designed to provide reasonable assurance that all lawyers in the firm will conform to the Rules of Professional Conduct. Such policies and procedures include those designed to detect and resolve conflicts of interest, identify dates by which actions must be taken in pending matters, account for client funds and property and ensure that inexperienced lawyers are properly supervised.

[3] Other measures that may be required to fulfill the responsibility prescribed in paragraph (a) can depend on the firm's structure and the nature of its practice. In a small firm of experienced lawyers, informal supervision and periodic review of compliance with the required systems ordinarily will suffice. In a large firm, or in practice situations in which difficult ethical problems frequently arise, more elaborate measures may be necessary. Some firms, for example, have a procedure whereby junior lawyers can make confidential referral of ethical problems directly to a designated senior partner or special committee. See Rule 5.2. Firms, whether large or small, may also rely on continuing legal education in professional ethics. In any event, the ethical atmosphere of a firm can influence the conduct of all its members, and the partners may not assume that all lawyers associated with the firm will inevitably conform to the Rules.

[4] Paragraph (c) expresses a general principle of personal responsibility for acts of another. See also Rule 8.4(a).

[5] Paragraph (c)(2) defines the duty of a partner or other lawyer having comparable managerial authority in a law firm, as well as a lawyer who has direct supervisory authority over performance of specific legal work by another lawyer. Whether a lawyer has supervisory authority in particular circumstances is a question of fact. Partners and lawyers with comparable authority have at least indirect responsibility for all work being done by the firm, while a partner or manager in charge of a particular matter ordinarily also has supervisory responsibility for the work of other firm lawyers engaged in the matter. Appropriate remedial action by a partner or managing lawyer would depend on the immediacy of that lawyer's involvement and the seriousness of the misconduct. A supervisor is required to intervene to prevent avoidable consequences of misconduct if the supervisor knows that the misconduct occurred. Thus,

if a supervising lawyer knows that a subordinate misrepresented a matter to an opposing party in negotiation, the supervisor as well as the subordinate has a duty to correct the resulting misapprehension.

[6] Professional misconduct by a lawyer under supervision could reveal a violation of paragraph (b) on the part of the supervisory lawyer even though it does not entail a violation of paragraph (c) because there was no direction, ratification or knowledge of the violation.

[7] Apart from this Rule and Rule 8.4(a), a lawyer does not have disciplinary liability for the conduct of a partner, associate or subordinate. Whether a lawyer may be liable civilly or criminally for another lawyer's conduct is a question of law beyond the scope of these Rules.

[8] The duties imposed by this Rule on managing and supervising lawyers do not alter the personal duty of each lawyer in a firm to abide by the Rules of Professional Conduct. See Rule 5.2(a).

Definitional Cross-References

"Firm" and "Law firm" *See* Rule 1.0(c)
"Knows" *See* Rule 1.0(f)
"Partner" *See* Rule 1.0(g)
"Reasonable" *See* Rule 1.0(h)

RULE 5.2: RESPONSIBILITIES OF A SUBORDINATE LAWYER

(a) A lawyer is bound by the Rules of Professional Conduct notwithstanding that the lawyer acted at the direction of another person.

(b) A subordinate lawyer does not violate the Rules of Professional Conduct if that lawyer acts in accordance with a supervisory lawyer's reasonable resolution of an arguable question of professional duty.

Comment

[1] Although a lawyer is not relieved of responsibility for a violation by the fact that the lawyer acted at the direction of a supervisor, that fact may be relevant in determining whether a lawyer had the knowledge required to render conduct a violation of the Rules. For example, if a subordinate filed a frivolous pleading at the direction of a supervisor, the subordinate would not be guilty of a professional violation unless the subordinate knew of the document's frivolous character.

[2] When lawyers in a supervisor-subordinate relationship encounter a matter involving professional judgment as to ethical duty, the supervisor may assume responsibility for making the judgment. Otherwise a consistent course of action or position could not be taken. If the question can reasonably be answered only one way, the duty of both lawyers is clear and they are equally responsible for fulfilling it. However, if the question is reasonably arguable, someone has to decide upon the course of action. That authority ordinarily reposes in the supervisor, and a subordinate may be guided accordingly. For example, if a question arises whether the interests of two clients conflict under Rule 1.7, the supervisor's reasonable resolution of the question should protect the subordinate professionally if the resolution is subsequently challenged.

Definitional Cross-References

"Reasonable" *See* Rule 1.0(h)

RULE 5.3: RESPONSIBILITIES REGARDING NONLAWYER ASSISTANCE

With respect to a nonlawyer employed or retained by or associated with a lawyer:

(a) a partner, and a lawyer who individually or together with other lawyers possesses comparable managerial authority in a law firm shall make reasonable efforts to ensure that the firm has in effect measures giving reasonable assurance that the person's conduct is compatible with the professional obligations of the lawyer;

(b) a lawyer having direct supervisory authority over the nonlawyer shall make reasonable efforts to ensure that the person's conduct is compatible with the professional obligations of the lawyer; and

(c) a lawyer shall be responsible for conduct of such a person that would be a violation of the Rules of Professional Conduct if engaged in by a lawyer if:

(1) the lawyer orders or, with the knowledge of the specific conduct, ratifies the conduct involved; or

(2) the lawyer is a partner or has comparable managerial authority in the law firm in which the person is employed, or has direct supervisory authority over the person, and knows of the conduct at a time when its consequences can be avoided or mitigated but fails to take reasonable remedial action.

Comment

[1] Paragraph (a) requires lawyers with managerial authority within a law firm to make reasonable efforts to ensure that the firm has in effect measures giving reasonable assurance that nonlawyers in the firm and nonlawyers outside the firm who work on firm matters act in a way compatible with the professional obligations of the lawyer. See Comment [6] to Rule 1.1 (retaining lawyers outside the firm) and Comment [1] to Rule 5.1 (responsibilities with respect to lawyers within a firm). Paragraph (b) applies to lawyers who have supervisory authority over such nonlawyers within or outside the firm. Paragraph (c) specifies the circumstances in which a lawyer is responsible for the conduct of such nonlawyers within or outside the firm that would be a violation of the Rules of Professional Conduct if engaged in by a lawyer.

Nonlawyers Within the Firm

[2] Lawyers generally employ assistants in their practice, including secretaries, investigators, law student interns, and paraprofessionals. Such assistants, whether employees or independent contractors, act for the lawyer in rendition of the lawyer's professional services. A lawyer must give such assistants appropriate instruction and supervision concerning the ethical aspects of their employment, particularly regarding the obligation not to disclose information relating to representation of the client, and should be responsible for their work product. The measures employed in supervising nonlawyers should take account of the fact that they do not have legal training and are not subject to professional discipline.

Nonlawyers Outside the Firm

[3] A lawyer may use nonlawyers outside the firm to assist the lawyer in rendering legal services to the client. Examples include the retention of an investigative or paraprofessional service, hiring a document management company to create and maintain a database for complex litigation, sending client documents to a third party for printing or scanning, and using an Internet-based service to store client information. When using such services outside the firm, a lawyer must make reasonable efforts to ensure that the services are provided in a manner that is compatible with the lawyer's professional obligations. The extent of this obligation will depend upon the circumstances, including the education, experience and reputation of the nonlawyer; the nature of the services involved; the terms of any arrangements concerning the protection of cli-

ent information; and the legal and ethical environments of the jurisdictions in which the services will be performed, particularly with regard to confidentiality. See also Rules 1.1 (competence), 1.2 (allocation of authority), 1.4 (communication with client), 1.6 (confidentiality), 5.4(a) (professional independence of the lawyer), and 5.5(a) (unauthorized practice of law). When retaining or directing a nonlawyer outside the firm, a lawyer should communicate directions appropriate under the circumstances to give reasonable assurance that the nonlawyer's conduct is compatible with the professional obligations of the lawyer.

[4] Where the client directs the selection of a particular nonlawyer service provider outside the firm, the lawyer ordinarily should agree with the client concerning the allocation of responsibility for monitoring as between the client and the lawyer. See Rule 1.2. When making such an allocation in a matter pending before a tribunal, lawyers and parties may have additional obligations that are a matter of law beyond the scope of these Rules.

Definitional Cross-References

"Firm" and "Law firm" *See* Rule 1.0(c)
"Knows" *See* Rule 1.0(f)
"Partner" *See* Rule 1.0(g)
"Reasonable" *See* Rule 1.0(h)

RULE 5.4: PROFESSIONAL INDEPENDENCE OF A LAWYER

(a) A lawyer or law firm shall not share legal fees with a nonlawyer, except that:

(1) an agreement by a lawyer with the lawyer's firm, partner, or associate may provide for the payment of money, over a reasonable period of time after the lawyer's death, to the lawyer's estate or to one or more specified persons;

(2) a lawyer who purchases the practice of a deceased, disabled, or disappeared lawyer may, pursuant to the provisions of Rule 1.17, pay to the estate or other representative of that lawyer the agreed-upon purchase price;

(3) a lawyer or law firm may include nonlawyer employees in a compensation or retirement plan, even though the plan is based in whole or in part on a profit-sharing arrangement; and

(4) a lawyer may share court-awarded legal fees with a nonprofit organization that employed, retained or recommended employment of the lawyer in the matter.

(b) A lawyer shall not form a partnership with a nonlawyer if any of the activities of the partnership consist of the practice of law.

(c) A lawyer shall not permit a person who recommends, employs, or pays the lawyer to render legal services for another to direct or regulate the lawyer's professional judgment in rendering such legal services.

(d) A lawyer shall not practice with or in the form of a professional corporation or association authorized to practice law for a profit, if:

(1) a nonlawyer owns any interest therein, except that a fiduciary representative of the estate of a lawyer may hold the stock or interest of the lawyer for a reasonable time during administration;

(2) a nonlawyer is a corporate director or officer thereof or occupies the position of similar responsibility in any form of association other than a corporation; or

(3) a nonlawyer has the right to direct or control the professional judgment of a lawyer.

Comment

[1] The provisions of this Rule express traditional limitations on sharing fees. These limitations are to protect the lawyer's professional independence of judgment. Where someone other than the client pays the lawyer's fee or salary, or recommends employment of the lawyer, that arrangement does not modify the lawyer's obligation to the client. As stated in paragraph (c), such arrangements should not interfere with the lawyer's professional judgment.

[2] This Rule also expresses traditional limitations on permitting a third party to direct or regulate the lawyer's professional judgment in rendering legal services to another. See also Rule 1.8(f) (lawyer may accept compensation from a third party as long as there is no interference with the lawyer's independent professional judgment and the client gives informed consent).

Definitional Cross-References

"Firm" and "Law firm" *See* Rule 1.0(c)
"Partner" *See* Rule 1.0(g)

Rule 5.5: Unauthorized Practice of Law; Multijurisdictional Practice of Law

(a) A lawyer shall not practice law in a jurisdiction in violation of the regulation of the legal profession in that jurisdiction, or assist another in doing so.

(b) A lawyer who is not admitted to practice in this jurisdiction shall not:

(1) except as authorized by these Rules or other law, establish an office or other systematic and continuous presence in this jurisdiction for the practice of law; or

(2) hold out to the public or otherwise represent that the lawyer is admitted to practice law in this jurisdiction.

(c) A lawyer admitted in another United States jurisdiction, and not disbarred or suspended from practice in any jurisdiction, may provide legal services on a temporary basis in this jurisdiction that:

(1) are undertaken in association with a lawyer who is admitted to practice in this jurisdiction and who actively participates in the matter;

(2) are in or reasonably related to a pending or potential proceeding before a tribunal in this or another jurisdiction, if the lawyer, or a person the lawyer is assisting, is authorized by law or order to appear in such proceeding or reasonably expects to be so authorized;

(3) are in or reasonably related to a pending or potential arbitration, mediation, or other alternative dispute resolution proceeding in this or another jurisdiction, if the services arise out of or are reasonably related to the lawyer's practice in a jurisdiction in which the lawyer is admitted to practice and are not services for which the forum requires pro hac vice admission; or

(4) are not within paragraphs (c)(2) or (c)(3) and arise out of or are reasonably related to the lawyer's practice in a jurisdiction in which the lawyer is admitted to practice.

(d) A lawyer admitted in another United States jurisdiction or in a foreign jurisdiction, and not disbarred or suspended from practice in any jurisdiction or the equivalent thereof, or a person otherwise lawfully practicing as an in-house counsel under the laws of a foreign jurisdiction, may provide legal services through an office or other systematic and continuous presence in this jurisdiction that:

(1) are provided to the lawyer's employer or its organizational affiliates; are not services for which the forum requires pro hac vice admission; and, when performed by a foreign lawyer and requires advice on the law of this or another jurisdiction or of the United States, such advice shall be based upon the advice of a lawyer who is duly licensed and authorized by the jurisdiction to provide such advice; or

(2) are services that the lawyer is authorized by federal law or other law or rule to provide in this jurisdiction.

(e) For purposes of paragraph (d):

(1) the foreign lawyer must be a member in good standing of a recognized legal profession in a foreign jurisdiction, the members of which are admitted to practice as lawyers or counselors at law or the equivalent, and subject to effective regulation and discipline by a duly constituted professional body or a public authority; or

(2) the person otherwise lawfully practicing as an in-house counsel under the laws of a foreign jurisdiction must be authorized to practice under this Rule by, in the exercise of its discretion, [the highest court of this jurisdiction].

Comment

[1] A lawyer may practice law only in a jurisdiction in which the lawyer is authorized to practice. A lawyer may be admitted to practice law in a jurisdiction on a regular basis or may be authorized by court rule or order or by law to practice for a limited purpose or on a restricted basis. Paragraph (a) applies to unauthorized practice of law by a lawyer, whether through the lawyer's direct action or by the lawyer assisting another person. For example, a lawyer may not assist a person in practicing law in violation of the rules governing professional conduct in that person's jurisdiction.

[2] The definition of the practice of law is established by law and varies from one jurisdiction to another. Whatever the definition, limiting the practice of law to members of the bar protects the public against rendition of legal services by unqualified persons. This Rule does not prohibit a lawyer from employing the services of paraprofessionals and delegating functions to them, so long as the lawyer supervises the delegated work and retains responsibility for their work. See Rule 5.3.

[3] A lawyer may provide professional advice and instruction to nonlawyers whose employment requires knowledge of the law; for example, claims adjusters, employees of financial or commercial institutions, social

workers, accountants and persons employed in government agencies. Lawyers also may assist independent nonlawyers, such as paraprofessionals, who are authorized by the law of a jurisdiction to provide particular law-related services. In addition, a lawyer may counsel nonlawyers who wish to proceed pro se.

[4] Other than as authorized by law or this Rule, a lawyer who is not admitted to practice generally in this jurisdiction violates paragraph (b)(1) if the lawyer establishes an office or other systematic and continuous presence in this jurisdiction for the practice of law. Presence may be systematic and continuous even if the lawyer is not physically present here. Such a lawyer must not hold out to the public or otherwise represent that the lawyer is admitted to practice law in this jurisdiction. See also Rule 7.1.

[5] There are occasions in which a lawyer admitted to practice in another United States jurisdiction, and not disbarred or suspended from practice in any jurisdiction, may provide legal services on a temporary basis in this jurisdiction under circumstances that do not create an unreasonable risk to the interests of their clients, the public or the courts. Paragraph (c) identifies four such circumstances. The fact that conduct is not so identified does not imply that the conduct is or is not authorized. With the exception of paragraphs (d)(1) and (d)(2), this Rule does not authorize a U.S. or foreign lawyer to establish an office or other systematic and continuous presence in this jurisdiction without being admitted to practice generally here.

[6] There is no single test to determine whether a lawyer's services are provided on a "temporary basis" in this jurisdiction, and may therefore be permissible under paragraph (c). Services may be "temporary" even though the lawyer provides services in this jurisdiction on a recurring basis, or for an extended period of time, as when the lawyer is representing a client in a single lengthy negotiation or litigation.

[7] Paragraphs (c) and (d) apply to lawyers who are admitted to practice law in any United States jurisdiction, which includes the District of Columbia and any state, territory or commonwealth of the United States. Paragraph (d) also applies to lawyers admitted in a foreign jurisdiction. The word "admitted" in paragraphs (c), (d) and (e) contemplates that the lawyer is authorized to practice in the jurisdiction in which the lawyer is admitted and excludes a lawyer who while technically admitted is not authorized to practice, because, for example, the lawyer is on inactive status.

[8] Paragraph (c)(1) recognizes that the interests of clients and the public are protected if a lawyer admitted only in another jurisdiction associates with a lawyer licensed to practice in this jurisdiction. For this paragraph to apply, however, the lawyer admitted to practice in this jurisdiction must actively participate in and share responsibility for the representation of the client.

[9] Lawyers not admitted to practice generally in a jurisdiction may be authorized by law or order of a tribunal or an administrative agency to appear before the tribunal or agency. This authority may be granted pursuant to formal rules governing admission pro hac vice or pursuant to informal practice of the tribunal or agency. Under paragraph (c)(2), a lawyer does not violate this Rule when the lawyer appears before a tribunal or agency pursuant to such authority. To the extent that a court rule or other law of this jurisdiction requires a lawyer who is not admitted to practice in this jurisdiction to obtain admission pro hac vice before appearing before a tribunal or administrative agency, this Rule requires the lawyer to obtain that authority.

[10] Paragraph (c)(2) also provides that a lawyer rendering services in this jurisdiction on a temporary basis does not violate this Rule when the lawyer engages in conduct in anticipation of a proceeding or hearing in a jurisdiction in which the lawyer is authorized to practice law or in which the lawyer reasonably expects to be admitted pro hac vice. Examples of such conduct include meetings with the client, interviews of potential witnesses, and the review of documents. Similarly, a lawyer admitted only in another jurisdiction may engage in conduct temporarily in this jurisdiction in connection with pending litigation in another jurisdiction in which the lawyer is or reasonably expects to be authorized to appear, including taking depositions in this jurisdiction.

[11] When a lawyer has been or reasonably expects to be admitted to appear before a court or administrative agency, paragraph (c)(2) also permits conduct by lawyers who are associated with that lawyer in the matter, but who do not expect to appear before the court or administrative agency. For example, subordinate lawyers may conduct research, review documents, and attend meetings with witnesses in support of the lawyer responsible for the litigation.

[12] Paragraph (c)(3) permits a lawyer admitted to practice law in another jurisdiction to perform services on a temporary basis in this jurisdiction if those services are in or reasonably related to a pending or po-

tential arbitration, mediation, or other alternative dispute resolution proceeding in this or another jurisdiction, if the services arise out of or are reasonably related to the lawyer's practice in a jurisdiction in which the lawyer is admitted to practice. The lawyer, however, must obtain admission pro hac vice in the case of a court-annexed arbitration or mediation or otherwise if court rules or law so require.

[13] Paragraph (c)(4) permits a lawyer admitted in another jurisdiction to provide certain legal services on a temporary basis in this jurisdiction that arise out of or are reasonably related to the lawyer's practice in a jurisdiction in which the lawyer is admitted but are not within paragraphs (c)(2) or (c)(3). These services include both legal services and services that nonlawyers may perform but that are considered the practice of law when performed by lawyers.

[14] Paragraphs (c)(3) and (c)(4) require that the services arise out of or be reasonably related to the lawyer's practice in a jurisdiction in which the lawyer is admitted. A variety of factors evidence such a relationship. The lawyer's client may have been previously represented by the lawyer, or may be resident in or have substantial contacts with the jurisdiction in which the lawyer is admitted. The matter, although involving other jurisdictions, may have a significant connection with that jurisdiction. In other cases, significant aspects of the lawyer's work might be conducted in that jurisdiction or a significant aspect of the matter may involve the law of that jurisdiction. The necessary relationship might arise when the client's activities or the legal issues involve multiple jurisdictions, such as when the officers of a multinational corporation survey potential business sites and seek the services of their lawyer in assessing the relative merits of each. In addition, the services may draw on the lawyer's recognized expertise developed through the regular practice of law on behalf of clients in matters involving a particular body of federal, nationally-uniform, foreign, or international law. Lawyers desiring to provide pro bono legal services on a temporary basis in a jurisdiction that has been affected by a major disaster, but in which they are not otherwise authorized to practice law, as well as lawyers from the affected jurisdiction who seek to practice law temporarily in another jurisdiction, but in which they are not otherwise authorized to practice law, should consult the [*Model Court Rule on Provision of Legal Services Following Determination of Major Disaster*].

[15] Paragraph (d) identifies two circumstances in which a lawyer who is admitted to practice in another United States or a foreign jurisdiction, and is not disbarred or suspended from practice in any jurisdiction, or the

equivalent thereof, may establish an office or other systematic and continuous presence in this jurisdiction for the practice of law. Pursuant to paragraph (c) of this Rule, a lawyer admitted in any U.S. jurisdiction may also provide legal services in this jurisdiction on a temporary basis. See also *Model Rule on Temporary Practice by Foreign Lawyers*. Except as provided in paragraphs (d)(1) and (d)(2), a lawyer who is admitted to practice law in another United States or foreign jurisdiction and who establishes an office or other systematic or continuous presence in this jurisdiction must become admitted to practice law generally in this jurisdiction.

[16] Paragraph (d)(1) applies to a U.S. or foreign lawyer who is employed by a client to provide legal services to the client or its organizational affiliates, i.e., entities that control, are controlled by, or are under common control with the employer. This paragraph does not authorize the provision of personal legal services to the employer's officers or employees. The paragraph applies to in-house corporate lawyers, government lawyers and others who are employed to render legal services to the employer. The lawyer's ability to represent the employer outside the jurisdiction in which the lawyer is licensed generally serves the interests of the employer and does not create an unreasonable risk to the client and others because the employer is well situated to assess the lawyer's qualifications and the quality of the lawyer's work. To further decrease any risk to the client, when advising on the domestic law of a United States jurisdiction or on the law of the United States, the foreign lawyer authorized to practice under paragraph (d)(1) of this Rule needs to base that advice on the advice of a lawyer licensed and authorized by the jurisdiction to provide it.

[17] If an employed lawyer establishes an office or other systematic presence in this jurisdiction for the purpose of rendering legal services to the employer, the lawyer may be subject to registration or other requirements, including assessments for client protection funds and mandatory continuing legal education. See *Model Rule for Registration of In-House Counsel*.

[18] Paragraph (d)(2) recognizes that a U.S. or foreign lawyer may provide legal services in a jurisdiction in which the lawyer is not licensed when authorized to do so by federal or other law, which includes statute, court rule, executive regulation or judicial precedent. See, e.g., *Model Rule on Practice Pending Admission*.

[19] A lawyer who practices law in this jurisdiction pursuant to paragraphs (c) or (d) or otherwise is subject to the disciplinary authority of this jurisdiction. See Rule 8.5(a).

[20] In some circumstances, a lawyer who practices law in this jurisdiction pursuant to paragraphs (c) or (d) may have to inform the client that the lawyer is not licensed to practice law in this jurisdiction. For example, that may be required when the representation occurs primarily in this jurisdiction and requires knowledge of the law of this jurisdiction. See Rule 1.4(b).

[21] Paragraphs (c) and (d) do not authorize communications advertising legal services in this jurisdiction by lawyers who are admitted to practice in other jurisdictions. Whether and how lawyers may communicate the availability of their services in this jurisdiction is governed by Rules 7.1 to 7.3.

Definitional Cross-References

"Reasonably" *See* Rule 1.0(h)
"Tribunal" *See* Rule 1.0(m)

RULE 5.6: RESTRICTIONS ON RIGHT TO PRACTICE

A lawyer shall not participate in offering or making:

(a) a partnership, shareholders, operating, employment, or other similar type of agreement that restricts the right of a lawyer to practice after termination of the relationship, except an agreement concerning benefits upon retirement; or

(b) an agreement in which a restriction on the lawyer's right to practice is part of the settlement of a client controversy.

Comment

[1] An agreement restricting the right of lawyers to practice after leaving a firm not only limits their professional autonomy but also limits the freedom of clients to choose a lawyer. Paragraph (a) prohibits such agreements except for restrictions incident to provisions concerning retirement benefits for service with the firm.

[2] Paragraph (b) prohibits a lawyer from agreeing not to represent other persons in connection with settling a claim on behalf of a client.

[3] This Rule does not apply to prohibit restrictions that may be included in the terms of the sale of a law practice pursuant to Rule 1.17.

RULE 5.7: RESPONSIBILITIES REGARDING LAW-RELATED SERVICES

(a) A lawyer shall be subject to the Rules of Professional Conduct with respect to the provision of law-related services, as defined in paragraph (b), if the law-related services are provided:

(1) by the lawyer in circumstances that are not distinct from the lawyer's provision of legal services to clients; or

(2) in other circumstances by an entity controlled by the lawyer individually or with others if the lawyer fails to take reasonable measures to assure that a person obtaining the law-related services knows that the services are not legal services and that the protections of the client-lawyer relationship do not exist.

(b) The term "law-related services" denotes services that might reasonably be performed in conjunction with and in substance are related to the provision of legal services, and that are not prohibited as unauthorized practice of law when provided by a nonlawyer.

Comment

[1] When a lawyer performs law-related services or controls an organization that does so, there exists the potential for ethical problems. Principal among these is the possibility that the person for whom the law-related services are performed fails to understand that the services may not carry with them the protections normally afforded as part of the client-lawyer relationship. The recipient of the law-related services may expect, for example, that the protection of client confidences, prohibitions against representation of persons with conflicting interests, and obligations of a lawyer to maintain professional independence apply to the provision of law-related services when that may not be the case.

[2] Rule 5.7 applies to the provision of law-related services by a lawyer even when the lawyer does not provide any legal services to the person for whom the law-related services are performed and whether the law-related services are performed through a law firm or a separate entity. The Rule identifies the circumstances in which all of the Rules of Professional Conduct apply to the provision of law-related services. Even when those circumstances do not exist, however, the conduct of a lawyer involved in the provision of law-related services is subject to those Rules

that apply generally to lawyer conduct, regardless of whether the conduct involves the provision of legal services. See, e.g., Rule 8.4.

[3] When law-related services are provided by a lawyer under circumstances that are not distinct from the lawyer's provision of legal services to clients, the lawyer in providing the law-related services must adhere to the requirements of the Rules of Professional Conduct as provided in paragraph (a)(1). Even when the law-related and legal services are provided in circumstances that are distinct from each other, for example through separate entities or different support staff within the law firm, the Rules of Professional Conduct apply to the lawyer as provided in paragraph (a)(2) unless the lawyer takes reasonable measures to assure that the recipient of the law-related services knows that the services are not legal services and that the protections of the client-lawyer relationship do not apply.

[4] Law-related services also may be provided through an entity that is distinct from that through which the lawyer provides legal services. If the lawyer individually or with others has control of such an entity's operations, the Rule requires the lawyer to take reasonable measures to assure that each person using the services of the entity knows that the services provided by the entity are not legal services and that the Rules of Professional Conduct that relate to the client-lawyer relationship do not apply. A lawyer's control of an entity extends to the ability to direct its operation. Whether a lawyer has such control will depend upon the circumstances of the particular case.

[5] When a client-lawyer relationship exists with a person who is referred by a lawyer to a separate law-related service entity controlled by the lawyer, individually or with others, the lawyer must comply with Rule 1.8(a).

[6] In taking the reasonable measures referred to in paragraph (a)(2) to assure that a person using law-related services understands the practical effect or significance of the inapplicability of the Rules of Professional Conduct, the lawyer should communicate to the person receiving the law-related services, in a manner sufficient to assure that the person understands the significance of the fact, that the relationship of the person to the business entity will not be a client-lawyer relationship. The communication should be made before entering into an agreement for provision of or providing law-related services, and preferably should be in writing.

[7] The burden is upon the lawyer to show that the lawyer has taken reasonable measures under the circumstances to communicate the desired understanding. For instance, a sophisticated user of law-related services, such as a publicly held corporation, may require a lesser ex-

planation than someone unaccustomed to making distinctions between legal services and law-related services, such as an individual seeking tax advice from a lawyer-accountant or investigative services in connection with a lawsuit.

[8] Regardless of the sophistication of potential recipients of law-related services, a lawyer should take special care to keep separate the provision of law-related and legal services in order to minimize the risk that the recipient will assume that the law-related services are legal services. The risk of such confusion is especially acute when the lawyer renders both types of services with respect to the same matter. Under some circumstances the legal and law-related services may be so closely entwined that they cannot be distinguished from each other, and the requirement of disclosure and consultation imposed by paragraph (a)(2) of the Rule cannot be met. In such a case a lawyer will be responsible for assuring that both the lawyer's conduct and, to the extent required by Rule 5.3, that of nonlawyer employees in the distinct entity that the lawyer controls complies in all respects with the Rules of Professional Conduct.

[9] A broad range of economic and other interests of clients may be served by lawyers' engaging in the delivery of law-related services. Examples of law-related services include providing title insurance, financial planning, accounting, trust services, real estate counseling, legislative lobbying, economic analysis, social work, psychological counseling, tax preparation, and patent, medical or environmental consulting.

[10] When a lawyer is obliged to accord the recipients of such services the protections of those Rules that apply to the client-lawyer relationship, the lawyer must take special care to heed the proscriptions of the Rules addressing conflict of interest (Rules 1.7 through 1.11, especially Rules 1.7(a)(2) and 1.8(a), (b) and (f)), and to scrupulously adhere to the requirements of Rule 1.6 relating to disclosure of confidential information. The promotion of the law-related services must also in all respects comply with Rules 7.1 through 7.3, dealing with advertising and solicitation. In that regard, lawyers should take special care to identify the obligations that may be imposed as a result of a jurisdiction's decisional law.

[11] When the full protections of all of the Rules of Professional Conduct do not apply to the provision of law-related services, principles of law external to the Rules, for example, the law of principal and agent, govern the legal duties owed to those receiving the services. Those other legal principles may establish a different degree of protection for the recipient with respect to confidentiality of information, conflicts of inter-

est and permissible business relationships with clients. See also Rule 8.4 (Misconduct).

Definitional Cross-References
"Knows" *See* Rule 1.0(f)
"Reasonable" *See* Rule 1.0(h)

PUBLIC SERVICE

RULE 6.1: VOLUNTARY PRO BONO PUBLICO SERVICE

Every lawyer has a professional responsibility to provide legal services to those unable to pay. A lawyer should aspire to render at least (50) hours of pro bono publico legal services per year. In fulfilling this responsibility, the lawyer should:

(a) provide a substantial majority of the (50) hours of legal services without fee or expectation of fee to:

(1) persons of limited means; or

(2) charitable, religious, civic, community, governmental and educational organizations in matters that are designed primarily to address the needs of persons of limited means; and

(b) provide any additional services through:

(1) delivery of legal services at no fee or substantially reduced fee to individuals, groups or organizations seeking to secure or protect civil rights, civil liberties or public rights, or charitable, religious, civic, community, governmental and educational organizations in matters in furtherance of their organizational purposes, where the payment of standard legal fees would significantly deplete the organization's economic resources or would be otherwise inappropriate;

(2) delivery of legal services at a substantially reduced fee to persons of limited means; or

(3) participation in activities for improving the law, the legal system or the legal profession.

In addition, a lawyer should voluntarily contribute financial support to organizations that provide legal services to persons of limited means.

Comment

[1] Every lawyer, regardless of professional prominence or professional work load, has a responsibility to provide legal services to those unable to pay, and personal involvement in the problems of the disadvantaged can be one of the most rewarding experiences in the life of a lawyer. The American Bar Association urges all lawyers to provide a minimum of 50 hours of pro bono services annually. States, however, may decide to choose a higher or lower number of hours of annual service (which may be expressed as a percentage of a lawyer's professional time) depending upon local needs and local conditions. It is recognized that in some years a lawyer may render greater or fewer hours than the annual standard specified, but during the course of his or her legal career, each lawyer should render on average per year, the number of hours set forth in this Rule. Services can be performed in civil matters or in criminal or quasi-criminal matters for which there is no government obligation to provide funds for legal representation, such as post-conviction death penalty appeal cases.

[2] Paragraphs (a)(1) and (2) recognize the critical need for legal services that exists among persons of limited means by providing that a substantial majority of the legal services rendered annually to the disadvantaged be furnished without fee or expectation of fee. Legal services under these paragraphs consist of a full range of activities, including individual and class representation, the provision of legal advice, legislative lobbying, administrative rule making and the provision of free training or mentoring to those who represent persons of limited means. The variety of these activities should facilitate participation by government lawyers, even when restrictions exist on their engaging in the outside practice of law.

[3] Persons eligible for legal services under paragraphs (a)(1) and (2) are those who qualify for participation in programs funded by the Legal Services Corporation and those whose incomes and financial resources are slightly above the guidelines utilized by such programs but nevertheless, cannot afford counsel. Legal services can be rendered to individuals or to organizations such as homeless shelters, battered women's centers and food pantries that serve those of limited means. The term "governmental organizations" includes, but is not limited to, public protection programs and sections of governmental or public sector agencies.

[4] Because service must be provided without fee or expectation of fee, the intent of the lawyer to render free legal services is essential for the

work performed to fall within the meaning of paragraphs (a)(1) and (2). Accordingly, services rendered cannot be considered pro bono if an anticipated fee is uncollected, but the award of statutory attorneys' fees in a case originally accepted as pro bono would not disqualify such services from inclusion under this section. Lawyers who do receive fees in such cases are encouraged to contribute an appropriate portion of such fees to organizations or projects that benefit persons of limited means.

[5] While it is possible for a lawyer to fulfill the annual responsibility to perform pro bono services exclusively through activities described in paragraphs (a)(1) and (2), to the extent that any hours of service remained unfulfilled, the remaining commitment can be met in a variety of ways as set forth in paragraph (b). Constitutional, statutory or regulatory restrictions may prohibit or impede government and public sector lawyers and judges from performing the pro bono services outlined in paragraphs (a)(1) and (2). Accordingly, where those restrictions apply, government and public sector lawyers and judges may fulfill their pro bono responsibility by performing services outlined in paragraph (b).

[6] Paragraph (b)(1) includes the provision of certain types of legal services to those whose incomes and financial resources place them above limited means. It also permits the pro bono lawyer to accept a substantially reduced fee for services. Examples of the types of issues that may be addressed under this paragraph include First Amendment claims, Title VII claims and environmental protection claims. Additionally, a wide range of organizations may be represented, including social service, medical research, cultural and religious groups.

[7] Paragraph (b)(2) covers instances in which lawyers agree to and receive a modest fee for furnishing legal services to persons of limited means. Participation in judicare programs and acceptance of court appointments in which the fee is substantially below a lawyer's usual rate are encouraged under this section.

[8] Paragraph (b)(3) recognizes the value of lawyers engaging in activities that improve the law, the legal system or the legal profession. Serving on bar association committees, serving on boards of pro bono or legal services programs, taking part in Law Day activities, acting as a continuing legal education instructor, a mediator or an arbitrator and engaging in legislative lobbying to improve the law, the legal system or the profession are a few examples of the many activities that fall within this paragraph.

[9] Because the provision of pro bono services is a professional responsibility, it is the individual ethical commitment of each lawyer. Nev-

ertheless, there may be times when it is not feasible for a lawyer to engage in pro bono services. At such times a lawyer may discharge the pro bono responsibility by providing financial support to organizations providing free legal services to persons of limited means. Such financial support should be reasonably equivalent to the value of the hours of service that would have otherwise been provided. In addition, at times it may be more feasible to satisfy the pro bono responsibility collectively, as by a firm's aggregate pro bono activities.

[10] Because the efforts of individual lawyers are not enough to meet the need for free legal services that exists among persons of limited means, the government and the profession have instituted additional programs to provide those services. Every lawyer should financially support such programs, in addition to either providing direct pro bono services or making financial contributions when pro bono service is not feasible.

[11] Law firms should act reasonably to enable and encourage all lawyers in the firm to provide the pro bono legal services called for by this Rule.

[12] The responsibility set forth in this Rule is not intended to be enforced through disciplinary process.

Definitional Cross-References

"Substantial" *See* Rule 1.0(l)

RULE 6.2: ACCEPTING APPOINTMENTS

A lawyer shall not seek to avoid appointment by a tribunal to represent a person except for good cause, such as:

(a) representing the client is likely to result in violation of the Rules of Professional Conduct or other law;

(b) representing the client is likely to result in an unreasonable financial burden on the lawyer; or

(c) the client or the cause is so repugnant to the lawyer as to be likely to impair the client-lawyer relationship or the lawyer's ability to represent the client.

Comment

[1] A lawyer ordinarily is not obliged to accept a client whose character or cause the lawyer regards as repugnant. The lawyer's freedom to select clients is, however, qualified. All lawyers have a responsibility to

assist in providing pro bono publico service. See Rule 6.1. An individual lawyer fulfills this responsibility by accepting a fair share of unpopular matters or indigent or unpopular clients. A lawyer may also be subject to appointment by a court to serve unpopular clients or persons unable to afford legal services.

Appointed Counsel

[2] For good cause a lawyer may seek to decline an appointment to represent a person who cannot afford to retain counsel or whose cause is unpopular. Good cause exists if the lawyer could not handle the matter competently, see Rule 1.1, or if undertaking the representation would result in an improper conflict of interest, for example, when the client or the cause is so repugnant to the lawyer as to be likely to impair the client-lawyer relationship or the lawyer's ability to represent the client. A lawyer may also seek to decline an appointment if acceptance would be unreasonably burdensome, for example, when it would impose a financial sacrifice so great as to be unjust.

[3] An appointed lawyer has the same obligations to the client as retained counsel, including the obligations of loyalty and confidentiality, and is subject to the same limitations on the client-lawyer relationship, such as the obligation to refrain from assisting the client in violation of the Rules.

Definitional Cross-References

"Tribunal" *See* Rule 1.0(m)

RULE 6.3: MEMBERSHIP IN LEGAL SERVICES ORGANIZATION

A lawyer may serve as a director, officer or member of a legal services organization, apart from the law firm in which the lawyer practices, notwithstanding that the organization serves persons having interests adverse to a client of the lawyer. The lawyer shall not knowingly participate in a decision or action of the organization:

(a) if participating in the decision or action would be incompatible with the lawyer's obligations to a client under Rule 1.7; or

(b) where the decision or action could have a material adverse effect on the representation of a client of the organization whose interests are adverse to a client of the lawyer.

Comment

[1] Lawyers should be encouraged to support and participate in legal service organizations. A lawyer who is an officer or a member of such an organization does not thereby have a client-lawyer relationship with persons served by the organization. However, there is potential conflict between the interests of such persons and the interests of the lawyer's clients. If the possibility of such conflict disqualified a lawyer from serving on the board of a legal services organization, the profession's involvement in such organizations would be severely curtailed.

[2] It may be necessary in appropriate cases to reassure a client of the organization that the representation will not be affected by conflicting loyalties of a member of the board. Established, written policies in this respect can enhance the credibility of such assurances.

Definitional Cross-References

"Law firm" *See* Rule 1.0(c)
"Knowingly" *See* Rule 1.0(f)

RULE 6.4: LAW REFORM ACTIVITIES AFFECTING CLIENT INTERESTS

A lawyer may serve as a director, officer or member of an organization involved in reform of the law or its administration notwithstanding that the reform may affect the interests of a client of the lawyer. When the lawyer knows that the interests of a client may be materially benefitted by a decision in which the lawyer participates, the lawyer shall disclose that fact but need not identify the client.

Comment

[1] Lawyers involved in organizations seeking law reform generally do not have a client-lawyer relationship with the organization. Otherwise, it might follow that a lawyer could not be involved in a bar association law reform program that might indirectly affect a client. See also Rule 1.2(b). For example, a lawyer specializing in antitrust litigation might be regarded as disqualified from participating in drafting revisions of rules governing that subject. In determining the nature and scope of participation in such activities, a lawyer should be mindful of obligations to clients under other Rules, particularly Rule 1.7. A lawyer is profession-

ally obligated to protect the integrity of the program by making an appropriate disclosure within the organization when the lawyer knows a private client might be materially benefitted.

Definitional Cross-References
"Knows" *See* Rule 1.0(f)

RULE 6.5: NONPROFIT AND COURT-ANNEXED LIMITED LEGAL SERVICES PROGRAMS

(a) A lawyer who, under the auspices of a program sponsored by a nonprofit organization or court, provides short-term limited legal services to a client without expectation by either the lawyer or the client that the lawyer will provide continuing representation in the matter:

(1) is subject to Rules 1.7 and 1.9(a) only if the lawyer knows that the representation of the client involves a conflict of interest; and

(2) is subject to Rule 1.10 only if the lawyer knows that another lawyer associated with the lawyer in a law firm is disqualified by Rule 1.7 or 1.9(a) with respect to the matter.

(b) Except as provided in paragraph (a)(2), Rule 1.10 is inapplicable to a representation governed by this Rule.

Comment

[1] Legal services organizations, courts and various nonprofit organizations have established programs through which lawyers provide short-term limited legal services—such as advice or the completion of legal forms—that will assist persons to address their legal problems without further representation by a lawyer. In these programs, such as legal-advice hotlines, advice-only clinics or pro se counseling programs, a client-lawyer relationship is established, but there is no expectation that the lawyer's representation of the client will continue beyond the limited consultation. Such programs are normally operated under circumstances in which it is not feasible for a lawyer to systematically screen for conflicts of interest as is generally required before undertaking a representation. See, e.g., Rules 1.7, 1.9 and 1.10.

[2] A lawyer who provides short-term limited legal services pursuant to this Rule must secure the client's informed consent to the limited scope

of the representation. See Rule 1.2(c). If a short-term limited representation would not be reasonable under the circumstances, the lawyer may offer advice to the client but must also advise the client of the need for further assistance of counsel. Except as provided in this Rule, the Rules of Professional Conduct, including Rules 1.6 and 1.9(c), are applicable to the limited representation.

[3] Because a lawyer who is representing a client in the circumstances addressed by this Rule ordinarily is not able to check systematically for conflicts of interest, paragraph (a) requires compliance with Rules 1.7 or 1.9(a) only if the lawyer knows that the representation presents a conflict of interest for the lawyer, and with Rule 1.10 only if the lawyer knows that another lawyer in the lawyer's firm is disqualified by Rules 1.7 or 1.9(a) in the matter.

[4] Because the limited nature of the services significantly reduces the risk of conflicts of interest with other matters being handled by the lawyer's firm, paragraph (b) provides that Rule 1.10 is inapplicable to a representation governed by this Rule except as provided by paragraph (a)(2). Paragraph (a)(2) requires the participating lawyer to comply with Rule 1.10 when the lawyer knows that the lawyer's firm is disqualified by Rules 1.7 or 1.9(a). By virtue of paragraph (b), however, a lawyer's participation in a short-term limited legal services program will not preclude the lawyer's firm from undertaking or continuing the representation of a client with interests adverse to a client being represented under the program's auspices. Nor will the personal disqualification of a lawyer participating in the program be imputed to other lawyers participating in the program.

[5] If, after commencing a short-term limited representation in accordance with this Rule, a lawyer undertakes to represent the client in the matter on an ongoing basis, Rules 1.7, 1.9(a) and 1.10 become applicable.

Definitional Cross-References

"Law firm" *See* Rule 1.0(c)
"Knows" *See* Rule 1.0(f)

INFORMATION ABOUT LEGAL SERVICES

RULE 7.1: COMMUNICATIONS CONCERNING A LAWYER'S SERVICES

A lawyer shall not make a false or misleading communication about the lawyer or the lawyer's services. A communication is false or misleading if it contains a material misrepresentation of fact or law, or omits a fact necessary to make the statement considered as a whole not materially misleading.

Comment

[1] This Rule governs all communications about a lawyer's services, including advertising. Whatever means are used to make known a lawyer's services, statements about them must be truthful.

[2] Misleading truthful statements are prohibited by this Rule. A truthful statement is misleading if it omits a fact necessary to make the lawyer's communication considered as a whole not materially misleading. A truthful statement is misleading if a substantial likelihood exists that it will lead a reasonable person to formulate a specific conclusion about the lawyer or the lawyer's services for which there is no reasonable factual foundation. A truthful statement is also misleading if presented in a way that creates a substantial likelihood that a reasonable person would believe the lawyer's communication requires that person to take further action when, in fact, no action is required.

[3] A communication that truthfully reports a lawyer's achievements on behalf of clients or former clients may be misleading if presented so as to lead a reasonable person to form an unjustified expectation that the same results could be obtained for other clients in similar matters without reference to the specific factual and legal circumstances of each client's case. Similarly, an unsubstantiated claim about a lawyer's or law firm's services or fees, or an unsubstantiated comparison of the lawyer's or law firm's services or fees with those of other lawyers or law firms, may be misleading if presented with such specificity as would lead a reasonable person to conclude that the comparison or claim can be substantiated. The inclusion of an appropriate disclaimer or qualifying language may preclude a finding that a statement is likely to create unjustified expectations or otherwise mislead the public.

[4] It is professional misconduct for a lawyer to engage in conduct involving dishonesty, fraud, deceit or misrepresentation. Rule 8.4(c). See also

Rule 8.4(e) for the prohibition against stating or implying an ability to improperly influence a government agency or official or to achieve results by means that violate the Rules of Professional Conduct or other law.

[5] Firm names, letterhead and professional designations are communications concerning a lawyer's services. A firm may be designated by the names of all or some of its current members, by the names of deceased members where there has been a succession in the firm's identity or by a trade name if it is not false or misleading. A lawyer or law firm also may be designated by a distinctive website address, social media username or comparable professional designation that is not misleading. A law firm name or designation is misleading if it implies a connection with a government agency, with a deceased lawyer who was not a former member of the firm, with a lawyer not associated with the firm or a predecessor firm, with a nonlawyer or with a public or charitable legal services organization. If a firm uses a trade name that includes a geographical name such as "Springfield Legal Clinic," an express statement explaining that it is not a public legal aid organization may be required to avoid a misleading implication.

[6] A law firm with offices in more than one jurisdiction may use the same name or other professional designation in each jurisdiction.

[7] Lawyers may not imply or hold themselves out as practicing together in one firm when they are not a firm, as defined in Rule 1.0(c), because to do so would be false and misleading.

[8] It is misleading to use the name of a lawyer holding a public office in the name of a law firm, or in communications on the law firm's behalf, during any substantial period in which the lawyer is not actively and regularly practicing with the firm.

RULE 7.2: COMMUNICATIONS CONCERNING A LAWYER'S SERVICES: SPECIFIC RULES

(a) A lawyer may communicate information regarding the lawyer's services through any media.

(b) A lawyer shall not compensate, give or promise anything of value to a person for recommending the lawyer's services except that a lawyer may:

(1) pay the reasonable costs of advertisements or communications permitted by this Rule;

(2) pay the usual charges of a legal service plan or a not-for-profit or qualified lawyer referral service;

(3) pay for a law practice in accordance with Rule 1.17;

(4) refer clients to another lawyer or a nonlawyer professional pursuant to an agreement not otherwise prohibited under these Rules that provides for the other person to refer clients or customers to the lawyer, if:

(i) the reciprocal referral agreement is not exclusive; and

(ii) the client is informed of the existence and nature of the agreement; and

(5) give nominal gifts as an expression of appreciation that are neither intended nor reasonably expected to be a form of compensation for recommending a lawyer's services.

(c) A lawyer shall not state or imply that a lawyer is certified as a specialist in a particular field of law, unless:

(1) the lawyer has been certified as a specialist by an organization that has been approved by an appropriate authority of the state or the District of Columbia or a U.S. Territory or that has been accredited by the American Bar Association; and

(2) the name of the certifying organization is clearly identified in the communication.

(d) Any communication made under this Rule must include the name and contact information of at least one lawyer or law firm responsible for its content.

Comment

[1] This Rule permits public dissemination of information concerning a lawyer's or law firm's name, address, email address, website, and telephone number; the kinds of services the lawyer will undertake; the basis on which the lawyer's fees are determined, including prices for specific services and payment and credit arrangements; a lawyer's foreign language ability; names of references and, with their consent, names of clients regularly represented; and other information that might invite the attention of those seeking legal assistance.

Paying Others to Recommend a Lawyer

[2] Except as permitted under paragraphs (b)(1)-(b)(5), lawyers are not permitted to pay others for recommending the lawyer's services. A communication contains a recommendation if it endorses or vouches for a lawyer's credentials, abilities, competence, character, or other professional qualities. Directory listings and group advertisements that list lawyers by

practice area, without more, do not constitute impermissible "recommendations."

[3] Paragraph (b)(1) allows a lawyer to pay for advertising and communications permitted by this Rule, including the costs of print directory listings, on-line directory listings, newspaper ads, television and radio airtime, domain-name registrations, sponsorship fees, Internet-based advertisements, and group advertising. A lawyer may compensate employees, agents and vendors who are engaged to provide marketing or client development services, such as publicists, public-relations personnel, business-development staff, television and radio station employees or spokespersons and website designers.

[4] Paragraph (b)(5) permits lawyers to give nominal gifts as an expression of appreciation to a person for recommending the lawyer's services or referring a prospective client. The gift may not be more than a token item as might be given for holidays, or other ordinary social hospitality. A gift is prohibited if offered or given in consideration of any promise, agreement or understanding that such a gift would be forthcoming or that referrals would be made or encouraged in the future.

[5] A lawyer may pay others for generating client leads, such as Internet-based client leads, as long as the lead generator does not recommend the lawyer, any payment to the lead generator is consistent with Rules 1.5(e) (division of fees) and 5.4 (professional independence of the lawyer), and the lead generator's communications are consistent with Rule 7.1 (communications concerning a lawyer's services). To comply with Rule 7.1, a lawyer must not pay a lead generator that states, implies, or creates a reasonable impression that it is recommending the lawyer, is making the referral without payment from the lawyer, or has analyzed a person's legal problems when determining which lawyer should receive the referral. See Comment [2] (definition of "recommendation"). See also Rule 5.3 (duties of lawyers and law firms with respect to the conduct of nonlawyers); Rule 8.4(a) (duty to avoid violating the Rules through the acts of another).

[6] A lawyer may pay the usual charges of a legal service plan or a not-for-profit or qualified lawyer referral service. A legal service plan is a prepaid or group legal service plan or a similar delivery system that assists people who seek to secure legal representation. A lawyer referral service, on the other hand, is any organization that holds itself out to the public as a lawyer referral service. Qualified referral services are consumer-oriented organizations that provide unbiased referrals to lawyers

with appropriate experience in the subject matter of the representation and afford other client protections, such as complaint procedures or malpractice insurance requirements. Consequently, this Rule only permits a lawyer to pay the usual charges of a not-for-profit or qualified lawyer referral service. A qualified lawyer referral service is one that is approved by an appropriate regulatory authority as affording adequate protections for the public. See, e.g., the American Bar Association's Model Rules Governing Lawyer Referral and Information Services.

[7] A lawyer who accepts assignments or referrals from a legal service plan or referrals from a lawyer referral service must act reasonably to assure that the activities of the plan or service are compatible with the lawyer's professional obligations. Legal service plans and lawyer referral services may communicate with the public, but such communication must be in conformity with these Rules. Thus, advertising must not be false or misleading, as would be the case if the communications of a group advertising program or a group legal services plan would mislead the public to think that it was a lawyer referral service sponsored by a state agency or bar association.

[8] A lawyer also may agree to refer clients to another lawyer or a nonlawyer professional, in return for the undertaking of that person to refer clients or customers to the lawyer. Such reciprocal referral arrangements must not interfere with the lawyer's professional judgment as to making referrals or as to providing substantive legal services. See Rules 2.1 and 5.4(c). Except as provided in Rule 1.5(e), a lawyer who receives referrals from a lawyer or nonlawyer professional must not pay anything solely for the referral, but the lawyer does not violate paragraph (b) of this Rule by agreeing to refer clients to the other lawyer or nonlawyer professional, so long as the reciprocal referral agreement is not exclusive and the client is informed of the referral agreement. Conflicts of interest created by such arrangements are governed by Rule 1.7. Reciprocal referral agreements should not be of indefinite duration and should be reviewed periodically to determine whether they comply with these Rules. This Rule does not restrict referrals or divisions of revenues or net income among lawyers within firms comprised of multiple entities.

Communications about Fields of Practice

[9] Paragraph (c) of this Rule permits a lawyer to communicate that the lawyer does or does not practice in particular areas of law. A lawyer is generally permitted to state that the lawyer "concentrates in" or is a "specialist," practices a "specialty," or "specializes in" particular fields based

on the lawyer's experience, specialized training or education, but such communications are subject to the "false and misleading" standard applied in Rule 7.1 to communications concerning a lawyer's services.

[10] The Patent and Trademark Office has a long-established policy of designating lawyers practicing before the Office. The designation of Admiralty practice also has a long historical tradition associated with maritime commerce and the federal courts. A lawyer's communications about these practice areas are not prohibited by this Rule.

[11] This Rule permits a lawyer to state that the lawyer is certified as a specialist in a field of law if such certification is granted by an organization approved by an appropriate authority of a state, the District of Columbia or a U.S. Territory or accredited by the American Bar Association or another organization, such as a state supreme court or a state bar association, that has been approved by the authority of the state, the District of Columbia or a U.S. Territory to accredit organizations that certify lawyers as specialists. Certification signifies that an objective entity has recognized an advanced degree of knowledge and experience in the specialty area greater than is suggested by general licensure to practice law. Certifying organizations may be expected to apply standards of experience, knowledge and proficiency to ensure that a lawyer's recognition as a specialist is meaningful and reliable. To ensure that consumers can obtain access to useful information about an organization granting certification, the name of the certifying organization must be included in any communication regarding the certification.

Required Contact Information

[12] This Rule requires that any communication about a lawyer or law firm's services include the name of, and contact information for, the lawyer or law firm. Contact information includes a website address, a telephone number, an email address or a physical office location.

Definitional Cross-References
"Reasonably" *See* Rule 1.0(h)
"Law firm" *See* Rule 1.0(c)

RULE 7.3: SOLICITATION OF CLIENTS

(a) "Solicitation" or "solicit" denotes a communication initiated by or on behalf of a lawyer or law firm that is directed to a specific person the lawyer knows or reasonably should know needs legal services in a particular matter and that offers to provide, or reasonably can be understood as offering to provide, legal services for that matter.

(b) A lawyer shall not solicit professional employment by live person-to-person contact when a significant motive for the lawyer's doing so is the lawyer's or law firm's pecuniary gain, unless the contact is with a:

(1) lawyer;

(2) person who has a family, close personal, or prior business or professional relationship with the lawyer or law firm; or

(3) person who routinely uses for business purposes the type of legal services offered by the lawyer.

(c) A lawyer shall not solicit professional employment even when not otherwise prohibited by paragraph (b), if:

(1) the target of the solicitation has made known to the lawyer a desire not to be solicited by the lawyer; or

(2) the solicitation involves coercion, duress or harassment.

(d) This Rule does not prohibit communications authorized by law or ordered by a court or other tribunal.

(e) Notwithstanding the prohibitions in this Rule, a lawyer may participate with a prepaid or group legal service plan operated by an organization not owned or directed by the lawyer that uses live person-to-person contact to enroll members or sell subscriptions for the plan from persons who are not known to need legal services in a particular matter covered by the plan.

Comment

[1] Paragraph (b) prohibits a lawyer from soliciting professional employment by live person-to-person contact when a significant motive for the lawyer's doing so is the lawyer's or the law firm's pecuniary gain. A lawyer's communication is not a solicitation if it is directed to the general public, such as through a billboard, an Internet banner advertisement, a website or a television commercial, or if it is in response to a request for information or is automatically generated in response to electronic searches.

[2] "Live person-to-person contact" means in-person, face-to-face, live telephone and other real-time visual or auditory person-to-person communications where the person is subject to a direct personal encounter without time for reflection. Such person-to-person contact does not include chat rooms, text messages or other written communications that

recipients may easily disregard. A potential for overreaching exists when a lawyer, seeking pecuniary gain, solicits a person known to be in need of legal services. This form of contact subjects a person to the private importuning of the trained advocate in a direct interpersonal encounter. The person, who may already feel overwhelmed by the circumstances giving rise to the need for legal services, may find it difficult to fully evaluate all available alternatives with reasoned judgment and appropriate selfinterest in the face of the lawyer's presence and insistence upon an immediate response. The situation is fraught with the possibility of undue influence, intimidation, and overreaching.

[3] The potential for overreaching inherent in live person-to-person contact justifies its prohibition, since lawyers have alternative means of conveying necessary information. In particular, communications can be mailed or transmitted by email or other electronic means that do not violate other laws. These forms of communications make it possible for the public to be informed about the need for legal services, and about the qualifications of available lawyers and law firms, without subjecting the public to live person-to-person persuasion that may overwhelm a person's judgment.

[4] The contents of live person-to-person contact can be disputed and may not be subject to thirdparty scrutiny. Consequently, they are much more likely to approach (and occasionally cross) the dividing line between accurate representations and those that are false and misleading.

[5] There is far less likelihood that a lawyer would engage in overreaching against a former client, or a person with whom the lawyer has a close personal, family, business or professional relationship, or in situations in which the lawyer is motivated by considerations other than the lawyer's pecuniary gain. Nor is there a serious potential for overreaching when the person contacted is a lawyer or is known to routinely use the type of legal services involved for business purposes. Examples include persons who routinely hire outside counsel to represent the entity; entrepreneurs who regularly engage business, employment law or intellectual property lawyers; small business proprietors who routinely hire lawyers for lease or contract issues; and other people who routinely retain lawyers for business transactions or formations. Paragraph (b) is not intended to prohibit a lawyer from participating in constitutionally protected activities of public or charitable legal-service organizations or bona fide political, social, civic, fraternal, employee or trade organizations whose purposes include providing or recommending legal services to their members or beneficiaries.

Rule 7.3

[6] A solicitation that contains false or misleading information within the meaning of Rule 7.1, that involves coercion, duress or harassment within the meaning of Rule 7.3(c)(2), or that involves contact with someone who has made known to the lawyer a desire not to be solicited by the lawyer within the meaning of Rule 7.3(c)(1) is prohibited. Live, person-to-person contact of individuals who may be especially vulnerable to coercion or duress is ordinarily not appropriate, for example, the elderly, those whose first language is not English, or the disabled.

[7] This Rule does not prohibit a lawyer from contacting representatives of organizations or groups that may be interested in establishing a group or prepaid legal plan for their members, insureds, beneficiaries or other third parties for the purpose of informing such entities of the availability of and details concerning the plan or arrangement which the lawyer or lawyer's firm is willing to offer. This form of communication is not directed to people who are seeking legal services for themselves. Rather, it is usually addressed to an individual acting in a fiduciary capacity seeking a supplier of legal services for others who may, if they choose, become prospective clients of the lawyer. Under these circumstances, the activity which the lawyer undertakes in communicating with such representatives and the type of information transmitted to the individual are functionally similar to and serve the same purpose as advertising permitted under Rule 7.2.

[8] Communications authorized by law or ordered by a court or tribunal include a notice to potential members of a class in class action litigation.

[9] Paragraph (e) of this Rule permits a lawyer to participate with an organization which uses personal contact to enroll members for its group or prepaid legal service plan, provided that the personal contact is not undertaken by any lawyer who would be a provider of legal services through the plan. The organization must not be owned by or directed (whether as manager or otherwise) by any lawyer or law firm that participates in the plan. For example, paragraph (e) would not permit a lawyer to create an organization controlled directly or indirectly by the lawyer and use the organization for the person-to-person solicitation of legal employment of the lawyer through memberships in the plan or otherwise. The communication permitted by these organizations must not be directed to a person known to need legal services in a particular matter, but must be designed to inform potential plan members generally of another means of affordable legal services. Lawyers who participate in a legal service plan must reasonably assure that the plan sponsors are in compliance with Rules 7.1, 7.2 and 7.3(c).

Definitional Cross-References

"Law firm" *See* Rule 1.0(c)
"Knows" *See* Rule 1.0(f)
"Reasonably should know" *See* Rule 1.0(j)
"Reasonably" *See* Rule 1.0(h)
"Known" *See* Rule 1.0(f)

RULE 7.4 (DELETED 2018)

RULE 7.5 (DELETED 2018)

RULE 7.6: POLITICAL CONTRIBUTIONS TO OBTAIN GOVERNMENT LEGAL ENGAGEMENTS OR APPOINTMENTS BY JUDGES

A lawyer or law firm shall not accept a government legal engagement or an appointment by a judge if the lawyer or law firm makes a political contribution or solicits political contributions for the purpose of obtaining or being considered for that type of legal engagement or appointment.

Comment

[1] Lawyers have a right to participate fully in the political process, which includes making and soliciting political contributions to candidates for judicial and other public office. Nevertheless, when lawyers make or solicit political contributions in order to obtain an engagement for legal work awarded by a government agency, or to obtain appointment by a judge, the public may legitimately question whether the lawyers engaged to perform the work are selected on the basis of competence and merit. In such a circumstance, the integrity of the profession is undermined.

[2] The term "political contribution" denotes any gift, subscription, loan, advance or deposit of anything of value made directly or indirectly to a candidate, incumbent, political party or campaign committee to influence or provide financial support for election to or retention in judicial or other government office. Political contributions in initiative and ref-

erendum elections are not included. For purposes of this Rule, the term "political contribution" does not include uncompensated services.

[3] Subject to the exceptions below, (i) the term "government legal engagement" denotes any engagement to provide legal services that a public official has the direct or indirect power to award; and (ii) the term "appointment by a judge" denotes an appointment to a position such as referee, commissioner, special master, receiver, guardian or other similar position that is made by a judge. Those terms do not, however, include (a) substantially uncompensated services; (b) engagements or appointments made on the basis of experience, expertise, professional qualifications and cost following a request for proposal or other process that is free from influence based upon political contributions; and (c) engagements or appointments made on a rotational basis from a list compiled without regard to political contributions.

[4] The term "lawyer or law firm" includes a political action committee or other entity owned or controlled by a lawyer or law firm.

[5] Political contributions are for the purpose of obtaining or being considered for a government legal engagement or appointment by a judge if, but for the desire to be considered for the legal engagement or appointment, the lawyer or law firm would not have made or solicited the contributions. The purpose may be determined by an examination of the circumstances in which the contributions occur. For example, one or more contributions that in the aggregate are substantial in relation to other contributions by lawyers or law firms, made for the benefit of an official in a position to influence award of a government legal engagement, and followed by an award of the legal engagement to the contributing or soliciting lawyer or the lawyer's firm would support an inference that the purpose of the contributions was to obtain the engagement, absent other factors that weigh against existence of the proscribed purpose. Those factors may include among others that the contribution or solicitation was made to further a political, social, or economic interest or because of an existing personal, family, or professional relationship with a candidate.

[6] If a lawyer makes or solicits a political contribution under circumstances that constitute bribery or another crime, Rule 8.4(b) is implicated.

Definitional Cross-References

"Law firm" *See* Rule 1.0(c)

MAINTAINING THE INTEGRITY OF THE PROFESSION

RULE 8.1: BAR ADMISSION AND DISCIPLINARY MATTERS

An applicant for admission to the bar, or a lawyer in connection with a bar admission application or in connection with a disciplinary matter, shall not:

(a) knowingly make a false statement of material fact; or

(b) fail to disclose a fact necessary to correct a misapprehension known by the person to have arisen in the matter, or knowingly fail to respond to a lawful demand for information from an admissions or disciplinary authority, except that this Rule does not require disclosure of information otherwise protected by Rule 1.6.

Comment

[1] The duty imposed by this Rule extends to persons seeking admission to the bar as well as to lawyers. Hence, if a person makes a material false statement in connection with an application for admission, it may be the basis for subsequent disciplinary action if the person is admitted, and in any event may be relevant in a subsequent admission application. The duty imposed by this Rule applies to a lawyer's own admission or discipline as well as that of others. Thus, it is a separate professional offense for a lawyer to knowingly make a misrepresentation or omission in connection with a disciplinary investigation of the lawyer's own conduct. Paragraph (b) of this Rule also requires correction of any prior misstatement in the matter that the applicant or lawyer may have made and affirmative clarification of any misunderstanding on the part of the admissions or disciplinary authority of which the person involved becomes aware.

[2] This Rule is subject to the provisions of the Fifth Amendment of the United States Constitution and corresponding provisions of state constitutions. A person relying on such a provision in response to a question, however, should do so openly and not use the right of nondisclosure as a justification for failure to comply with this Rule.

[3] A lawyer representing an applicant for admission to the bar, or representing a lawyer who is the subject of a disciplinary inquiry or proceeding, is governed by the Rules applicable to the client-lawyer relationship, including Rule 1.6 and, in some cases, Rule 3.3.

Definitional Cross-References

"Knowingly" and "Known" *See* Rule 1.0(f)

RULE 8.2: JUDICIAL AND LEGAL OFFICIALS

(a) A lawyer shall not make a statement that the lawyer knows to be false or with reckless disregard as to its truth or falsity concerning the qualifications or integrity of a judge, adjudicatory officer or public legal officer, or of a candidate for election or appointment to judicial or legal office.

(b) A lawyer who is a candidate for judicial office shall comply with the applicable provisions of the Code of Judicial Conduct.

Comment

[1] Assessments by lawyers are relied on in evaluating the professional or personal fitness of persons being considered for election or appointment to judicial office and to public legal offices, such as attorney general, prosecuting attorney and public defender. Expressing honest and candid opinions on such matters contributes to improving the administration of justice. Conversely, false statements by a lawyer can unfairly undermine public confidence in the administration of justice.

[2] When a lawyer seeks judicial office, the lawyer should be bound by applicable limitations on political activity.

[3] To maintain the fair and independent administration of justice, lawyers are encouraged to continue traditional efforts to defend judges and courts unjustly criticized.

Definitional Cross-References

"Knows" *See* Rule 1.0(f)

RULE 8.3: REPORTING PROFESSIONAL MISCONDUCT

(a) A lawyer who knows that another lawyer has committed a violation of the Rules of Professional Conduct that raises a substantial question as to that lawyer's honesty, trustworthiness or fitness as a lawyer in other respects, shall inform the appropriate professional authority.

(b) A lawyer who knows that a judge has committed a violation of applicable rules of judicial conduct that raises a substantial question as to the judge's fitness for office shall inform the appropriate authority.

(c) This Rule does not require disclosure of information otherwise protected by Rule 1.6 or information gained by a lawyer or judge while participating in an approved lawyers assistance program.

Comment

[1] Self-regulation of the legal profession requires that members of the profession initiate disciplinary investigation when they know of a violation of the Rules of Professional Conduct. Lawyers have a similar obligation with respect to judicial misconduct. An apparently isolated violation may indicate a pattern of misconduct that only a disciplinary investigation can uncover. Reporting a violation is especially important where the victim is unlikely to discover the offense.

[2] A report about misconduct is not required where it would involve violation of Rule 1.6. However, a lawyer should encourage a client to consent to disclosure where prosecution would not substantially prejudice the client's interests.

[3] If a lawyer were obliged to report every violation of the Rules, the failure to report any violation would itself be a professional offense. Such a requirement existed in many jurisdictions but proved to be unenforceable. This Rule limits the reporting obligation to those offenses that a self-regulating profession must vigorously endeavor to prevent. A measure of judgment is, therefore, required in complying with the provisions of this Rule. The term "substantial" refers to the seriousness of the possible offense and not the quantum of evidence of which the lawyer is aware. A report should be made to the bar disciplinary agency unless some other agency, such as a peer review agency, is more appropriate in the circumstances. Similar considerations apply to the reporting of judicial misconduct.

[4] The duty to report professional misconduct does not apply to a lawyer retained to represent a lawyer whose professional conduct is in question. Such a situation is governed by the Rules applicable to the client-lawyer relationship.

[5] Information about a lawyer's or judge's misconduct or fitness may be received by a lawyer in the course of that lawyer's participation in an approved lawyers or judges assistance program. In that circumstance, pro-

viding for an exception to the reporting requirements of paragraphs (a) and (b) of this Rule encourages lawyers and judges to seek treatment through such a program. Conversely, without such an exception, lawyers and judges may hesitate to seek assistance from these programs, which may then result in additional harm to their professional careers and additional injury to the welfare of clients and the public. These Rules do not otherwise address the confidentiality of information received by a lawyer or judge participating in an approved lawyers assistance program; such an obligation, however, may be imposed by the rules of the program or other law.

Definitional Cross-References
"Knows" *See* Rule 1.0(f)
"Substantial" *See* Rule 1.0(l)

RULE 8.4: MISCONDUCT

It is professional misconduct for a lawyer to:

(a) violate or attempt to violate the Rules of Professional Conduct, knowingly assist or induce another to do so, or do so through the acts of another;

(b) commit a criminal act that reflects adversely on the lawyer's honesty, trustworthiness or fitness as a lawyer in other respects;

(c) engage in conduct involving dishonesty, fraud, deceit or misrepresentation;

(d) engage in conduct that is prejudicial to the administration of justice;

(e) state or imply an ability to influence improperly a government agency or official or to achieve results by means that violate the Rules of Professional Conduct or other law;

(f) knowingly assist a judge or judicial officer in conduct that is a violation of applicable rules of judicial conduct or other law; or

(g) engage in conduct that the lawyer knows or reasonably should know is harassment or discrimination on the basis of race, sex, religion, national origin, ethnicity, disability, age, sexual orientation, gender identity, marital status or socioeconomic status in conduct related to the practice of law. This paragraph does not limit the ability of a lawyer to accept, decline or withdraw from a representation in accordance with Rule 1.16. This paragraph does not preclude legitimate advice or advocacy consistent with these Rules.

Comment

[1] Lawyers are subject to discipline when they violate or attempt to violate the Rules of Professional Conduct, knowingly assist or induce another to do so or do so through the acts of another, as when they request or instruct an agent to do so on the lawyer's behalf. Paragraph (a), however, does not prohibit a lawyer from advising a client concerning action the client is legally entitled to take.

[2] Many kinds of illegal conduct reflect adversely on fitness to practice law, such as offenses involving fraud and the offense of willful failure to file an income tax return. However, some kinds of offenses carry no such implication. Traditionally, the distinction was drawn in terms of offenses involving "moral turpitude." That concept can be construed to include offenses concerning some matters of personal morality, such as adultery and comparable offenses, that have no specific connection to fitness for the practice of law. Although a lawyer is personally answerable to the entire criminal law, a lawyer should be professionally answerable only for offenses that indicate lack of those characteristics relevant to law practice. Offenses involving violence, dishonesty, breach of trust, or serious interference with the administration of justice are in that category. A pattern of repeated offenses, even ones of minor significance when considered separately, can indicate indifference to legal obligation.

[3] Discrimination and harassment by lawyers in violation of paragraph (g) undermine confidence in the legal profession and the legal system. Such discrimination includes harmful verbal or physical conduct that manifests bias or prejudice towards others. Harassment includes sexual harassment and derogatory or demeaning verbal or physical conduct. Sexual harassment includes unwelcome sexual advances, requests for sexual favors, and other unwelcome verbal or physical conduct of a sexual nature. The substantive law of antidiscrimination and antiharassment statutes and case law may guide application of paragraph (g).

[4] Conduct related to the practice of law includes representing clients; interacting with witnesses, coworkers, court personnel, lawyers and others while engaged in the practice of law; operating or managing a law firm or law practice; and participating in bar association, business or social activities in connection with the practice of law. Lawyers may engage in conduct undertaken to promote diversity and inclusion without violating this Rule by, for example, implementing initiatives aimed at recruiting, hiring, retaining and advancing diverse employees or sponsoring diverse law student organizations.

[5] A trial judge's finding that peremptory challenges were exercised on a discriminatory basis does not alone establish a violation of paragraph (g). A lawyer does not violate paragraph (g) by limiting the scope or subject matter of the lawyer's practice or by limiting the lawyer's practice to members of underserved populations in accordance with these Rules and other law. A lawyer may charge and collect reasonable fees and expenses for a representation. Rule 1.5(a). Lawyers also should be mindful of their professional obligations under Rule 6.1 to provide legal services to those who are unable to pay, and their obligation under Rule 6.2 not to avoid appointments from a tribunal except for good cause. See Rule 6.2(a), (b) and (c). A lawyer's representation of a client does not constitute an endorsement by the lawyer of the client's views or activities. See Rule 1.2(b).

[6] A lawyer may refuse to comply with an obligation imposed by law upon a good faith belief that no valid obligation exists. The provisions of Rule 1.2(d) concerning a good faith challenge to the validity, scope, meaning or application of the law apply to challenges of legal regulation of the practice of law.

[7] Lawyers holding public office assume legal responsibilities going beyond those of other citizens. A lawyer's abuse of public office can suggest an inability to fulfill the professional role of lawyers. The same is true of abuse of positions of private trust such as trustee, executor, administrator, guardian, agent and officer, director or manager of a corporation or other organization.

Definitional Cross-References

"Fraud" *See* Rule 1.0(d)
"Knowingly and knows" *See* Rule 1.0(f)
"Reasonably should know" *See* Rule 1.0(j)

RULE 8.5: DISCIPLINARY AUTHORITY; CHOICE OF LAW

(a) Disciplinary Authority. A lawyer admitted to practice in this jurisdiction is subject to the disciplinary authority of this jurisdiction, regardless of where the lawyer's conduct occurs. A lawyer not admitted in this jurisdiction is also subject to the disciplinary authority of this jurisdiction if the lawyer provides or offers to provide any legal services in this jurisdiction.

A lawyer may be subject to the disciplinary authority of both this jurisdiction and another jurisdiction for the same conduct.

(b) Choice of Law. In any exercise of the disciplinary authority of this jurisdiction, the rules of professional conduct to be applied shall be as follows:

(1) for conduct in connection with a matter pending before a tribunal, the rules of the jurisdiction in which the tribunal sits, unless the rules of the tribunal provide otherwise; and

(2) for any other conduct, the rules of the jurisdiction in which the lawyer's conduct occurred, or, if the predominant effect of the conduct is in a different jurisdiction, the rules of that jurisdiction shall be applied to the conduct. A lawyer shall not be subject to discipline if the lawyer's conduct conforms to the rules of a jurisdiction in which the lawyer reasonably believes the predominant effect of the lawyer's conduct will occur.

Comment
Disciplinary Authority

[1] It is longstanding law that the conduct of a lawyer admitted to practice in this jurisdiction is subject to the disciplinary authority of this jurisdiction. Extension of the disciplinary authority of this jurisdiction to other lawyers who provide or offer to provide legal services in this jurisdiction is for the protection of the citizens of this jurisdiction. Reciprocal enforcement of a jurisdiction's disciplinary findings and sanctions will further advance the purposes of this Rule. See, Rules 6 and 22, ABA *Model Rules for Lawyer Disciplinary Enforcement*. A lawyer who is subject to the disciplinary authority of this jurisdiction under Rule 8.5(a) appoints an official to be designated by this court to receive service of process in this jurisdiction. The fact that the lawyer is subject to the disciplinary authority of this jurisdiction may be a factor in determining whether personal jurisdiction may be asserted over the lawyer for civil matters.

Choice of Law

[2] A lawyer may be potentially subject to more than one set of rules of professional conduct which impose different obligations. The lawyer may be licensed to practice in more than one jurisdiction with differing rules, or may be admitted to practice before a particular court with rules that differ from those of the jurisdiction or jurisdictions in which the lawyer is licensed to practice. Additionally, the lawyer's conduct may involve significant contacts with more than one jurisdiction.

[3] Paragraph (b) seeks to resolve such potential conflicts. Its premise is that minimizing conflicts between rules, as well as uncertainty about which rules are applicable, is in the best interest of both clients and the profession (as well as the bodies having authority to regulate the profession). Accordingly, it takes the approach of (i) providing that any particular conduct of a lawyer shall be subject to only one set of rules of professional conduct, (ii) making the determination of which set of rules applies to particular conduct as straightforward as possible, consistent with recognition of appropriate regulatory interests of relevant jurisdictions, and (iii) providing protection from discipline for lawyers who act reasonably in the face of uncertainty.

[4] Paragraph (b)(1) provides that as to a lawyer's conduct relating to a proceeding pending before a tribunal, the lawyer shall be subject only to the rules of professional conduct of that tribunal. As to all other conduct, including conduct in anticipation of a proceeding not yet pending before a tribunal, paragraph (b)(2) provides that a lawyer shall be subject to the rules of the jurisdiction in which the lawyer's conduct occurred, or, if the predominant effect of the conduct is in another jurisdiction, the rules of that jurisdiction shall be applied to the conduct. In the case of conduct in anticipation of a proceeding that is likely to be before a tribunal, the predominant effect of such conduct could be where the conduct occurred, where the tribunal sits or in another jurisdiction.

[5] When a lawyer's conduct involves significant contacts with more than one jurisdiction, it may not be clear whether the predominant effect of the lawyer's conduct will occur in a jurisdiction other than the one in which the conduct occurred. So long as the lawyer's conduct conforms to the rules of a jurisdiction in which the lawyer reasonably believes the predominant effect will occur, the lawyer shall not be subject to discipline under this Rule. With respect to conflicts of interest, in determining a lawyer's reasonable belief under paragraph (b)(2), a written agreement between the lawyer and client that reasonably specifies a particular jurisdiction as within the scope of that paragraph may be considered if the agreement was obtained with the client's informed consent confirmed in the agreement.

[6] If two admitting jurisdictions were to proceed against a lawyer for the same conduct, they should, applying this rule, identify the same governing ethics rules. They should take all appropriate steps to see that they do apply the same rule to the same conduct, and in all events should avoid proceeding against a lawyer on the basis of two inconsistent rules.

[7] The choice of law provision applies to lawyers engaged in transnational practice, unless international law, treaties or other agreements between competent regulatory authorities in the affected jurisdictions provide otherwise.

Definitional Cross-References
"Reasonably believes" *See* Rule 1.0(i)
"Tribunal" *See* Rule 1.0(m)

Appendix A

Subject Guide

A

Abuse of process,
Rule 3.1 (Comment)

Accepting appointments,
Rule 6.2

Accounting for funds,
Rule 1.15

Acquiring interest in litigation,
Rule 1.8(i)

contingent fee,
Rule 1.8(i)(2)

Adjudicative officers,

negotiating for private employment,
Rule 1.12(b)

disqualification of former,
Rule 1.12(a)

Administration of justice,

conduct prejudicial to,
Rule 8.4(d)

interference with,
Rule 8.4 (Comment)

lawyer's duty to seek improvement in,
Preamble

Administration of law,

participation in,
Rule 6.4

Administrative agencies and tribunals,

appearance before,
Rule 3.9

Administrator,

fee for representation of,
Rule 1.5 (Comment)

Admiralty practice,

communication of,
Rule 7.2(c) (Comment)

Admission to practice,
Rule 8.1

Advance fee payments,

propriety of,
Rule 1.5 (Comment)

deposit of,
Rule 1.15(c)

Adversary system,

duty of lawyer to,
Preamble

Adverse legal authority,

lawyer's duty to disclose,
Rule 3.3(a)(2)

Advertising. (*See also* Solicitation, Letterheads, Firm name.)

class action members, to notify,
Rule 7.3(d) (Comment)

communications concerning a lawyer's services, generally,
Rule 7.1

comparisons with services of other lawyers,
Rule 7.1 (Comment)

fields of practice,
Rule 7.2

mail,
Rule 7.2(a)
Rule 7.3 (Comment)

permitted forms,
Rule 7.2
prior results,
Rule 7.1 (Comment)
specialization,
Rule 7.2(c)
Advice to client,
candor, duty of,
Rule 2.1
legal services program,
Rule 6.5 (Comment)
used to engage in criminal or fraudulent conduct,
Rule 1.2 (Comment)
when lawyer not competent in area,
Rule 1.1 (Comment)
Advice to unrepresented person,
Rule 4.3
Advisor,
lawyer as,
Preamble, Rule 2.1
Advocate,
in nonadjudicative proceedings,
Rule 3.9
lawyer as,
Preamble
Alteration of documents,
Rule 3.4(a)
Alternative dispute resolution,
Rule 2.4 (Comment)
duty to inform of,
Rule 2.1 (Comment)
Ancillary businesses (or services),
Rule 5.7

Appeal,
advising client of possibility,
Rule 1.3 (Comment)
contingent fee,
Rule 1.5 (Comment)
government lawyer's authority,
Scope
Appointed counsel,
accepting appointments,
Rule 6.2
discharge by client,
Rule 1.16 (Comment)
endorsement of client's views,
Rule 1.2(b)
requirement of competence,
Rule 1.1 (Comment)
withdrawal by,
Rule 1.16 (Comment)
Arbitration,
fee disputes,
Rule 1.5 (Comment)
Arbitrator,
codes of ethics,
Rule 1.12 (Comment),
Rule 2.4 (Comment)
conflict of interest,
Rule 1.12
former, negotiating for private employment,
Rule 1.12(b)
lawyer as,
Rule 2.4
partisan in multimember panel,
Rule 1.12(d)
Area of practice,
sale of,
Rule 1.17

APPENDIX A: SUBJECT GUIDE

Association with
competent lawyer,
    Rule 1.1 (Comment)

Associations, unincorporated,
    Rule 1.13 (Comment)

Attorney-client privilege,
  common representation,
    Rule 1.7 (Comment)
  dispute resolution,
    Rule 2.4 (Comment)
  distinguished from
  confidentiality rule,
    Rule 1.6 (Comment)

Attorney general,
  authority of,
    Scope

Auditors' requests for
information,
    Rule 2.3 (Comment)

Authority of lawyer,
  decision-making authority,
    Rule 1.2(a)
  government lawyer,
    Scope

Autonomy of legal profession,
    Preamble

B

Bank charges,
    Rule 1.15(b)

Belief,
  defined,
    Rule 1.0(a)

Beneficiary,
  fiduciary client, lawyer's
  obligation toward,
    Rule 1.2 (Comment)

Board of directors,
  lawyer member,
    Rule 1.7 (Comment)
  organization as client,
    Rule 1.13

Bodily harm,
  client's intent to commit
  serious,
    Rule 1.6(b)(1)

Breach of trust,
offense involving,
    Rule 8.4 (Comment)

Bribery,
  of officials,
    Rule 3.5(a)
  of witness,
    Rule 3.4(b)
  remediation,
    Rule 3.3 (Comment)

Business affairs of lawyer,
  adverse to client,
    Rule 1.8(a)
  conflict of interest,
    Rule 1.7 (Comment)
  duty to conduct in
  compliance with law,
    Preamble
  law-related services,
    Rule 5.7

C

Campaign contributions,
    Rule 7.6

Candid advice,
    Rule 2.1

Candidate for judicial office,
    Rule 8.2(b)

Candidate for public office,
   contributions to,
      Rule 7.6
Candor toward tribunal,
   Rule 3.3
Cause of action,
   violation of Rules as basis for,
      Scope
Certification,
   as specialist,
      Rule 7.2(c)
Champerty, law of,
   Rule 1.8 (Comment)
Child client,
   Rule 1.14
   communication with,
      Rule 1.4 (Comment)
Child of lawyer,
   gift to,
      Rule 1.8(c)
   client of,
      Rule 1.7 (Comment)
Choice of law,
   Rule 8.5(b)
Citizen, lawyer as,
   Preamble
Civil disobedience,
   Rule 1.2 (Comment)
Civil liability,
   violation of Rules as basis for,
      Scope
Class actions,
   conflict of interest,
      Rule 1.7 (Comment)

fee determination,
   Rule 1.5 (Comment)
notice to members,
   Rule 7.3(d) (Comment)
Client-lawyer relationship,
   existence of defined by substantive law,
      Scope
   informed understanding, lawyer's role,
      Preamble
   law-related services,
      Rule 5.7(a)(2)
Client's identity,
   duty to disclose,
      Rule 1.13(f)
   government agency,
      Rule 1.11 (Comment),
      Rule 1.13 (Comment)
   organizational client,
      Rule 1.0 (Comment),
      Rule 1.13 (Comment)
Clinic, legal,
   Rule 6.5 (Comment)
Code of Judicial Conduct,
   Rule 1.12 (Comment),
   Rule 3.5 (Comment),
   Rule 8.2(b)
Comments,
   do not expand lawyer's responsibilities,
      Scope
Common representation,
   Rule 1.7 (Comment),
   Rule 1.9 (Comment)
Communication,
   concerning lawyer's services,
      Rule 7.1

APPENDIX A: SUBJECT GUIDE

duty to maintain with client,
  Preamble, Rule 1.4
safeguarding confidentiality,
  Rule 1.6 (Comment)
with represented party,
  Rule 4.2
with third persons,
  Rule 4.1
with unrepresented persons,
  Rule 4.3
withholding information
from client,
  Rule 1.4 (Comment)
Competence,
  Preamble,
  Rule 1.16 (Comment)
Competent representation,
  requirements of,
    Rule 1.1
  prosecutors,
    Rule 3.8 (Comment)
Compliance with Rules,
  Preamble, Scope
Concealment,
  duty to avoid,
    Rule 1.2 (Comment)
  of documents,
    Rule 3.3 (Comment),
    Rule 3.4(a)
Confidences of client,
  attachment of duty,
    Scope
  common representation,
    Rule 1.7 (Comment)
  consent required to reveal,
    Rule 1.6(a)
  corporate client,
    Rule 1.13 (Comment)

disclosure of,
  Preamble, Rule 1.6(b)
disclosure to disciplinary
authorities,
  Rule 8.1(b),
  Rule 8.3 (Comment)
duty to preserve,
  Preamble, Rule 1.6(a)
evaluation, information
used in preparing,
  Rule 2.3(c)
former client,
  Rule 1.9(c)
government client,
  Rule 1.11(c)
imputed to members of firm,
  Rule 1.0 (Comment)
inadvertent or unauthorized
disclosure,
  Rule 1.6(c)
lawyer assistance program,
  Rule 8.3(c)
perjury by client,
  Rule 3.3(c)
prospective client,
  Rule 1.18(b)
public interest in preserving,
  Preamble,
  Rule 1.6 (Comment)
with diminished capacity,
  Rule 1.14(c)
withdrawal, facts constituting
explanation for,
  Rule 1.16 (Comment)
Confirmed in writing,
  defined,
    Rule 1.0(b)

Conflict of interest,
  acquiring interest in litigation,
    Rule 1.8(i)
  advocate, when acting as,
    Rule 1.7 (Comment)
  aggregate agreements,
    Rule 1.8(g)
  arising from lawyer's change of employment,
    Rule 1.6(b)
  business interests of lawyer,
    Rule 1.7 (Comment)
  business transaction with client,
    Rule 1.8(a)
  consent of client to,
    Rule 1.7(b)(4), Rule 1.8(a)(3), Rule 1.8(b), Rule 1.8(f)(1), Rule 1.8(g), Rule 1.9(a), Rule 1.9(b), Rule 1.11(a)(2), Rule 1.12(a), Rule 1.18(d)(1)
  co-parties, representation of,
    Rule 1.7 (Comment)
  current client, concurrent conflict,
    Rule 1.7
  declining employment because of,
    Rule 1.7 (Comment)
  estate planning or administration,
    Rule 1.7 (Comment)
  fee paid by one other than client,
    Rule 1.7 (Comment), Rule 1.8(f), Rule 5.4(c)
  former client,
    Rule 1.9
  former judge or other neutral,
    Rule 1.12
  government client,
    Rule 1.11
  imputation,
    Rule 1.10
  interest of lawyer adverse to client,
    Rule 1.7(a)(2)
  lawyer as third party neutral,
    Rule 2.4 (Comment)
  legal services corporation, director of,
    Rule 6.3
  legal services program,
    Rule 6.5
  "matter" defined,
    Rule 1.11(e)
  negotiation,
    Rule 1.7 (Comment)
  prospective client,
    Rule 1.18(c)
  responsibility for firm,
    Rule 5.1 (Comment)
  screening,
    Rule 1.10(a)(2)
  sexual relations with client,
    Rule 1.8(j)
  third person, interest adverse to client,
    Rule 1.7(a)(2)
  unrelated matters,
    Rule 1.7 (Comment)
  waiver of future,
    Rule 1.7 (Comment)
  withdrawal because of,
    Rule 1.7 (Comment)

APPENDIX A: SUBJECT GUIDE

Conflicting responsibilities,
Preamble

Conscience,
Preamble

Consent by client,
communication regarding decisions requiring,
Rule 1.4(a)(1)

to common representation,
Rule 1.7 (Comment)

to conflict of interest,
Rule 1.7(b)(4), Rule 1.8(a)(3), Rule 1.8(b), Rule 1.8(f)(1), Rule 1.8(g), Rule 1.9(a), Rule 1.9(b), Rule 1.11(a)(2), Rule 1.12(a), Rule 1.18(d)(1)

to disclosure of professional misconduct,
Rule 8.3 (Comment)

to evaluation for use by third persons,
Rule 2.3(b)

to limited representation,
Rule 1.2(c), Rule 6.5 (Comment)

to retaining or contracting with other lawyers outside the firm,
Rule 1.1 (Comment)

to reveal confidences,
Rule 1.6(a)

Constitutional law,
governing authority of government lawyer,
Scope

Consultation,
duty,
Rule 1.2(a), Rule 1.4(a)(2)

Contingent fee,
civil cases,
Rule 1.8(i)(2)

costs and expenses advanced by lawyer,
Rule 1.8(e)(1)

criminal cases,
Rule 1.5(d)(2)

domestic relations cases,
Rule 1.5(d)(1)

expert witness,
Rule 3.4 (Comment)

prohibited representations,
Rule 1.5(d)

requirements of,
Rule 1.5(c)

Continuing legal education,
Rule 1.1 (Comment)

Corporate legal department,
Rule 1.0(c),
Rule 1.10 (Comment)

Corporate representation.
(*See* Organization, representation of.)

Costs advanced to client,
Rule 1.8(e)(1)

Court. (*See also* Tribunal.)
authority over legal profession,
Preamble

candor, duty of,
Rule 3.3

legal services program,
Rule 6.5

offering false evidence to,
Rule 3.3(a)(3)

Court order,
> allowing communication with represented person, Rule 4.2
> disclosure of client confidences pursuant to, Rule 1.6(b)(4)

Court rules, relation to Rules, Scope

Creditors of client,
> claim funds of client, Rule 1.15 (Comment)

Crime,
> client's use of lawyer's services, Rule 1.6,(b)(2)(3)

Criminal conduct,
> by lawyer, Rule 8.4(b)
> counselling or assisting client to engage in, Rule 1.2(d), Rule 3.3(b), Rule 4.1(b)
> withdrawal when client persists in, Rule 1.2 (Comment), Rule 1.6 (Comment), Rule 1.13(c), Rule 1.16(a)(4), Rule 1.16(b)(2), Rule 3.3 (Comment), Rule 4.1 (Comment)

Criminal representation,
> aggregate plea bargain on behalf of multiple defendants, Rule 1.8(g)
> codefendants, representation of, Rule 1.7 (Comment)
> contingent fee for, Rule 1.5(d)(2)
> decision-making authority, Rule 1.2(a)
> frivolous defense, Rule 3.1
> perjury by client, Rule 3.3(a)(3)
> trial publicity, Rule 3.6

D

Deceased lawyer,
> avoiding neglect of matters of, Rule 1.3 (Comment)
> payments to estate of, Rule 5.4(a)(2)

Deceit by lawyer, Rule 8.4(c)

Declining representation,
> causes, Rule 1.16(a)
> conflict of interest, Rule 1.7 (Comment)
> refusing to accept appointment, Rule 6.2
> when political contributions have been made, Rule 7.6

Decorum of tribunal, Rule 3.5

Delay, Rule 4.4(a)

Delivery of funds or property, Rule 1.15(d)

Deposition,
> disruption, Rule 3.5 (Comment)

APPENDIX A: SUBJECT GUIDE

false statement,
    Rule 3.3 (Comment)
Derivative actions,
    Rule 1.13 (Comment)
Destruction of
potential evidence,
    Rule 3.3 (Comment),
    Rule 3.4(a)
Dilatory practices,
    Rule 3.2 (Comment)
Diligence,
    Preamble, Rule 1.3
Diminished capacity of client,
    Rule 1.2 (Comment),
    Rule 1.4 (Comment),
    Rule 1.14
  discharge of lawyer,
    Rule 1.16 (Comment)
Diminished capacity of lawyer,
    Rule 1.16(a)(2)
  avoiding neglect of
  client matters,
    Rule 1.3 (Comment)
Direct contact with
prospective clients,
    Rule 7.3
Directors of organization,
    Rule 1.13
Disaffirmation,
    Rule 1.2 (Comment),
    Rule 1.6 (Comment),
    Rule 4.1 (Comment)
Discharge of lawyer,
    Rule 1.16(a)(3)
Disciplinary authority,
    Rule 8.5(a)
Disciplinary proceedings,
  disclosure of client confidences
    in connection with,
    Rule 1.6(b)(3)
  failure to comply with
  requests for information,
    Rule 8.1(b)
  jurisdiction,
    Rule 8.5
  reporting professional
  misconduct,
    Rule 8.3
Discipline,
    violation of Rules as basis for,
    Scope
Disclosure of,
  client confidences,
    Rule 1.6(b)
  client's criminal conduct,
    Rule 3.3(b)
  client's diminished capacity,
    Rule 1.14 (Comment)
  client's interests when lawyer
  participates in law reform
  activities,
    Rule 6.4
  fee division,
    Rule 1.5(e)(2)
  material fact to avoid assisting
  client crime or fraud,
    Rule 4.1(b)
  wrongful conviction,
    Rule 3.8(g) and (h)
Discovery,
  obstructive tactics,
    Rule 3.4(d)
Discretion of lawyer,
    Preamble, Scope
Discrimination, conduct involving,
    Rule 8.4(g)

Dishonesty, conduct involving,
  Rule 8.4(c)
Disruptive conduct,
  Rule 3.5(d)
Disputes with client,
  confidentiality exception,
    Rule 1.6(b)(3)
  fees,
    Rule 1.5 (Comment)
Disqualification. (*See also* Imputed disqualification.)
  former judge,
    Rule 1.12(a)
  violation of Rules not necessarily warranting,
    Scope
  waiver by client,
    Rule 1.9 (Comment),
    Rule 1.10(d)
Division of fees,
  requirements of,
    Rule 1.5(e)
  with nonlawyer,
    Rule 5.4(a)
Documents,
  alteration of,
    Rule 3.3 (Comment),
    Rule 3.4(a)
  inadvertent receipt of,
    Rule 4.4(b)
Domestic relations,
  contingent fee in,
    Rule 1.5(d)(1)
Dual representation of organization and constituent,
  Rule 1.13(g)

E

Economic factors relevant to client's situation,
  Rule 2.1
Education, legal,
  Preamble
Electronically stored information,
  inadvertent receipt of,
    Rule 4.4(b)
Embarrassing third persons,
  Rule 4.4(a)
Emergency,
  advice in matter,
    Rule 1.1 (Comment)
Employees of client,
  Rule 1.13, Rule 3.4(f)(1)
Employees of lawyer,
  imputation of conflicts,
    Rule 1.10 (Comment)
  responsibility for,
    Rule 5.3
Employment agreement restricting right to practice,
  Rule 5.6(a)
Escrow agent,
  Rule 1.15 (Comment)
Estate planning,
  conflicts of interest in,
    Rule 1.7 (Comment)
Evaluation for use by third person,
  Rule 2.3
Evaluator,
  lawyer as,
    Preamble,
    Rule 2.4 (Comment)

APPENDIX A: SUBJECT GUIDE

Evidence,
   destruction of,
      Rule 3.4(a)
   methods of obtaining,
      Rule 4.4(a)
   obstructing access to,
      Rule 3.4(a)
   offering false,
      Rule 3.3(a)(3)

Ex parte communications with member of tribunal,
      Rule 3.5(b)

Ex parte proceedings,
      Rule 3.3(d)

Executor,
   lawyer's fee for representation of,
      Rule 1.5 (Comment)

Expediting litigation,
      Rule 3.2

Expenses of litigation,
   client's right to determine,
      Rule 1.2 (Comment)
   contingent fee,
      Rule 1.5(c)
   lawyer advancing to client,
      Rule 1.8(e)(1)
   indigent client, paying on behalf of,
      Rule 1.8(e)(2)
   reasonableness,
      Rule 1.5(a)
   termination of representation,
      Rule 1.16(d)

Expert witness. (*See* Witness.)

Expertise,
   competent representation,
      Rule 1.1 (Comment)

F

Failure to disclose adverse legal authority,
      Rule 3.3(a)(2)

Fairness to opposing party and counsel,
      Rule 3.4

False communications concerning lawyer's services,
      Rule 7.1

False statement to tribunal,
      Rule 3.3(a)(1)

Falsification of evidence,
      Rule 3.3 (Comment),
      Rule 3.4(b)

Family of client with diminished capacity,
      Rule 1.14 (Comment)

Family of lawyer,
   gift to,
      Rule 1.8(c)
   client of lawyer-relative,
      Rule 1.7 (Comment)

Fees,
   acquiring ownership interest in enterprise as,
      Rule 1.5 (Comment)
   advance fee payments,
      Rule 1.5 (Comment)
   advertising of,
      Rule 7.1 (Comment)
   arbitration of,
      Rule 1.5 (Comment)
   communication to client,
      Rule 1.5(b)
   contingent, prohibited representations,
      Rule 1.5(d)

contingent, requirements of,
Rule 1.5(c)
determination of,
Rule 1.5(a)
disclosure of confidential information to collect,
Rule 1.6(b)(3)
division with lawyer,
Rule 1.5(e)
division with nonlawyer,
Rule 5.4(a)
division with nonprofit organization,
Rule 5.4(a)(4)
former government lawyer,
Rule 1.11(b)(1), Rule 1.11(c)
paid by one other than client,
Rule 1.7 (Comment),
Rule 1.8(f), Rule 5.4(c)
reasonableness,
Rule 1.5(a)
termination of representation,
Rule 1.16(d)

Fiduciary,
lawyer's obligation toward beneficiary,
Rule 1.2 (Comment)
standard for holding property of others,
Rule 1.15 (Comment)

Field of practice,
communication of,
Rule 7.2(c)

Fifth Amendment in bar admission and disciplinary matters,
Rule 8.1 (Comment)

Financial assistance to client,
Rule 1.8(e)

Firm. (*See* Law firm.)

Former client. (*See* Conflict of interest.)

Former government lawyer,
"confidential government information" defined,
Rule 1.11(c)
conflict of interest,
Rule 1.7 (Comment), Rule 1.11
"matter" defined,
Rule 1.11(e)

Former judge. (*See* Judges.)

Fraud,
client's use of lawyer's services,
Rule 1.6(b)(2)(3)
defined,
Rule 1.0(d)

Fraudulent conduct,
counselling or assisting client to engage in,
Rule 1.2(d), Rule 4.1(b)
engaging in,
Rule 8.4(c)
remediation,
Rule 3.3 (Comment)
withdrawal when client persists in,
Rule 1.2 (Comment),
Rule 1.6 (Comment),
Rule 1.13(c), Rule 1.16(a)(4),
Rule 1.16(b)(2)

Frivolous claims and defenses,
Rule 3.1

Frivolous discovery request,
Rule 3.4(d)

Funds of client,
handling of,
Rule 1.15

APPENDIX A: SUBJECT GUIDE

lawyer claims interest in,
Rule 1.15(e)

responsibility of firm,
Rule 5.1 (Comment)

G

Gift from lawyer to client,
Rule 1.8(e)

Gift to lawyer by client,
Rule 1.8(c)

Government agency,
appearance before,
Rule 3.9

communication with,
Rule 4.2 (Comment)

conflict of interest,
Rule 1.11

constitutes firm,
Rule 1.0 (Comment),
Rule 5.1 (Comment)

improper influence on,
Rule 8.4(e)

representation of,
Rule 1.13 (Comment)

Government lawyer,
authority of,
Scope

communication with accused by,
Rule 4.2 (Comment)

conflict of interest,
Rule 1.11(d)

duties of,
Rule 1.13 (Comment)

representing multiple clients,
Scope

subject to Rules,
Rule 1.11 (Comment)

supervisory responsibilities,
Rule 5.1 (Comment)

Guardian of client with diminished capacity,
acting adversely to ward,
Rule 1.14 (Comment)

appointment of,
Rule 1.14(b)

H

Harassment,
Preamble,
Rule 8.4(g)

Harm,
client's intent to commit serious bodily,
Rule 1.6(b)(1)

Hearing officers.
(*See* Adjudicative officers.)

Homicide,
client's intent to commit,
Rule 1.6(b)(1)

Hotlines,
Rule 6.5 (Comment)

Hypotheticals,
Rule 1.6 (Comment)

I

Identity of client,
conflicts of interest,
Rule 1.0 (Comment)

explaining,
Rule 1.13(d)

government agency,
Rule 1.11 (Comment)

organization,
Rule 1.13 (Comment)

Impartiality and decorum of tribunal,
Rule 3.5

Imperatives in rules,
Scope

Imputed disqualification,
   firm of former judge or
   other neutral,
      Rule 1.12(c)
   firm of political contributor,
      Rule 7.6
   former client,
      Rule 1.9 (Comment)
   general rule,
      Rule 1.10
   government lawyers,
      Rule 1.11(b)
   legal services program,
      Rule 6.5(a)(2), Rule 6.5(b)
   prospective client,
      Rule 1.18(c)
   types of conflicts,
      Rule 1.8(k)
   witness, when member
   of firm serves as,
      Rule 3.7(b)
Incompetent client,
   appointment of guardian for,
      Rule 1.14(b)
   representation of,
      Rule 1.14(a)
Independence of legal profession,
   Preamble, Rule 5.4
Independent professional
judgment,
   Rule 2.1, Rule 5.4(c),
   Rule 5.4(d)(3)
Indigent client,
   court costs and expenses of,
      Rule 1.8(e)(2)
   legal representation,
      Preamble,
      Rule 1.2 (Comment),
      Rule 6.1

Information,
   used to disadvantage
   of client,
      Rule 1.8(b)
   prevention of inadvertent
   or unauthorized disclosure
   relating to representation,
      Rule 1.6(c)
   withholding from client,
      Rule 1.4 (Comment)
Informed consent,
   defined,
      Rule 1.0(e)
Injury,
   client's intent to commit
   serious bodily,
      Rule 1.6(b)(1)
Interest, acquisition by lawyer,
   adverse to client,
      Rule 1.8(a)
   in litigation,
      Rule 1.8(i)
Internet-based client leads,
   Rule 7.2 (Comment)
Intimidation,
   Preamble,
   Rule 3.3 (Comment)
Investigation of client's affairs,
   Rule 2.1 (Comment)

J

Judgment, exercise of,
   Preamble
Judges,
   contributions to,
      Rule 7.6
   duty to show respect for,
      Preamble

APPENDIX A: SUBJECT GUIDE

ex parte communication with,
Rule 3.5(b)
former judge,
disqualification,
Rule 1.12
improper influence on,
Rule 3.3 (Comment),
Rule 3.5(a)
misconduct by,
Rule 8.3(b), Rule 8.4(f)
statements about,
Rule 8.2(a)
Juror,
communication with,
Rule 3.5(b), Rule 3.5(c)
improper influence on,
Rule 3.3 (Comment),
Rule 3.5(a)
Jury trial,
client's right to waive,
Rule 1.2(a)

K

Knowledge,
defined,
Rule 1.0(f)
factors,
Rule 1.1 (Comment)
lawyer's role,
Preamble
of client's intent to
commit homicide or
serious bodily harm,
Rule 1.6 (Comment)

L

Law clerk,
negotiating for private
employment,
Rule 1.12(b)

Law firm,
defined,
Rule 1.0(c),
Rule 1.10 (Comment)
disclosure of client
information in,
Rule 1.6 (Comment)
disqualification,
Rule 1.10(a), Rule 1.10(b)
former government lawyer,
disqualification,
Rule 1.11(b), Rule 1.11(c)
former judge or arbitrator,
disqualification,
Rule 1.12(c)
legal services program,
disqualification,
Rule 6.5(b)
name,
Rule 7.1 (Comment)
nonlawyer assistants,
Rule 1.10 (Comment),
Rule 5.3
partner, manager or
supervisory lawyer,
Rule 5.1
political contributions by,
Rule 7.6
prospective client,
disqualification,
Rule 1.18(c)
subordinate lawyer,
Rule 5.2
Law reform activities,
affecting clients' interests,
Rule 6.4
Law-related services,
Rule 5.7

Lawyer admitted in another jurisdiction, approved legal services,
    Rule 5.5(c) and (d)
  authorized by other law or rule,
    Rule 5.5(d)
  in association with admitted lawyer,
    Rule 5.5(c)(1)
  provided to lawyer's employer,
    Rule 5.5(d)
  related to pending or potential proceeding before tribunal,
    Rule 5.5(c)(2)
  related to pro hac vice admission,
    Rule 5.5(c)(3)
  related to practice,
    Rule 5.5(c)(4)

Lawyer as witness,
    Rule 3.7

Lawyer assistance program,
    Rule 8.3(c)

Lawyer not admitted to practice in jurisdiction,
    Rule 5.5(b)
  establishing office or continuous presence,
    Rule 5.5(b)
  holding out to public,
    Rule 5.5(b)

Lawyer outside the firm,
  retaining or contracting with,
    Rule 1.1 (Comment)

Lawyer referral services,
  costs of,
    Rule 7.2(b)(2)

Lawyer's fund for client protection,
    Rule 1.15 (Comment)

Lawyer's services,
  recommending,
    Rule 7.2(b)

Learned profession,
  lawyer as member of,
    Preamble

Legal advice,
  disclosure of client confidences when seeking,
    Rule 1.6(b)(2)

Legal aid,
  constitutes law firm,
    Rule 1.0 (Comment),
    Rule 1.10 (Comment)

Legal assistants,
  conflict of interest,
    Rule 1.10 (Comment)
  responsibilities of lawyer,
    Rule 5.3

Legal education,
    Preamble

Legal representative of client with diminished capacity,
    Rule 1.14 (Comment)

Legal services organization,
  constitutes law firm,
    Rule 1.0 (Comment),
    Rule 1.10 (Comment),
    Rule 5.1 (Comment)
  limited legal services,
    Rule 6.5 (Comment)

APPENDIX A: SUBJECT GUIDE

membership in,
  Rule 6.3
Legal service plan,
  cost of,
    Rule 7.2(b)(2)
  participation in,
    Rule 7.3(e)
Legislature,
  appearance before,
    Rule 3.9
Letterheads,
  false or misleading,
    Rule 7.1 (Comment)
  public officials,
    Rule 7.1 (Comment)
Liability to client,
  agreements limiting,
    Rule 1.8(h)
Licensure statutes,
  relation to Rules,
    Scope
Lien to secure fees and expenses,
    Rule 1.8(i)(1)
Limited legal services,
    Rule 6.5
Literary rights concerning representation,
    Rule 1.8(d)
Litigation,
  acquiring interest in,
    Rule 1.8(i)
  conflict of interest,
    Rule 1.7(b)(3)
  expedite, duty to,
    Rule 3.2

information,
  Rule 1.4 (Comment)
Loyalty to client,
  Rule 1.7 (Comment)

M

Mail contact with prospective clients,
    Rule 7.2(a),
    Rule 7.3 (Comment)
Maintenance, law of,
    Rule 1.8 (Comment)
Malpractice,
  limiting liability to client for,
    Rule 1.8(h)
Mandatory withdrawal,
    Rule 1.16(a)
Matter,
    Rule 1.11(e)
  substantially related,
    Rule 1.9 (Comment)
Media rights concerning representation,
    Rule 1.8(d)
Mediation of fee disputes,
    Rule 1.5 (Comment)
Mediator,
  lawyer as,
    Rule 2.4
  codes of ethics,
    Rule 1.12 (Comment),
    Rule 2.4 (Comment)
  disqualification of former,
    Rule 1.12
Mental impairment of client,
    Rule 1.14(a)

client decisions,
Rule 1.2 (Comment)

communication with client,
Rule 1.4 (Comment)

Mental impairment of lawyer,
Rule 1.16(a)(2)

avoiding neglect of client matters,
Rule 1.3 (Comment)

Meritorious claims and contentions,
Rule 3.1

Military lawyers,

duties of,
Rule 1.13 (Comment)

representation of adverse interests,
Rule 1.9 (Comment)

Minor client,
Rule 1.14 (Comment)

Misconduct,

forms of,
Rule 8.4

reporting,
Rule 8.3

Misrepresentation,

advertisements,
Rule 7.1

bar admission and disciplinary matters,
Rule 8.1

firm names and letterhead,
Rule 7.1 (Comment)

misconduct,
Rule 8.4(c)

negligent,
Rule 1.0(d)

to court,
Rule 3.3

to third person,
Rule 4.1(a)

Model Court Rule on Provision of Legal Services Following Determination of Major Disaster,
Rule 5.5 (Comment)

Model Rule on Practice Pending Admission,
Rule 5.5 (Comment)

Model Rule for Registration of In-House Counsel,
Rule 5.5 (Comment)

Model Rule on Temporary Practice by Foreign Lawyers,
Rule 5.5 (Comment)

Moral factors relevant to client's situation,
Rule 2.1

Moral turpitude offenses,
Rule 8.4 (Comment)

Multijurisdictional practice,
Rule 5.5

Multiple representation.
(*See* Common representation.)

N

Negotiation,

conflicting interests, representation of,
Rule 1.7 (Comment)

statements made during,
Rule 4.1 (Comment)

Negotiator,

lawyer as,
Preamble

APPENDIX A: SUBJECT GUIDE

Nonadjudicative proceedings,
Rule 3.9

Nonlawyer assistants,
conflict of interest,
Rule 1.10 (Comment)
responsibilities of lawyer,
Rule 5.3

Nonlawyers,
division of fees with,
Rule 5.4(a)
partnership,
Rule 5.4(b)
professional corporation,
Rule 5.4(d)

Nonprofit legal services program,
Rule 6.5

Nonprofit organization,
division of fees with,
Rule 5.4(a)(4)

Notice of receipt of funds
or other property,
Rule 1.15(d)

O

Objectives of the representation,
client's right to determine,
Rule 1.2(a)

Obstruction of party's access
to evidence,
Rule 3.3 (Comment),
Rule 3.4(a)

Officer of legal system,
Preamble

Opinions,
evaluation for use by
third persons,
Rule 2.3

limit on malpractice liability,
Rule 1.8 (Comment)

Opposing party,
communication with
represented party,
Rule 4.2
communication with
unrepresented party,
Rule 4.3
duty of fairness to,
Rule 3.4

Optional withdrawal,
Rule 1.16(b)

Organization, representation of,
board of directors, lawyer on,
Rule 1.7 (Comment)
communication with,
Rule 1.4 (Comment)
communication with
constituents of,
Rule 4.2 (Comment)
conflict of interest,
Rule 1.7 (Comment)
intended conduct,
Rule 1.6 (Comment)
constituents, representing,
Rule 1.13(g)
identity of client,
Rule 1.13(a), Rule 1.13(f)
law department of,
Rule 1.0 (Comment),
Rule 1.10 (Comment),
Rule 5.1 (Comment)
misconduct, client
engaged in,
Rule 1.13(b)

officers of,
  Rule 1.13
violation of law,
  Rule 1.13

P

Papers, retention of,
  Rule 1.16(d)
Parent of lawyer,
  gift to,
    Rule 1.8(c)
  client of,
    Rule 1.7 (Comment)
Partner,
  defined,
    Rule 1.0(g)
  nonlawyer,
    Rule 5.4(b)
  supervision of lawyers,
    Rule 5.1
  supervision of nonlawyers,
    Rule 5.3
Partnership,
  agreement restricting right to practice,
    Rule 5.6(a)
  name,
    Rule 7.1 (Comment)
Patent practice,
  advertising,
    Rule 7.2(c) (Comment)
Peer approval,
  Preamble
Peer review agency,
reporting misconduct to,
  Rule 8.3 (Comment)

Perjury,
  criminal defendant,
    Rule 3.3 (Comment)
  disclosure of,
    Rule 3.3(a)(3)
Permissive rules,
  Scope
Personal affairs of lawyer,
  duty to conduct in compliance with law,
    Preamble
Physical condition of lawyer,
  Rule 1.16(a)(2)
Plea bargain,
  client's right to accept or reject,
    Rule 1.2(a)
Pleadings,
  verification of,
    Rule 3.3 (Comment)
Political contributions,
  by lawyers to public officials' campaigns,
    Rule 7.6
Political factors relevant to client's situation,
  Rule 2.1
Practice area,
  sale of,
    Rule 1.17
Preamble, role of,
  Scope
Precedent,
  failure to disclose to court,
    Rule 3.3(a)(2)

APPENDIX A: SUBJECT GUIDE

Prepaid legal services,
  advertising for,
    Rule 7.2 (Comment),
    Rule 7.3(e) (Comment)
Pro bono publico service,
  Rule 6.1
Procedural law,
  Preamble, Scope
Procedural use of Rules,
  Scope
Procrastination,
  Rule 1.3 (Comment)
Professional corporation,
  defined as firm,
    Rule 1.0(c)
  formation of,
    Rule 5.4(d)
  shareholders' responsibilities,
    Rule 5.1 (Comment)
Professional role,
  Scope
Promptness,
  Preamble
Property of client,
  payment for services,
    Rule 1.5 (Comment)
  prospective client,
    Rule 1.18 (Comment)
  return upon termination of representation,
    Rule 1.16(d)
  safekeeping,
    Rule 1.15
Prosecutor,
  communication with accused,
    Rule 4.2 (Comment) and Rule 3.8 (Comment)
  representing former defendant,
    Rule 1.9 (Comment)
  special responsibilities of,
    Rule 3.8
  trial publicity,
    Rule 3.6, Rule 3.8(f)
Prospective client,
  Rule 1.18
Protective order,
  Rule 1.6 (Comment)
Psychiatrist,
  withholding diagnosis,
    Rule 1.4 (Comment)
Public interest in preserving client confidences,
  Preamble,
  Rule 1.6 (Comment)
Public citizen,
  lawyer's duty as,
    Preamble
Public interest legal services. (*See* Pro bono publico service.)
Public office,
  abuse of,
    Rule 8.4 (Comment)
  negotiating private employment while holding,
    Rule 1.11(d)(2)(ii)
Public officials,
  firm's use of name,
    Rule 7.1 (Comment)
  improper influence,
    Rule 8.4(e)
  lawyers' contributions to election campaigns of,
    Rule 7.6

respect for,
    Preamble
Public service,
    Preamble
Publicity, trial,
    Rule 3.6(g)
    special responsibilities of prosecutor,
        Rule 3.8(f)

Q

Quality of service, improvement,
    Preamble

R

Reasonable,
    defined,
        Rule 1.0(h)
Recordkeeping,
    property of client,
        Rule 1.15(a)
Referral,
    to other professionals,
        Rule 7.2(b)(4)
    when lawyer not competent to handle matter,
        Rule 1.1 (Comment)
Referral services,
    costs of,
        Rule 7.2(b)(2)
Referees. (*See* Adjudicative officers.)
Reform of the law,
    Preamble, Rule 6.4
Regulation,
    validity or interpretation,
        Rule 1.2 (Comment)

Regulation of legal profession,
    self-governance,
        Preamble
Remedial measures when false evidence offered,
    Rule 3.3(a)(3)
Reporting misconduct,
    Rule 8.3
Representation of client,
    decision-making authority of lawyer and client,
        Rule 1.2(a)
    declining or terminating,
        Rule 1.2 (Comment),
        Rule 1.16
    scope, lawyer's right to limit,
        Rule 1.2(c)
Representative of client,
    lawyer as,
        Preamble,
        Rule 2.4 (Comment)
Representative, legal, of client with diminished capacity,
    Rule 1.14 (Comment)
Represented party, communication with,
    Rule 4.2
Responsibility for observing Rules,
    Preamble
Restrictions on right to practice,
    partnership or employment agreement,
        Rule 5.6(a)
    settlement agreement,
        Rule 5.6(b)
Rule of reason,
    Scope

APPENDIX A: SUBJECT GUIDE

S

Safekeeping property,
Rule 1.15
Sale of law practice,
Rule 1.17
Sanction,
severity of,
Scope
Scope of representation,
Rule 1.1 (Comment),
Rule 1.2
Screened,
defined,
Rule 1.0(k)
Screening,
disqualified former government lawyer,
Rule 1.11(b)(1)
disqualified former judge or other neutral,
Rule 1.12(c)
disqualified lawyer associated with new firm,
Rule 1.10(a)(2)
nonlawyer assistants,
Rule 1.10 (Comment)
prospective client,
Rule 1.18(d)(2)
Securities, safekeeping,
Rule 1.15 (Comment)
Self-regulation,
Preamble
Settlement,
aggregate,
Rule 1.8(g)
client's right to refuse,
Rule 1.2(a)

contingent fee,
Rule 1.5(c)
government lawyer's authority,
Scope
informing client of settlement offers,
Rule 1.4 (Comment)
restricting right to practice,
Rule 5.6(b)
Sexual relations with client,
Rule 1.8(j)
Shareholders of organization,
Rule 1.13
Sibling of lawyer,
gift to,
Rule 1.8(c)
client of,
Rule 1.7 (Comment)
Signed,
defined,
Rule 1.0(n)
Solicitation of clients,
Rule 7.3
Special masters.
(*See* Adjudicative officers.)
Specialization, communication of,
Rule 7.1 (Comment)
Spouse of lawyer,
gift to,
Rule 1.8(c)
client of,
Rule 1.7 (Comment)
State's attorney,
authority of,
Scope

Statute of limitations,
    Rule 1.3 (Comment)
Statutes,
    conflict of interest,
    agency consent to,
        Rule 1.11 (Comment)
    shape lawyer's role,
        Scope
    validity or interpretation,
        Rule 1.2 (Comment)
Subordinate lawyer,
    responsibilities of,
        Rule 5.2
Substantive law,
    defines existence of client-lawyer relationship,
        Scope
    lawyer's professional responsibilities prescribed by,
        Preamble
    relation to Rules,
        Scope
Supervision,
    of lawyer,
        Rule 5.1
    of nonlawyer,
        Rule 5.3

T

Taxation,
    escaping liability,
        Rule 1.2 (Comment)
Technology,
    maintaining competence,
        Rule 1.1 (Comment)
Termination of representation,
    Rule 1.2 (Comment),
    Rule 1.16

records of funds and other property,
    Rule 1.15(a)
Testamentary gifts,
    Rule 1.8(c)
Testimony of client in criminal trial,
    false,
        Rule 3.3(a)(3)
    right to decide to give,
        Rule 1.2(a)
Testimony of lawyer.
    (*See* Lawyer as witness.)
Third-party neutral,
    Preamble, Rule 1.12,
    Rule 2.4
Third persons,
    evaluation for use by,
        Rule 2.3
    respect for rights of,
        Rule 4.4
    statements to,
        Rule 4.1
Trade names,
    Rule 7.1 (Comment)
Transactions with persons other than client. (*See* Third persons.)
Trial conduct,
    allusion to irrelevant or inadmissible evidence,
        Rule 3.4(e)
    disruptive conduct,
        Rule 3.5(d)
Trial publicity,
    Rule 3.6
    special responsibilities of prosecutor,
        Rule 3.8(f)

APPENDIX A: SUBJECT GUIDE

Tribunal,
   continued representation
   ordered by,
      Rule 1.16(c)
   defined,
      Rule 1.0(m)
   disobeying obligation of,
      Rule 3.4(c)
   impartiality and decorum of,
      Rule 3.5

Trust accounts,
     Rule 1.15
   responsibility for firm,
      Rule 5.1 (Comment)

Truthfulness in statements
to third persons,
     Rule 4.1

U

Unauthorized practice of law,
   assisting in,
      Rule 5.5(a)
   engaging in,
      Rule 5.5(a)

Unrepresented person,
   dealing with,
      Rule 4.3
   in alternative dispute
   resolution,
      Rule 2.4(b)

Unincorporated associations,
     Rule 1.13 (Comment)

V

Violation of Rules of Professional
Conduct. (*See also* Misconduct.)
   declining or terminating
   representation,
      Rule 1.16(a)(1)

Violence,
     Rule 8.4 (Comment)

W

Waiver,
   future conflict of interest,
      Rule 1.7 (Comment)
   prosecutor obtaining from
   criminal defendant,
      Rule 3.8(c)

Withdrawal,
     Rule 1.16
   conflict of interest,
      Rule 1.7 (Comment)
   discharge,
      Rule 1.16(a)(3)
   incapacity,
      Rule 1.16(a)(2)
   mandatory,
      Rule 1.16(a)
   method of,
      Rule 1.3 (Comment)
   notice of,
      Rule 1.6 (Comment)
   optional,
      Rule 1.16(b)
   property of client,
      Rule 1.16(d)
   when client persists in
   criminal or fraudulent
   conduct,
      Rule 1.2 (Comment),
      Rule 1.6 (Comment),
      Rule 1.13(c), Rule 1.16(a)(4),
      Rule 1.16(b)(2),
      Rule 3.3 (Comment),
      Rule 4.1 (Comment)

Withholding information
from client,
     Rule 1.4 (Comment)

Witness,
  bribing,
    Rule 3.3 (Comment),
    Rule 3.4(b)
  client's right to decide whether to testify,
    Rule 1.2(a)
  expenses, payment of,
    Rule 3.4 (Comment)
  expert, payment of,
    Rule 3.4 (Comment)
  lawyer as,
    Rule 1.6 (Comment),
    Rule 3.7
Work load management,
    Rule 1.3 (Comment)
Work product privilege,
  confidentiality rule,
    Rule 1.6 (Comment)
Writing,
  defined,
    Rule 1.0(n)
Wrongful conviction,
  prosecutor's knowledge of,
    Rule 3.8(g) and (h)

Z

Zealous representation,
  opposing party well represented,
    Preamble
  requirement of,
    Rule 1.3 (Comment)

Appendix B

Correlation Tables

Tables A and B: Related Sections in the ABA Model Code of Professional Responsibility

Table A*

ABA MODEL RULES	ABA MODEL CODE
Competence	
Rule 1.1	EC 1-1, EC 1-2, EC 6-1, EC 6-2, EC 6-3, EC 6-4, EC 6-5, DR 6-101(A)
Scope of Representation and Allocation of Authority between Client and Lawyer	
Rule 1.2(a)	EC 5-12, EC 7-7, EC 7-8, DR 7-101(A)(1)
Rule 1.2(b)	EC 7-17
Rule 1.2(c)	EC 7-8, EC 7-9, DR 7-101(B)(1)
Rule 1.2(d)	EC 7-1, EC 7-2, EC 7-5, EC 7-22, DR 7-102(A)(6), (7), & (8), DR 7-106
Diligence	
Rule 1.3	EC 2-31, EC 6-4, EC 7-1, EC 7-38, DR 6-101(A)(3), DR 7-101(A)(1) & (3)
Communication	
Rule 1.4(a)	EC 7-8, EC 9-2, DR 2-110(C)(1)(c), DR 6-101(A)(3), DR 9-102(B)(1)
Rule 1.4(b)	EC 7-8
Fees	
Rule 1.5(a)	EC 2-16, EC 2-17, EC 2-18, DR 2-106(A) & (B)
Rule 1.5(b)	EC 2-19
Rule 1.5(c)	EC 2-20, EC 5-7
Rule 1.5(d)	EC 2-20, DR 2-106(C)
Rule 1.5(e)	EC 2-22, DR 2-107(A)

---

* Table A provides cross-references to related provisions, but only in the sense that the provisions consider substantially similar subject matter or reflect similar concerns. A cross-reference does not indicate that a provision of the ABA Model Code of Professional Responsibility has been incorporated by the provision of a Model Rule. The Canons of the Code are not cross-referenced.

ABA MODEL RULES

ABA MODEL RULES	ABA MODEL CODE
Confidentiality of Information	
Rule 1.6(a)	EC 4-1, EC 4-2, EC 4-3, EC 4-4, DR 4-101(A), (B), & (C)
Rule 1.6(b)(1)	EC 4-2, DR 4-101(C)(3), DR 7-102(B)
Rule 1.6(b)(2)	DR 4-101(C)(3)
Rule 1.6(b)(3)	None
Rule 1.6(b)(4)	None
Rule 1.6(b)(5)	DR 4-101(C)(4)
Rule 1.6(b)(6)	DR 4-101(C)(2)
Rule 1.6(b)(7)	None
Rule 1.6(c)	None
Conflict of Interest: Current Clients	
Rule 1.7(a)	EC 2-21, EC 5-1, EC 5-2, EC 5-3, EC 5-9, EC 5-11, EC 5-13, EC 5-14, EC 5-15, EC 5-17, EC 5-21, EC 5-22, EC 5-23, DR 5-101(A) & (B), DR 5-102, DR 5-104(A), DR 5-105(A) & (B), DR 5-107(A) & (B)
Rule 1.7(b)	EC 2-21, EC 5-15, EC 5-16, EC 5-17, EC 5-19, EC 5-23, DR 5-101(A) & (B), DR 5-102, DR 5-104(A), DR 5-105(C), DR 5-107(A)
Conflict of Interest: Current Clients: Specific Rules	
Rule 1.8(a)	EC 5-3, EC 5-5, DR 5-104(A)
Rule 1.8(b)	EC 4-5, DR 4-101(B)
Rule 1.8(c)	EC 5-1, EC 5-2, EC 5-5, EC 5-6
Rule 1.8(d)	EC 5-1, EC 5-3, EC 5-4, DR 5-104(B)
Rule 1.8(e)	EC 5-1, EC 5-3, EC 5-7, EC 5-8, DR 5-103(B)
Rule 1.8(f)	EC 2-21, EC 5-1, EC 5-22, EC 5-23, DR 5-107(A) & (B)
Rule 1.8(g)	EC 5-1, DR 5-106(A)
Rule 1.8(h)	EC 6-6, DR 6-102(A)
Rule 1.8(i)	EC 5-1, EC 5-7, DR 5-101(A), DR 5-103(A)
Rule 1.8(j)	None
Rule 1.8(k)	None
Duties to Former Clients	
Rule 1.9(a)	DR 5-105(C)
Rule 1.9(b)	EC 4-5, EC 4-6
Rule 1.9(c)	None
Imputation of Conflicts of Interest: General Rule	
Rule 1.10(a)	EC 4-5, DR 5-105(D)
Rule 1.10(b)	EC 4-5, DR 5-105(D)

APPENDIX B: CORRELATION TABLES

ABA MODEL RULES	ABA MODEL CODE
Rule 1.10(c)	DR 5-105(A)
Rule 1.10(d)	None

Special Conflicts of Interest for Former and Current Government Officers and Employees

Rule 1.11(a)	EC 9-3, DR 9-101(B)
Rule 1.11(b)	None
Rule 1.11(c)	None
Rule 1.11(d)	EC 8-8
Rule 1.11(e)	None

Former Judge, Arbitrator, Mediator or Other Third-Party Neutral

Rule 1.12(a)&(b)	EC 5-20, EC 9-3, DR 9-101(A) & (B)
Rule 1.12(c)	DR 5-105(D)
Rule 1.12(d)	None

Organization as Client

Rule 1.13(a)	EC 5-18, EC 5-24
Rule 1.13(b)	EC 5-18, EC 5-24, DR 5-107(B)
Rule 1.13(c)	EC 5-18, EC 5-24, DR 5-105(D), DR 5-107(B)
Rule 1.13(d)	None
Rule 1.13(e)	None
Rule 1.13(f)	EC 5-16
Rule 1.13(g)	EC 4-4, EC 5-16, DR 5-105(B) & (C)

Client with Diminished Capacity

Rule 1.14(a)	EC 7-11, EC 7-12
Rule 1.14(b)	EC 7-12
Rule 1.14(c)	None

Safekeeping Property

Rule 1.15	EC 5-7, EC 9-5, EC 9-7, DR 5-103(A)(1), DR 9-102

Declining or Terminating Representation

Rule 1.16(a)(1)	EC 2-30, EC 2-31, EC 2-32, DR 2-103(E), DR 2-104(A), DR 2-109(A), DR 2-110(B)(1) & (2)
Rule 1.16(a)(2)	EC 1-6, EC 2-30, EC 2-31, EC 2-32, DR 2-110(B)(3), DR 2-110(C)(4)
Rule 1.16(a)(3)	EC 2-31, EC 2-32, DR 2-110(B)(4)
Rule 1.16(a)(4)	None
Rule 1.16(b)(1)	EC 2-32, DR 2-110(A)(2), DR 2-110(C)(5)
Rule 1.16(b)(2)	EC 2-31, EC 2-32, DR 2-110(C)(1)(b) & (c), DR 2-110(C)(2)

ABA MODEL RULES

ABA MODEL RULES	ABA MODEL CODE
Rule 1.16(b)(3)	EC 2-31, EC 2-32, DR 2-110(C)(2)
Rule 1.16(b)(4)	EC 2-30, EC 2-31, EC 2-32, DR 2-110(C)(1)(d)
Rule 1.16(b)(5)	EC 2-31, EC 2-32, DR 2-110(C)(1)(f)(i)(j)
Rule 1.16(b)(6)	EC 2-32, DR 2-110(C)(1)(d) & (e)
Rule 1.16(b)(7)	EC 2-32, DR 2-110(C)(6)
Rule 1.16(c)	EC 2-32, DR 2-110(A)(1)
Rule 1.16(d)	EC 2-32, DR 2-110(A)(2) & (3)

Sale of Law Practice

Rule 1.17	None

Duties to Prospective Client

Rule 1.18	EC 4-1

Advisor

Rule 2.1	EC 5-11, EC 7-3, EC 7-8, DR 5-107(B)

Evaluation for Use by Third Persons

Rule 2.3	None

Lawyer Serving as Third-Party Neutral

Rule 2.4	EC 5-20

Meritorious Claims and Contentions

Rule 3.1	EC 7-1, EC 7-4, EC 7-5, EC 7-14, EC 7-25, DR 5-102(A)(5), DR 2-109(A)(B)(1), DR 7-102(A)(1) & (2)

Expediting Litigation

Rule 3.2	EC 7-20, DR 1-102(A)(5), DR 7-101(A)(1) & (2)

Candor toward the Tribunal

Rule 3.3(a)(1)	EC 7-4, EC 7-26, EC 7-32, EC 8-5, DR 1-102(A)(4) & (5), DR 7-102(A)(4) & (5)
Rule 3.3(a)(2)	EC 7-23, DR 1-102(A)(5), DR 7-106(B)(1)
Rule 3.3(a)(3)	EC 7-5, EC 7-6, EC 7-26, EC 8-5, DR 1-102(A)(4) & (5), DR 7-102(A)(4), (6), & (7), DR 7-102(B)(1) & (2)
Rule 3.3(b)	EC 7-5, EC 7-26, EC 7-27, EC 7-32, EC 8-5, DR 1-102(A)(4) & (5), DR 7-102(A)(4), (6), & (7), DR 7-102(B)(1) & (2), DR 7-108(G), DR 7-109(A) & (B)
Rule 3.3(c)	EC 8-5, DR 7-102(B)
Rule 3.3(d)	EC 7-24, EC 7-27

APPENDIX B: CORRELATION TABLES

ABA MODEL RULES	ABA MODEL CODE

Fairness to Opposing Party and Counsel

Rule 3.4(a)	EC 7-6, EC 7-27, DR 1-102(A)(4) & (5), DR 7-106(C)(7), DR 7-109(A) & (B)
Rule 3.4(b)	EC 7-6, EC 7-28, DR 1-102(A)(4), (5), & (6), DR 7-102(A)(6), DR 7-109(C)
Rule 3.4(c)	EC 7-22, EC 7-25, EC 7-38, DR 1-102(A)(5), DR 7-106(A), DR 7-106(C)(5) & (7)
Rule 3.4(d)	DR 1-102(A)(5), DR 7-106(A), DR 7-106(C)(7)
Rule 3.4(e)	EC 7-24, EC 7-25, DR 1-102(A)(5), DR 7-106(C)(1), (2), (3), & (4)
Rule 3.4(f)	EC 7-27, DR 1-102(A)(5), DR 7-104(A)(2), DR 7-109(B)

Impartiality and Decorum of the Tribunal

Rule 3.5(a)	EC 7-20, EC 7-29, EC 7-31, EC 7-32, EC 7-34, DR 7-106, DR 7-108, DR 7-109, DR 7-110, DR 8-101(A)
Rule 3.5(b)	EC 7-35, DR 7-108, DR 7-110(A) & (B)
Rule 3.5(c)	EC 7-29, EC 7-30, EC 7-31, EC 7-32, DR 7-108
Rule 3.5(d)	EC 7-20, EC 7-25, EC 7-36, EC 7-37, DR 7-101(A)(1), DR 7-106(C)(6)

Trial Publicity

Rule 3.6	EC 7-25, EC 7-33, DR 7-107

Lawyer as Witness

Rule 3.7(a)	EC 5-9, EC 5-10, DR 5-101(B)(1) & (2), DR 5-102
Rule 3.7(b)	EC 5-9, DR 5-101(B), DR 5-102

Special Responsibilities of a Prosecutor

Rule 3.8(a)	EC 7-11, EC 7-13, EC 7-14, DR 7-103(A)
Rule 3.8(b)	EC 7-11, EC 7-13
Rule 3.8(c)	EC 7-11, EC 7-13, EC 7-18
Rule 3.8(d)	EC 7-11, EC 7-13, DR 7-103(B)
Rule 3.8(e)	None
Rule 3.8(f)	EC 7-14
Rule 3.8(g)	None
Rule 3.8(h)	None

Advocate in Nonadjudicative Proceedings

Rule 3.9	EC 7-11, EC 7-15, EC 7-16, EC 8-4, EC 8-5, DR 7-106(B)(2), DR 9-101(C)

ABA MODEL RULES

ABA MODEL RULES	ABA MODEL CODE

Truthfulness in Statements to Others

Rule 4.1	EC 7-5, DR 7-102(A)(3), (4), (5), & (7), DR 7-102(B)

Communication with Person Represented by Counsel

Rule 4.2	EC 2-30, EC 7-18, DR 7-104(A)(1)

Dealing with Unrepresented Person

Rule 4.3	EC 2-3, EC 7-18, DR 7-104(A)(2)

Respect for Rights of Third Persons

Rule 4.4(a)	EC 7-10, EC 7-14, EC 7-21, EC 7-25, EC 7-29, EC 7-30, EC 7-37, DR 2-110(B)(1), DR 7-101(A)(1), DR 7-102(A)(1), DR 7-106(C)(2), DR 7-107(D), (E), & (F), DR 7-108(D), (E), & (F)
Rule 4.4(b)	None

Responsibilities of Partners, Managers, and Supervisory Lawyers

Rule 5.1(a)&(b)	EC 4-5, DR 4-101(D), DR 7-107(J)
Rule 5.1(c)	DR 1-102(A)(2), DR 1-103(A), DR 7-108(E)

Responsibilities of a Subordinate Lawyer

Rule 5.2	None

Responsibilities regarding Nonlawyer Assistance

Rule 5.3(a)	EC 3-6, EC 4-2, EC 4-5, EC 7-28, DR 4-101(D), DR 7-107(J)
Rule 5.3(b)	DR 1-102(A)(2), DR 7-107(J), DR 7-108(B), DR 7-108(E)
Rule 5.3(c)	None

Professional Independence of a Lawyer

Rule 5.4(a)	EC 2-33, EC 3-8, EC 5-24, DR 2-103(D)(1), DR 2-103(D)(2), DR 2-103(D)(4)(a), (d), (e), & (f), DR 3-102(A), DR 5-107(C)(3)
Rule 5.4(b)	EC 2-33, EC 3-8, DR 3-103(A)
Rule 5.4(c)	EC 2-33, EC 5-22, EC 5-23, DR 2-103(C), DR 5-107(B)
Rule 5.4(d)	EC 2-33, EC 3-8, DR 5-107(C)

Unauthorized Practice of Law; Multijurisdictional Practice of Law

Rule 5.5(a)	DR 3-101(A) & (B)
Rule 5.5(b)	None
Rule 5.5(c)	None

APPENDIX B: CORRELATION TABLES

ABA MODEL RULES	ABA MODEL CODE
Rule 5.5(d)	None
Rule 5.5(e)	None

Restrictions on Right to Practice

Rule 5.6	DR 2-108

Responsibilities regarding Law-Related Services

Rule 5.7	None

Voluntary Pro Bono Publico Service

Rule 6.1	EC 1-2, EC 1-4, EC 2-1, EC 2-2, EC 2-16, EC 2-24, EC 2-25, EC 6-2, EC 8-1, EC 8-2, EC 8-3, EC 8-7, EC 8-9

Accepting Appointments

Rule 6.2 (a)	EC 2-1, EC 2-25, EC 2-27, EC 2-28, EC 2-29, EC 8-3
Rule 6.2(b)	EC 2-16, EC 2-25, EC 2-29, EC 2-30
Rule 6.2(c)	EC 2-25, EC 2-27, EC 2-29, EC 2-30

Membership in Legal Services Organization

Rule 6.3	EC 2-33, DR 5-101(A)

Law Reform Activities Affecting Client Interests

Rule 6.4	EC 2-33, DR 5-101(A), DR 8-101

Nonprofit and Court-Annexed Limited Legal Services Programs

Rule 6.5	None

Communications Concerning a Lawyer's Services

Rule 7.1	EC 2-8, EC 2-9, EC 2-10, DR 2-101(A), (B), (C), (E), (F), & (G), DR 2-102(E)

Firm Names and Letterheads

Rule 7.1 (Comment)	EC 2-11, EC 2-12, EC 2-13, DR 2-102(A)(4), DR 2-102(B), (C), (D), & (E), DR 2-105

Advertising

Rule 7.2(a)	EC 2-1, EC 2-2, EC 2-6, EC 2-7, EC 2-8, EC 2-15, DR 2-101(B) & (H), DR 2-102(A) & (B), DR 2-103(B), DR 2-104(A)(4) & (5)
Rule 7.2(b)	EC 2-8, EC 2-15, DR 2-101(I), DR 2-103(B), (C), & (D)
Rule 7.2(c)	EC 2-8, EC 2-14, DR 2-105(A)(2) & (3)
Rule 7.2(d)	None

ABA MODEL RULES	ABA MODEL CODE

Communication of Fields of Practice and Specialization
  Rule 7.2(c)   EC 2-1, EC 2-7, EC 2-8, EC 2-14, DR 2-101(B)(2),
                    DR 2-102(A)(3), DR 2-102(E), DR 2-105(A)

Solicitation of Clients
  Rule 7.3   EC 2-3, EC 2-4, EC 5-6, DR 2-103(A),
                    DR 2-103(C)(1), DR 2-103(D)(4)(b) & (c),
                    DR 2-104(A)(1), (2), (3), & (5)

Political Contributions to Obtain Government Legal Engagements or Appointments by Judges
  Rule 7.6   None

Bar Admission and Disciplinary Matters
  Rule 8.1(a)   EC 1-1, EC 1-2, EC 1-3, DR 1-101(A) & (B)
  Rule 8.1(b)   DR 1-102(A)(5), DR 1-103(B)

Judicial and Legal Officials
  Rule 8.2(a)   EC 8-6, DR 8-102
  Rule 8.2(b)   DR 8-103

Reporting Professional Misconduct
  Rule 8.3   EC 1-3, DR 1-103(A)

Misconduct
  Rule 8.4(a)   EC 1-5, EC 1-6, EC 9-6, DR 1-102(A)(1) & (2),
                    DR 2-103(E), DR 7-102(A) & (B)
  Rule 8.4(b)   EC 1-5, DR 1-102(A)(3) & (6), DR 7-102(A)(8),
                    DR 8-101(A)(3)
  Rule 8.4(c)   EC 1-5, EC 9-4, DR 1-102(A)(4), DR 8-101(A)(3)
  Rule 8.4(d)   EC 3-9, EC 8-3, DR 1-102(A)(5), DR 3-101(B)
  Rule 8.4(e)   EC 1-5, EC 9-2, EC 9-4, EC 9-6, DR 9-101(C)
  Rule 8.4(f)   EC 1-5, EC 7-34, EC 9-1, DR 1-102(A)(3), (4), (5),
                    & (6), DR 7-110(A), DR 8-101(A)(2)
  Rule 8.4(g)   None

Disciplinary Authority; Choice of Law
  Rule 8.5   None

Table B*

ABA MODEL CODE	ABA MODEL RULES

Canon 1: Integrity of Profession

EC 1-1	Rules 1.1, 8.1(a)
EC 1-2	Rules 1.1, 6.1, 8.1(a)
EC 1-3	Rules 8.1(a), 8.3
EC 1-4	Rule 6.1
EC 1-5	Rule 8.4(a), (b), (c), (e), & (f)
EC 1-6	Rules 1.16(a)(2), 8.4(a)
DR 1-101	Rule 8.1(a)
DR 1-102(A)(1)	Rule 8.4(a)
DR 1-102(A)(2)	Rules 5.1(c), 5.3(b), 8.4(a)
DR 1-102(A)(3)	Rule 8.4(b) & (f)
DR 1-102(A)(4)	Rules 3.3(a)(1), (3), & (b), 3.4(a) & (b), 8.4(c) & (f)
DR 1-102(A)(5)	Rules 3.1, 3.2, 3.3(a) & (b), 3.4, 8.4(d) & (f)
DR 1-102(A)(6)	Rules 3.4(b), 8.4(b) & (f)
DR 1-103(A)	Rules 5.1(c), 8.3
DR 1-103(B)	Rule 8.1(b)

Canon 2: Making Counsel Available

EC 2-1	Rules 6.1, 6.2(a), 7.2(a), 7.2(c)
EC 2-2	Rules 6.1, 7.2(a)
EC 2-3	Rules 4.3, 7.3
EC 2-4	Rule 7.3
EC 2-5	None
EC 2-6	Rule 7.2(a)
EC 2-7	Rules 7.2(a), 7.2(c)
EC 2-8	Rules 7.1, 7.2(a) & (b), 7.4
EC 2-9	Rule 7.1
EC 2-10	Rule 7.1
EC 2-11	Rule 7.1 (Comment)
EC 2-12	Rule 7.1 (Comment)
EC 2-13	Rule 7.1 (Comment)
EC 2-14	Rule 7.2(c)
EC 2-15	Rule 7.2(a) & (b)
EC 2-16	Rules 1.5(a), 6.1, 6.2(b)

** Table B provides cross-references to related provisions, but only in the sense that the provisions consider substantially similar subject matter or reflect similar concerns. A cross-reference does not indicate that a provision of the ABA Model Code of Professional Responsibility has been incorporated by the provision of a Model Rule. The Canons of the Code are not cross-referenced.

ABA MODEL RULES

ABA MODEL CODE	ABA MODEL RULES
EC 2-17	Rule 1.5(a)
EC 2-18	Rule 1.5(a)
EC 2-19	Rule 1.5(b)
EC 2-20	Rule 1.5(c) & (d)
EC 2-21	Rules 1.7(a), 1.8(f)
EC 2-22	Rule 1.5(e)
EC 2-23	None
EC 2-24	Rule 6.1
EC 2-25	Rules 6.1, 6.2
EC 2-26	None
EC 2-27	Rule 6.2(a) & (c)
EC 2-28	Rule 6.2(a)
EC 2-29	Rule 6.2
EC 2-30	Rules 1.16(a)(1) & (2), 1.16(b)(4), 4.2, 6.2(b) & (c)
EC 2-31	Rules 1.3, 1.16(a) & (b)
EC 2-32	Rule 1.16
EC 2-33	Rules 5.4, 6.3, 6.4
DR 2-101(A)	Rule 7.1
DR 2-101(B)	Rules 7.1, 7.2(a)
DR 2-101(C)	Rule 7.1
DR 2-101(D)	None
DR 2-101(E)	Rule 7.1
DR 2-101(F)	Rule 7.1
DR 2-101(G)	Rule 7.1
DR 2-101(H)	Rule 7.2
DR 2-101(I)	Rule 7.2(b)
DR 2-102(A)	Rules 7.2(a), 7.2(c)
DR 2-102(B)	Rules 7.2(a), 7.1 (Comment)
DR 2-102(C)	Rule 7.1 (Comment)
DR 2-102(D)	Rule 7.1 (Comment)
DR 2-102(E)	Rules 7.1, 7.2(c)
DR 2-103(A)	Rule 7.3
DR 2-103(B)	Rule 7.2(a) & (b)
DR 2-103(C)	Rules 5.4(a), 7.2(b), 7.3
DR 2-103(D)	Rules 1.16(a)(1), 5.4(a), 7.2(b), 7.3
DR 2-103(E)	Rules 1.16(a), 7.2(a), 7.3
DR 2-104	Rules 1.16(a), 7.3
DR 2-105	Rule 7.2(c)
DR 2-106(A)	Rule 1.5(a)

APPENDIX B: CORRELATION TABLES

ABA MODEL CODE	ABA MODEL RULES
DR 2-106(B)	Rule 1.5(a)
DR 2-106(C)	Rule 1.5(d)
DR 2-107(A)	Rule 1.5(e)
DR 2-107(B)	Rule 5.4(a)(1)
DR 2-108(A)	Rule 5.6
DR 2-108(B)	Rule 5.6
DR 2-109(A)	Rules 1.16(a)(1), 3.1
DR 2-110(A)	Rule 1.16(b)(1), (c), & (d)
DR 2-110(B)	Rules 1.16(a), 3.1, 4.4(a)
DR 2-110(C)	Rules 1.4(a)(5), 1.16(a) & (b)

Canon 3: Unauthorized Practice

EC 3-1	None
EC 3-2	None
EC 3-3	Rule 8.4(e)
EC 3-4	None
EC 3-5	None
EC 3-6	Rule 5.3(a)
EC 3-7	None
EC 3-8	Rule 5.4(a), (b), & (d)
EC 3-9	Rule 8.4(d)
DR 3-101(A)	Rule 5.5(a)
DR 3-101(B)	Rules 5.5(a), 8.4(d)
DR 3-102	Rule 5.4(a)
DR 3-103	Rule 5.4(b)

Canon 4: Confidences and Secrets

EC 4-1	Rules 1.6(a), 1.18
EC 4-2	Rules 1.6(a) & (b)(1), 5.3(a)
EC 4-3	Rule 1.6(a)
EC 4-4	Rules 1.6(a), 1.13(g)
EC 4-5	Rules 1.8(b), 1.9(b), 1.10(a) & (b), 5.1(a) & (c), 5.3(a)
EC 4-6	Rule 1.9(b)
DR 4-101(A)	Rule 1.6(a)
DR 4-101(B)	Rules 1.6(a), 1.8(b), 1.9(b)
DR 4-101(C)	Rule 1.6(a) & (b)
DR 4-101(D)	Rules 5.1(a) & (b), 5.3(a) & (b)

ABA MODEL CODE	ABA MODEL RULES

Canon 5: Independent Judgment

EC 5-1	Rules 1.7(a), 1.8(c), (d), (e), (f), (g), & (i)
EC 5-2	Rules 1.7(a), 1.8(c)
EC 5-3	Rules 1.7, 1.8(a), (d), & (e)
EC 5-4	Rule 1.8(d)
EC 5-5	Rule 1.8(a) & (c)
EC 5-6	Rules 1.8(c), 7.3
EC 5-7	Rules 1.5(c), 1.8(e) & (i), 1.15
EC 5-8	Rule 1.8(e)
EC 5-9	Rules 1.7(a), 3.7
EC 5-10	Rule 3.7(a)
EC 5-11	Rules 1.7(a), 2.1
EC 5-12	Rule 1.2(a)
EC 5-13	Rule 1.7(a)
EC 5-14	Rule 1.7(a)
EC 5-15	Rule 1.7
EC 5-16	Rules 1.7(b), 1.13(f) & (g)
EC 5-17	Rule 1.7
EC 5-18	Rule 1.13(a), (b), & (c)
EC 5-19	Rule 1.7(b)
EC 5-20	Rules 1.12(a) & (b), 2.4
EC 5-21	Rule 1.7
EC 5-22	Rule 1.7
EC 5-23	Rules 1.7(a), 1.8(f), 5.4(c)
EC 5-24	Rules 1.13(a), (b), & (c), 5.4(a)
DR 5-101(A)	Rules 1.7, 1.8(i), 6.3, 6.4
DR 5-101(B)	Rules 1.7, 3.7
DR 5-102(A)	Rules 1.7, 3.7
DR 5-102(B)	Rules 1.7(b), 3.7
DR 5-103(A)	Rules 1.8(i), 1.15
DR 5-103(B)	Rule 1.8(e)
DR 5-104(A)	Rules 1.7, 1.8(a)
DR 5-104(B)	Rule 1.8(d)
DR 5-105(A)	Rules 1.7, 1.10(c)
DR 5-105(B)	Rules 1.7, 1.13(g)
DR 5-105(C)	Rules 1.7(b), 1.13(g), 1.9(a)
DR 5-105(D)	Rules 1.10(a), 1.12(c), 1.13(c)
DR 5-106	Rule 1.8(g)
DR 5-107(A)	Rules 1.7(b), 1.8(f)

APPENDIX B: CORRELATION TABLES

ABA MODEL CODE	ABA MODEL RULES
DR 5-107(B)	Rules 1.7(a), 1.8(f), 1.13(b) & (c), 2.1, 5.4(c)
DR 5-107(C)	Rule 5.4(a) & (d)

Canon 6: Competence

EC 6-1	Rule 1.1
EC 6-2	Rules 1.1, 5.1(a) & (b), 6.1
EC 6-3	Rule 1.1
EC 6-4	Rules 1.1, 1.3
EC 6-5	Rule 1.1
EC 6-6	Rule 1.8(h)
DR 6-101	Rules 1.1, 1.3, 1.4(a)
DR 6-102	Rule 1.8(h)

Canon 7: Zeal Within the Law

EC 7-1	Rules 1.2(d), 1.3, 3.1
EC 7-2	Rule 1.2(d)
EC 7-3	Rule 2.1
EC 7-4	Rules 3.1, 3.3(a)(1)
EC 7-5	Rules 1.2(d), 3.1, 3.3(a)(3) & (b), 4.1
EC 7-6	Rule 3.4(a) & (b)
EC 7-7	Rule 1.2(a)
EC 7-8	Rules 1.2(a) & (c), 1.4, 2.1
EC 7-9	Rule 1.2(c)
EC 7-10	Rule 4.4(a)
EC 7-11	Rules 1.14(a), 3.8(a), (b), (c), & (d), 3.9
EC 7-12	Rule 1.14
EC 7-13	Rule 3.8
EC 7-14	Rules 3.1, 3.8(a) & (f), 4.4(a)
EC 7-15	Rule 3.9
EC 7-16	Rule 3.9
EC 7-17	Rule 1.2(b)
EC 7-18	Rules 3.8(c), 4.2, 4.3
EC 7-19	None
EC 7-20	Rules 3.2, 3.5(a) & (d)
EC 7-21	Rule 4.4(a)
EC 7-22	Rules 1.2(d), 3.4(c)
EC 7-23	Rule 3.3(a)(2)
EC 7-24	Rules 3.3(d), 3.4(e)
EC 7-25	Rules 3.1, 3.4(c) & (e), 3.5(d), 3.6, 4.4(a)
EC 7-26	Rule 3.3(a)(3) & (b)

ABA MODEL RULES

ABA MODEL CODE	ABA MODEL RULES
EC 7-27	Rules 3.3(b) & (d), 3.4(a) & (f)
EC 7-28	Rules 3.4(b), 5.3(a)
EC 7-29	Rules 3.5(a) & (c), 4.4(a)
EC 7-30	Rules 3.5(c), 4.4(a)
EC 7-31	Rule 3.5(a) & (c)
EC 7-32	Rules 3.3(a)(1) & (b), 3.5(a) & (c)
EC 7-33	Rule 3.6
EC 7-34	Rules 3.5(a), 8.4(f)
EC 7-35	Rule 3.5(b)
EC 7-36	Rule 3.5(d)
EC 7-37	Rules 3.5(d), 4.4(a)
EC 7-38	Rules 1.3, 3.4(c)
EC 7-39	None
DR 7-101(A)	Rules 1.2(a), 1.3, 3.2, 3.5(d), 4.4(a)
DR 7-101(B)	Rules 1.2(b), 1.16(b)
DR 7-102(A)(1)	Rules 3.1, 4.4(a)
DR 7-102(A)(2)	Rule 3.1
DR 7-102(A)(3)	Rules 3.3(a)(1), (a)(3), & (b), 4.1
DR 7-102(A)(4)	Rules 3.3(a) & (b), 4.1
DR 7-102(A)(5)	Rules 3.3(a)(1), 4.1
DR 7-102(A)(6)	Rules 1.2(d), 3.3(b), 3.4(b)
DR 7-102(A)(7)	Rules 1.2(d), 3.3(a)(3) & (b), 4.1
DR 7-102(A)(8)	Rules 1.2(d), 8.4(a) & (b)
DR 7-102(B)	Rules 1.6(b)(1), 3.3(b) & (c), 4.1
DR 7-103(A)	Rule 3.8(a)
DR 7-103(B)	Rule 3.8(d)
DR 7-104	Rules 3.4(f), 4.2, 4.3
DR 7-105	None
DR 7-106(A)	Rules 1.2(d), 3.4(c) & (d), 3.5(a)
DR 7-106(B)	Rules 3.3(a)(2), 3.9
DR 7-106(C)	Rules 3.4(a), (c), (d), & (e), 3.5(d), 4.4(a)
DR 7-107(A)–(I)	Rule 3.6
DR 7-107(D)–(F)	Rule 4.4(a)
DR 7-107(J)	Rules 5.1(a) & (b), 5.3(a) & (b)
DR 7-108(A)	Rule 3.5(a), (b), & (c)
DR 7-108(B)	Rules 3.5(a), (b), & (c), 5.3(b)
DR 7-108(C)	Rule 3.5(a), (b), & (c)
DR 7-108(D)	Rules 3.5(c)(3), 4.4(a)
DR 7-108(E)	Rules 3.5(a), (b), & (c), 4.4(a), 5.1(c), 5.3(b)

APPENDIX B: CORRELATION TABLES

ABA MODEL CODE	ABA MODEL RULES
DR 7-108(F)	Rules 3.5(a), (b), & (c), 4.4(a)
DR 7-108(G)	Rules 3.3(b), 3.5(c)
DR 7-109(A)	Rules 3.3(a)(1), (a)(3), & (b), 3.4(a)
DR 7-109(B)	Rules 3.3(b), 3.4(a) & (f)
DR 7-109(C)	Rule 3.4(b)
DR 7-110(A)	Rules 3.5(a), 8.4(f)
DR 7-110(B)	Rule 3.5(a) & (b)

Canon 8: Improving Legal System

EC 8-1	Rule 6.1
EC 8-2	Rule 6.1
EC 8-3	Rules 6.1, 6.2(a), 8.4(d)
EC 8-4	Rule 3.9
EC 8-5	Rules 3.3(a)(1), (a)(3), & (b), 3.9
EC 8-6	Rule 8.2(a)
EC 8-7	Rule 6.1
EC 8-8	Rule 1.11(d)
EC 8-9	Rule 6.1
DR 8-101	Rules 3.5, 8.4(b), (c), & (f)
DR 8-102	Rule 8.2(a)
DR 8-103	Rule 8.2(b)

Canon 9: Appearance of Impropriety

EC 9-1	Rule 8.4(f)
EC 9-2	Rules 1.4(a), 8.4(e)
EC 9-3	Rules 1.11(a), 1.12(a) & (b)
EC 9-4	Rule 8.4(c) & (e)
EC 9-5	Rule 1.15
EC 9-6	Preamble, Rule 8.4(e)
EC 9-7	Rule 1.15
DR 9-101(A)	Rule 1.12(a) & (b)
DR 9-101(B)	Rules 1.11(a), 1.12(a) & (b)
DR 9-101(C)	Rules 1.4(a)(5), 3.9, 8.4(e)
DR 9-102	Rules 1.4(a), 1.15

Appendix C

ABA Standing Committee On Ethics and Professional Responsibility

COMPOSITION AND JURISDICTION

The Standing Committee on Ethics and Professional Responsibility, which consists of ten members, may:

(1) by the concurrence of a majority of its members, express its opinion on proper professional or judicial conduct, either on its own initiative or when requested to do so by a member of the bar or the judiciary;

(2) periodically publish its issued opinions to the profession in summary or complete form and, on request, provide copies of opinions to members of the bar, the judiciary and the public;

(3) provide under its supervision informal responses to ethics inquiries the answers to which are substantially governed by applicable ethical codes and existing written opinions;

(4) on request, advise or otherwise assist professional organizations and courts in their activities relating to the development, modification and interpretation of statements of the ethical standards of the profession such as the Model Rules of Professional Conduct, the predecessor Model Code of Professional Responsibility and the Model Code of Judicial Conduct;

(5) recommend amendments to or clarifications of the Model Rules of Professional Conduct or the Model Code of Judicial Conduct; and

(6) adopt rules relating to the procedures to be used in issuing opinions, effective when approved by the Board of Governors.

[The above Composition and Jurisdiction statement is found at §31.7 of the Bylaws of the Association. The Rules of Procedure are not incorporated into the Bylaws.]

RULES OF PROCEDURE

1. The Committee may express its opinion on questions of proper professional and judicial conduct. The Model Rules of Professional Conduct and the Model Code of Judicial Conduct, as they may be amended or superseded, contain the standards to be applied. For as long as a significant number of jurisdictions continue to base their professional standards on the predecessor Model Code of Professional Responsibility, the Committee will continue to refer also to the Model Code in its opinions.

2. The Committee may issue an opinion on its own initiative or upon a request from a member of the bar or the judiciary or from a professional organization or a court.

3. The Committee may issue opinions of two kinds: Formal Opinions and Informal Opinions. Formal Opinions are those upon subjects the Committee determines to be of widespread interest or unusual importance. Other opinions are Informal Opinions. The Committee will assign to each opinion a non-duplicative identifying number, with distinction between Formal Opinions and Informal Opinions.

4. The Committee will not usually issue an opinion on a question that is known to be pending before a court in a proceeding in which the requestor is involved. The Committee's published opinions will not identify the person who was the requestor or whose conduct is the subject of the opinion. The Committee will not issue an opinion on a question of law.

5. The Committee may invite or accept written information relevant to a particular opinion from a person or persons interested in such an opinion before the Committee begins its work on an opinion. Ordinarily, the Committee will not invite anyone to make an oral presentation or argument in support of that position.

6. When a Committee or staff member receives an inquiry about the status of a draft opinion from anyone outside the Committee, the member may inform the inquirer that the Committee is considering the question. Draft opinions may, in appropriate circumstances, be shown to other interested ABA Committees and entities. Committee and staff members shall not, absent unusual circumstances, discuss the substance of pending opinions with the public, but may mention topics related to pending opinions in a general fashion.

7. Before issuing an opinion with respect to judicial conduct the Committee will submit the proposed opinion to the Judges' Advisory Committee and consider any objection or comment from the Judges' Advisory

APPENDIX C: RULES OF PROCEDURE

Committee and any member of it. The Committee may assume that the Judges' Advisory Committee and its members have no objection or comment if none is received by the Committee within 30 days after the submission.

8. If the Committee decides not to issue a requested opinion the requestor will be promptly notified.

9. The Committee will issue an opinion only with the concurrence of six members in a vote taken at a meeting or in a telephone conference call. When a Committee member votes against a position declaring a Committee policy, that vote may be recorded in the minutes, which may include the name of the dissenting Committee member. The minutes shall not reflect the names of Committee members voting for or against any non-Committee policy question except that a member's vote shall be recorded and identified at the member's request. When drafting an opinion, policy statement or other document to be publicly disseminated, the Committee shall make every effort to reach a consensus. When, after a full examination of the issue and an exchange of views, the Committee cannot reach a consensus, a dissenting opinion may be appropriate to express the views of a Committee member or members. A member may place a statement of dissent in the Committee file or request that the dissent be published with the opinion.

10. The Chair may assign to one or more members the responsibility of preparing a proposed opinion for consideration by the Committee. The Committee will issue a requested opinion as promptly as feasible.

11. A Formal Opinion overrules an earlier Formal Opinion or Informal Opinion to the extent of conflict. An Informal Opinion overrules an earlier Informal Opinion to the extent of conflict but does not overrule an earlier Formal Opinion.

12. Opinions of the Committee issued before the effective dates of the Model Rules of Professional Conduct, the predecessor Model Code of Professional Responsibility and the Model Code of Judicial Conduct continue in effect to the extent not inconsistent with those standards and not overruled or limited by later opinions.

13. The Committee will make opinions and/or summaries of opinions available for publication in the American Bar Association journal. The Committee will cause Formal Opinions and Informal Opinions to be published in looseleaf form.

14. The Committee may through its staff arrange to provide informal responses to ethics inquiries the answers to which are substantially gov-

erned by applicable ethical codes and opinions of this Committee or other ethics committees. The staff will maintain a log of such inquiries that will periodically be reviewed by the Committee.

15. Information contained in Committee files relating to requests for opinions that would disclose the identity of the inquirer or the person whose conduct is the subject of the opinion will not voluntarily be disclosed by the Association without the consent of the affected persons.

Appendix D

ABA Special Committee on Implementation of the Model Rules of Professional Conduct (1983–1987)

MICHAEL FRANCK, *Chair*
Lansing, Michigan

EDWARD L. BENOIT
Twin Falls, Idaho

ROGER BROSNAHAN
Minneapolis, Minnesota

WAYNE A. BUDD
Boston, Massachusetts

RICHARD M. COLEMAN
Los Angeles, California

JOHN C. ELAM
Columbus, Ohio

JOSEPH E. GALLAGHER
Scranton, Pennsylvania

ROBERT O. HETLAGE
St. Louis, Missouri

W. STELL HUIE
Atlanta, Georgia

JAMES T. JENNINGS
Roswell, New Mexico

CAROLYN B. LAMM
Washington, D.C.

LLOYD LOCHRIDGE
Austin, Texas

LEON SILVERMAN
New York, New York

E.C. WARD
Natchez, Mississippi

BEN J. WEAVER
Indianapolis, Indiana

Appendix E

Amendments to the Model Rules of Professional Conduct (By Rule)

Preamble
Amended 2002 per Midyear Meeting Report 401.

Scope
Amended 2002 per Midyear Meeting Report 401.

Rule 1.0
Amended 2002 per Midyear Meeting Report 401.
Amended 2009 per Midyear Meeting Report 109.
Amended 2012 per Annual Meeting Report 105A.

Rule 1.1
Amended 2002 per Midyear Meeting Report 401.
Amended 2012 per Annual Meeting Reports 105A and C.

Rule 1.2
Amended 2002 per Midyear Meeting Report 401.

Rule 1.3
Amended 2002 per Midyear Meeting Report 401.

Rule 1.4
Amended 2002 per Midyear Meeting Report 401.
Amended 2012 per Annual Meeting Report 105A.

Rule 1.5
Amended 2002 per Midyear Meeting Report 401.

Rule 1.6
Amended 2002 per Midyear Meeting Report 401.
Amended 2003 per Annual Meeting Report 119A.
Amended 2012 per Annual Meeting Reports 105A and F.

Rule 1.7
Amended 1987 per Midyear Meeting Report 121.
Amended 2002 per Midyear Meeting Report 401.

Rule 1.8
Amended 1987 per Midyear Meeting Report 121.
Amended 2002 per Midyear Meeting Report 401.
Amended 2020 per Annual Meeting Report 107.

Rule 1.9
Amended 1987 per Midyear Meeting Report 121.
Amended 1989 per Midyear Meeting Report 120A.
Amended 2002 per Midyear Meeting Report 401.

Rule 1.10
Amended 1989 per Midyear Meeting Report 120A.
Amended 2002 per Midyear Meeting Report 401.
Amended 2009 per Midyear Meeting Report 109.
Amended 2009 per Annual Meeting Report 109.

Rule 1.11
Amended 1987 per Midyear Meeting Report 121.
Amended 2002 per Midyear Meeting Report 401.

Rule 1.12
Amended 1987 per Midyear Meeting Report 121.
Amended 2002 per Midyear Meeting Report 401.

Rule 1.13
Amended 2002 per Midyear Meeting Report 401.
Amended 2003 per Annual Meeting Report 119B.

Rule 1.14
Amended 1997 per Midyear Meeting Report 113.
Amended 2002 per Midyear Meeting Report 401.

Rule 1.15
Amended 2002 per Midyear Meeting Report 401.

Rule 1.16
Amended 2002 per Midyear Meeting Report 401.
Amended 2023 per Annual Meeting Report 100

Rule 1.17
Added 1990 per Midyear Meeting Report 8A.
Amended 2002 per Midyear Meeting Report 401.
Amended 2012 per Annual Meeting Report 105F.

Rule 1.18
Added 2002 per Midyear Meeting Report 401.
Amended 2012 per Annual Meeting Report 105B.

APPENDIX E: AMENDMENTS TO THE MODEL RULES

Rule 2.1
Amended 2002 per Midyear Meeting Report 401.

Rule 2.2
Deleted 2002 per Midyear Meeting Report 401.

Rule 2.3
Amended 2002 per Midyear Meeting Report 401.

Rule 2.4
Added 2002 per Midyear Meeting Report 401.

Rule 3.1
Amended 2002 per Midyear Meeting Report 401.

Rule 3.2
Amended 2002 per Midyear Meeting Report 401.

Rule 3.3
Amended 2002 per Midyear Meeting Report 401.

Rule 3.4
Amended 2002 per Midyear Meeting Report 401.

Rule 3.5
Amended 2002 per Midyear Meeting Report 401.

Rule 3.6
Amended 1994 per Annual Meeting Report 100.
Amended 2002 per Midyear Meeting Report 401.

Rule 3.7
Amended 2002 per Midyear Meeting Report 401.

Rule 3.8
Amended 1990 per Midyear Meeting Report 118.
Amended 1994 per Annual Meeting Report 100.
Amended 1995 per Annual Meeting Report 101.
Amended 2002 per Midyear Meeting Report 401.
Amended 2008 per Midyear Meeting Report 105B.

Rule 3.9
Amended 2002 per Midyear Meeting Report 401.

Rule 4.1
Amended 2002 per Midyear Meeting Report 401.

Rule 4.2
Amended 1995 per Annual Meeting Report 100.
Amended 2002 per Midyear Meeting Report 401.

Rule 4.3
Amended 2002 per Midyear Meeting Report 401.

Rule 4.4
Amended 2002 per Midyear Meeting Report 401.
Amended 2012 per Annual Meeting Report 105A.

Rule 5.1
Amended 2002 per Midyear Meeting Report 401.

Rule 5.3
Amended 2002 per Midyear Meeting Report 401.
Amended 2012 per Annual Meeting Report 105C.

Rule 5.4
Amended 1990 per Midyear Meeting Report 8A.
Amended 2002 per Midyear Meeting Report 401.

Rule 5.5
Amended 2002 per Annual Meeting Report 201B.
Amended 2007 per Midyear Meeting Report 104.
Amended 2012 per Annual Meeting Reports 105 B and C.
Amended 2013 per Midyear Meeting Report 107A.
Amended 2016 per Midyear Meeting Report 103.

Rule 5.6
Amended 1990 per Midyear Meeting Report 8A.
Amended 2002 per Midyear Meeting Report 401.

Rule 5.7
Added 1994 per Midyear Meeting Report 113.
Amended 2002 per Midyear Meeting Report 401.

Rule 6.1
Amended 1993 per Midyear Meeting Report 8A.
Amended 2002 per Midyear Meeting Report 401.

Rule 6.3
Amended 1987 per Midyear Meeting Report 121.

Rule 6.5
Added 2002 per Midyear Meeting Report 401.

APPENDIX E: AMENDMENTS TO THE MODEL RULES

Rule 7.1
Amended 2002 per Midyear Meeting Report 401.
Amended 2012 per Annual Meeting Report 105B.
Amended 2018 per Annual Meeting Report 101.

Rule 7.2
Amended 1989 per Midyear Meeting Report 120B.
Amended 1990 per Midyear Meeting Report 8A.
Amended 2002 per Midyear Meeting Report 401.
Amended 2002 per Annual Meeting Report 114.
Amended 2012 per Annual Meeting Report 105B.
Amended 2018 per Annual Meeting Report 101.

Rule 7.3
Amended 1989 per Midyear Meeting Reports 115 and 120B.
Amended 2002 per Midyear Meeting Report 401.
Amended 2012 per Annual Meeting Report 105B.
Amended 2018 per Annual Meeting Report 101.

Rule 7.4
Deleted 2018 per Annual Meeting Report 101.

Rule 7.5
Deleted 2018 per Annual Meeting Report 101.

Rule 7.6
Added 2000 per Midyear Meeting Report 110.

Rule 8.1
Amended 2002 per Midyear Meeting Report 401.

Rule 8.3
Amended 1991 per Midyear Meeting Report 108C.
Amended 2002 per Midyear Meeting Report 401.

Rule 8.4
Amended 1998 per Annual Meeting Report 117.
Amended 2002 per Midyear Meeting Report 401.
Amended 2016 per Annual Meeting Report 109.

Rule 8.5
Amended 1993 per Annual Meeting Report 114.
Amended 2002 per Annual Meeting Report 201C.
Amended 2013 per Midyear Meeting Report 107D.

Amendments to the Model Rules of Professional Conduct (By Date)

1987 Midyear Meeting
Rules 1.7, 1.8, 1.9, 1.11, 1.12 and 6.3

1989 Midyear Meeting
Rules 1.9, 1.10, 7.2, 7.3 and 7.4

1990 Midyear Meeting
Rules 1.17, 3.8, 5.4, 5.6 and 7.2

1991 Midyear Meeting
Rule 8.3

1992 Annual Meeting
Rule 7.4

1993 Midyear Meeting
Rule 6.1

1993 Annual Meeting
Rule 8.5

1994 Midyear Meeting
Rule 5.7

1994 Annual Meeting
Rules 3.6, 3.8 and 7.4

1995 Annual Meeting
Rules 3.8 and 4.2

1997 Midyear Meeting
Rule 1.14

1998 Annual Meeting
Rule 8.4

2000 Midyear Meeting
Rule 7.6

APPENDIX E: AMENDMENTS TO THE MODEL RULES

2002 Midyear Meeting
Preamble, Scope, Rules 1.0, 1.1, 1.2, 1.3, 1.4, 1.5, 1.6, 1.7, 1.8, 1.9, 1.10, 1.11, 1.12, 1.13, 1.14, 1.15, 1.16, 1.17, 1.18, 2.1, 2.2, 2.3, 2.4, 3.1, 3.2, 3.3, 3.4, 3.5, 3.6, 3.7, 3.8, 3.9, 4.1, 4.2, 4.3, 4.4, 5.1, 5.3. 5.4, 5.6, 5.7, 6.1, 6.5, 7.1, 7.2, 7.3, 7.4, 7.5, 8.1, 8.3 and 8.4

2002 Annual Meeting
Rules 5.5, 7.2, 7.5 and 8.5

2003 Annual Meeting
Rules 1.6 and 1.13

2007 Midyear Meeting
Rule 5.5

2008 Midyear Meeting
Rule 3.8

2009 Midyear Meeting
Rules 1.0 and 1.10

2009 Annual Meeting
Rule 1.10

2012 Annual Meeting
Rules 1.0, 1.1, 1.4, 1.6, 1.17, 1.18, 4.4, 5.3, 5.5, 7.1, 7.2 and 7.3

2013 Midyear Meeting
Rules 5.5 and 8.5

2016 Midyear Meeting
Rule 5.5

2016 Annual Meeting
Rule 8.4

2018 Annual Meeting
Rules 7.1, 7.2, 7.3, 7.4, and 7.5

2020 Annual Meeting
Rule 1.8

2023 Annual Meeting
Rule 1.16

APPENDIX F

FORMAL ETHICS OPINIONS

AMERICAN BAR ASSOCIATION
STANDING COMMITTEE ON ETHICS AND PROFESSIONAL RESPONSIBILITY

Formal Opinion 504 March 1, 2023
Choice of Law

When a lawyer practices the law of more than one jurisdiction, choice-of-law questions arise concerning which jurisdiction's ethics rules the lawyer must follow. Model Rule 8.5 provides that when a lawyer's conduct is in connection with a matter pending before a tribunal, the lawyer must comply with the ethics rules of the jurisdiction in which the tribunal sits, unless otherwise provided. For all other conduct, including conduct in anticipation of litigation not yet filed, a lawyer must comply with the ethics rules of the jurisdiction in which the lawyer's conduct occurs. However, if the predominant effect of the lawyer's conduct is in a different jurisdiction, then the lawyer must comply with the ethics rules of that jurisdiction.

Introduction

Lawyers frequently are admitted to practice law or are authorized to practice the law of more than one jurisdiction. When jurisdictions have differing ethical requirements, the lawyer must determine which jurisdiction's ethics rules govern the lawyer's actions in the representation.[1] This Formal Opinion addresses several scenarios applying ABA Model Rule of Professional Conduct 8.5, Disciplinary Authority; Choice of Law, to determine which jurisdiction's rules govern the situation, including: 1) fee agreements; 2) law firm ownership; 3) reporting professional misconduct; 4) confidentiality duties; and 5) screening lawyers who leave one firm to join another (referred to as "lateral" lawyers).

ABA Model Rule of Professional Conduct 8.5, Disciplinary Authority; Choice of Law—An Overview

Pursuant to ABA Model Rule of Professional Conduct 8.5(a), lawyers are subject to the disciplinary authority of the jurisdiction(s) in which they are

---

1. This opinion is based on the ABA Model Rules of Professional Conduct as amended by the ABA House of Delegates through February 2023. The laws, court rules, regulations, rules of professional conduct, and opinions promulgated in individual jurisdictions are controlling.

licensed regardless of where their conduct occurred. Lawyers also are subject to the disciplinary authority of the jurisdiction(s) in which they are offering to provide or are providing legal services regardless of whether they are admitted to practice or licensed by that jurisdiction. For example, lawyers practicing pursuant to a jurisdiction's in-house counsel rule, or pro hac vice rule, or providing legal services temporarily pursuant to Model Rule 5.5, are all subject to the disciplinary authority of the jurisdiction in which they are providing legal services. Finally, a lawyer "may be subject to the disciplinary authority of *both this jurisdiction and another jurisdiction for the same conduct.*"[2]

ABA Model Rule of Professional Conduct 8.5(b) determines which jurisdiction's ethics rules apply to a lawyer's conduct. In answering the choice of law question, Rule 8.5(b) addresses litigation matters and non-litigation matters differently.

For litigation matters, Rule 8.5(b)(1) provides: "In any exercise of the disciplinary authority of this jurisdiction, the rules of professional conduct to be applied shall be as follows: (1) for conduct in connection with a matter pending before a tribunal, the rules of the jurisdiction in which the tribunal sits, unless the rules of the tribunal provide otherwise[.]"

For "any other conduct," Rule 8.5(b)(2) explains that the ethics rules of the jurisdiction where the lawyer's conduct occurred will govern unless the "predominant effect" of that conduct is in a different jurisdiction, in which case, the "rules of that jurisdiction shall be applied to the conduct."

For litigation matters, a key question is what does Rule 8.5(b)(1)'s phrase "in connection with a matter pending before a tribunal" mean? Does it apply to the fee agreement entered into before the matter is filed in court or to the ownership structure of a law firm in a different jurisdiction than the tribunal?

Another key question is what does Rule 8.5(b)(2)'s phrase "any other conduct" mean? Does it apply to transactional matters and/or conduct that is *not* involving a tribunal—such as the fee agreement or conduct occurring before a case is filed?

Comment [4] is instructive, explaining that the phrase "any other conduct" includes "all other conduct, including conduct in anticipation of a proceeding not yet pending before a tribunal."

Rule 8.5(b)(2) provides a safe harbor for a lawyer's "predominant effect" determination: "A lawyer shall not be subject to discipline if the lawyer's conduct conforms to the rules of a jurisdiction in which the lawyer reasonably believes the predominant effect of the lawyer's conduct will occur." This safe harbor from disciplinary action is not without limits. The lawyer's belief about the jurisdiction of the predominant effect of the lawyer's conduct must be a reasonable belief. Reasonable belief is a defined term and "denotes

---

2. MODEL RULES OF PROF'L CONDUCT R. 8.5(a) (emphasis added).

that the lawyer believes the matter in question and that the circumstances are such that the belief is reasonable."[3]

Although Rule 8.5 does not provide lawyers guidance on what factors the lawyer should consider when determining where the predominant effect of the lawyer's conduct occurs, the Committee believes lawyers should look to the following factors:

- the client's location, residence, and/or principal place of business;
- where the transaction may occur;
- which jurisdiction's substantive law applies to the transaction;
- the location of the lawyer's principal office;
- where the lawyer is admitted;
- the location of the opposing party and other relevant third parties (residence and/or principal place of business);[4] and
- the jurisdiction with the greatest interest in the lawyer's conduct.[5]

When a choice of law question concerning the applicable conflict of interest rules arises and a regulatory authority must determine whether the lawyer's belief—that a specific jurisdiction's rules applied because the predominant effect of that lawyer's conduct occurred in that jurisdiction—was reasonable, then a written agreement between the lawyer and client that explains a particular jurisdiction's conflict of interest rules will apply may be considered, at least if certain requirements are satisfied.

Specifically, the ABA added to the last sentence of Comment [5] to Rule 8.5 in 2013 to address this concept:

[5] When a lawyer's conduct involves significant contacts with more than one jurisdiction, it may not be clear whether the predominant effect of the lawyer's conduct will occur in a jurisdiction other than the one in which the conduct occurred. So long as the lawyer's conduct conforms to the rules of a jurisdiction in which the lawyer reasonably believes the predominant effect will occur, the lawyer shall not be subject to discipline under this Rule. *With respect to conflicts of interest, in determining a lawyer's reasonable belief under paragraph (b)(2), a written agreement between the lawyer and client that reasonably speci-*

---

3. MODEL RULES OF PROF'L CONDUCT R. 1.0(i).

4. *See, e.g.,* N.Y. State Bar Ass'n Comm. on Prof'l Ethics Op. 1027 (2014) (noting that factors for determining "predominant effect" may include where client resides, where funds will be deposited, where the services will be performed, and where the business will operate).

5. For example, conduct permitted in one jurisdiction that has little or no relationship to the client and legal matter may be the subject of discipline if the conduct is prohibited in another jurisdiction that has a greater nexus with the matter.

fies a particular jurisdiction as within the scope of that paragraph may be considered if the agreement was obtained with the client's informed consent confirmed in the agreement. (emphasis added)[6]

To offer guidance to lawyers on these important choice-of-law principles, the following scenarios illustrate how Rule 8.5 applies when a lawyer may be subject to more than one jurisdiction's ethics rules.

Scenario 1: Fee Agreements

Lawyer is admitted in State X and enters into a client-lawyer relationship with Client who resides in State X. Lawyer will work from Lawyer's office in State X on Client's matter. Litigation is to be filed in State Y. In drafting the terms of the fee agreement,[7] should Lawyer adhere to the Rules of Professional Conduct of State X or State Y?

---

6. Ethics 20/20 Commission Report and Resolution 107D that recommended adding the last sentence to this Comment explained "[l]awyers and clients can resolve some of the unavoidable uncertainties of Rule 8.5(b)(2) in the same way choice of law issues are resolved in other contexts: through choice of law agreements ... They may also be useful to disciplinary authorities who are asked to consider whether a lawyer's determination of the applicable jurisdiction's conflict of interest rule was 'reasonable' ... These kinds of agreements are analogous to waivers of future conflicts, which are already authorized in Comment [22] of Rule 1.7, and will have a similar effect.". *See* ETHICS 20/20 COMMISSION REPORT AND RESOLUTION 107D (2013), *available at* 20121112_ethics_20_20_choice_of_rule_resolution_and_report_final.pdf (americanbar.org).

The Ethics 20/20 Commission specifically limited any contractual authorization between lawyers and clients to conflicts of interest considerations. *See* Resolution and Report 107D (2013) at p.3. A lawyer and client cannot contract around Rule 8.5(b)(1)'s choice of law conclusion for conduct "in connection with a matter pending before a tribunal." The report noted that "[d]espite the advantages of these agreements, the Commission concluded that they should be subject to several limitations. First, such agreements should only be used in the context of conflicts of interest; they should not be used to specify the rules of a jurisdiction on other issues, such as the duty of confidentiality. The Commission did not want to authorize parties to contract around rules intended to protect adverse parties or tribunals. To ensure the limited use of the agreements, the proposed Comment language begins with the phrase 'With respect to conflicts of interest...'" This "essentially permits a lawyer and client to enter into a choice-of-law agreement regarding the applicable conflict-of-interest rules, although the agreement is not binding on a court or disciplinary authority." ABA ANNOTATED MODEL RULES OF PROFESSIONAL CONDUCT 748 (2019).

7. "Principles of substantive law external to these Rules determine whether a client-lawyer relationship exists." MODEL RULES OF PROFESSIONAL CONDUCT, Scope [17]. Once the client-lawyer relationship is formed, Rule 1.5(b) states that the scope of representation and how fees and costs will be charged "shall be communicated to the client, preferably in writing, [. . .]". Many jurisdictions' versions of Rule 1.5(b) require written fee agreements for all representations. Rule 1.5(c) and (e) require specific written disclosures for contingent fee agreements and situations where lawyers in different firms will be sharing a fee.

APPENDIX F: FORMAL ETHICS OPINIONS

As noted above, Rule 8.5(b)(1) will apply the rules of the jurisdiction of the tribunal for conduct "in connection with a matter pending before a tribunal" but Comment [4] to the Rule expressly recognizes:

> [. . .] As to all other conduct, including conduct in anticipation of a proceeding not yet pending before a tribunal, paragraph (b)(2) provides that a lawyer shall be subject to the rules of the jurisdiction in which the lawyer's conduct occurred, or, if the predominant effect of the conduct is in another jurisdiction, the rules of that jurisdiction shall be applied to the conduct.[. . .]

Securing a fee agreement is "conduct in anticipation of a proceeding not yet pending before a tribunal" and, therefore, Rule 8.5(b)(2) applies. Applying the factors set forth above to determine the jurisdiction in which the "predominant effect" of the lawyer's conduct occurs, a lawyer admitted in State X, who is hired to represent a resident of State X, may reasonably conclude that State X's rules apply to the terms of the fee agreement both because the Lawyer's conduct, executing the fee agreement and accepting the representation, and the predominant effect of the agreement to represent the Client take place in State X.[8]

The agreement is signed in State X, where Lawyer's office is located, where Lawyer is admitted to practice, where Lawyer will research and prepare for the matter (even if done virtually), and where Client resides. Therefore, State X's version of Rule 1.5 would apply to the fee agreement including whether the fee agreement must be in writing, whether it must be signed by a client if it is a contingent fee agreement, and whether the fee may be divided with lawyers in different firms who assume joint responsibility.

Certainly, from a client protection perspective, the jurisdiction where the lawyer is licensed and/or the jurisdiction where the client resides has a significant interest in requiring certain provisions in the fee agreement, and therefore, application of that jurisdiction's version of Rule 1.5 is most appropriate.[9]

---

8. This Opinion is limited to analyzing which jurisdiction's rules of professional conduct apply to a fee agreement and does not opine on which state's substantive contract laws would apply.

9. The Committee recognizes that Mass. Bar Ass'n Op. 12-02 (2012) comes to a different conclusion as to which state's rules apply in a dispute over a fee agreement. Massachusetts' version of Rule 8.5 is different than the ABA Model Rule and the issue presented involved the reasonableness of the fee charged in litigation, not the formation of the agreement. The Committee's position is consistent with Bernick v. Frost, 510 A.2d 56 (N.J. 1986), construing contract law to find that New Jersey—the state in which the lawyer was licensed, and the client lived—was the appropriate venue for a dispute between a lawyer and client over the engagement agreement for a matter litigated in New York. *But see In re* Schiller, 808 S.E.2d 378 (S.C. 2017) applying rules of professional conduct of North Carolina, the state in which litigation was filed, to South Carolina licensed lawyer fee agreement.

To avoid ambiguity, a lawyer may want to identify in the fee agreement the lawyer's belief as to which jurisdiction's rules of professional conduct will apply to the fee agreement. That fee agreement may list the factors considered by the lawyer in reasonably concluding where the lawyer's conduct will occur and where the predominant effect of the fee agreement will occur.[10]

Of course, there must be some reasonable relationship between the jurisdiction whose rules of professional conduct are selected to govern the fee agreement and where the lawyer is admitted to practice, as well as the other factors listed above.[11] It would not be reasonable for a lawyer to conclude that the applicable ethics rules would be those of a jurisdiction in which the lawyer is not admitted to practice or a jurisdiction for which there is no reasonable basis to find the "predominant effect" of the lawyer's conduct occurred.

The ethics rules that apply to fee agreements between lawyers and clients may include not just Rule 1.5 but also the ethics rules regulating what the lawyer may then do with those fees such as rules governing with whom the lawyer may share or divide a legal fee.[12]

This hypothetical demonstrates the relevance of the final sentence of Model Rule 8.5(b)(2): "A lawyer shall not be subject to discipline if the lawyer's conduct conforms to the rules of a jurisdiction in which the lawyer reasonably believes the predominant effect of the lawyer's conduct will occur." Thus, a lawyer who reasonably believes that the predominant effect of the fee agreement will be in a specific jurisdiction should not be subject to discipline, even if the scope of representation contemplates filing a case for the client in a different jurisdiction.

Scenario 2: Law Firm Ownership

State A permits Lawyer to have nonlawyer partners in the law firm, while State B follows Model Rule 5.4, which does not permit nonlawyer partners in law firms. Lawyer is admitted to practice law only in State A and has a law firm formed in State A with a nonlawyer partner. Lawyer seeks to appear in a case *pro hac vice* pending before a tribunal in State B. Will State B's Rules of Professional Conduct prohibit Lawyer from sharing the fees earned on the case pending before State B tribunal with Lawyer's nonlawyer partners?[13]

---

10. In addition to Rule 1.5 applying to fee agreements, Rules 1.15 and 5.4 also may be relevant.

11. *See In re Wyatt*, 159 N.H. 285 (2009) (lawyer cannot use another state's rules as defense to disciplinary charges where lawyer was not licensed or admitted pro hac vice).

12. For instance, a lawyer admitted in jurisdiction X and practicing law in jurisdiction X will have the fee agreement enforced and interpreted by the Rules of Professional Conduct in jurisdiction X, which might, for instance, permit paying referral fees or permit jurisdiction X lawyers to have nonlawyer partners. Compare MODEL RULES OF PROF'L CONDUCT R. 5.4 with Ariz. Rule 1.5 Cmt [9].

13. There is no ethical concern for Lawyer's local counsel who is admitted to practice law only in State B in sharing fees with Lawyer under a co-counsel agreement so long as

APPENDIX F: FORMAL ETHICS OPINIONS

Can one jurisdiction in essence reach into a law firm in another jurisdiction and find that jurisdiction's permissible firm structure to be unethical and subject lawyers from another jurisdiction to discipline?

When a lawyer seeks to appear before a tribunal by *pro hac vice* admission the lawyer agrees to be bound by the rules of the tribunal, and Rule 8.5(b)(1) provides that the ethics rules of that tribunal apply to "conduct in connection with a matter pending before a tribunal." Under the ABA Model Rules on Pro Hac Vice Admission, the tribunal has the discretion to admit the out-of-state lawyer and Rule 1.D.3 provides:

> [. . .] An application ordinarily should be granted unless the court or agency finds reason to believe that such admission:
>
> a. may be detrimental to the prompt, fair and efficient administration of justice,
>
> b. may be detrimental to legitimate interests of parties to the proceedings other than the client(s) the applicant proposes to represent,
>
> c. one or more of the clients the applicant proposes to represent may be at risk of receiving inadequate representation and cannot adequately appreciate that risk, or
>
> d. the applicant has engaged in such frequent appearances as to constitute regular practice in this state.

Thus, the Model Rule on Pro Hac Vice Admission defaults to permitting admission unless there is some fact to suggest the admission would be detrimental to the administration of justice, or competent representation of the client is an issue, or the lawyer is too frequently appearing in the court. There is nothing in the Model Rules on Pro Hac Vice Admission that says the tribunal should inquire into the Lawyer's business model particularly when it is permitted by the Lawyer's home licensing jurisdiction. Nor is there any indication that the business model permitted in the Lawyer's home jurisdiction would be detrimental to the "prompt, fair and efficient administration of justice."

Even so, a Lawyer admitted pro hac vice agrees to be bound by the ethics rules of the tribunal and Rule 8.5(b)(1) provides that the Rules of Professional

---

local counsel is in a separate firm and not part of Lawyer's State A law firm. ABA Comm. on Ethics & Prof'l Responsibility, Formal Op. 464 (2013); *See also* N.Y. City Bar Formal Op. 2020-1 (2020) (finding that New York lawyer may share fees with Arizona lawyer who has separate firm from New York lawyer and Arizona firm has nonlawyer owners); Fla. Bar Op. 17-1 (2017); Phila. Bar Ass'n Op. 2010-7 (2010).

Conduct of that tribunal apply to "conduct in connection with a matter pending before a tribunal [. . .]".[14] Certainly, the tribunal's ethics rules with respect to the Lawyer's conduct in representing the client in the proceeding, in dealing with the tribunal, and dealing with the opposing party and counsel will be governed by tribunal's Rules of Professional Conduct. Model Rule 8.5(b) expressly chooses the tribunal's ethics rules regarding the lawyer's "conduct in connection with a matter pending before a tribunal"—suggesting that the tribunal has a relevant interest in assuring the Lawyer's conduct *in that tribunal's matter* complies with the tribunal's Rules.

But does Model Rule 8.5 make the Lawyer who is licensed in State A—which allows nonlawyer partners in firms—subject to discipline for having nonlawyer partners when the Lawyer is admitted pro have vice to represent a client in a matter pending in a tribunal, in State B which does not allow nonlawyer partners?

The Lawyer's law firm is in State A, where the Lawyer is admitted to practice and has an office, and that firm structure is not "conduct in connection with a matter pending before a tribunal." The firm is not located in State B—the partnership conduct is occurring in State A, not State B where the tribunal sits.

Therefore, Rule 8.5(b)(2), not (b)(1), governs which ethics rules regulate the structure of the firm. Lawyer's conduct—establishing a firm structure—and the "predominant effect" of Lawyer's partnership with a nonlawyer is in State A, not State B. Thus, even if the Lawyer is admitted before a tribunal in State B, pro hac vice, Lawyer's law firm ownership in State A is governed by State A's ethics rules and not State B's.

Scenario 3: Reporting Professional Misconduct

Lawyer is admitted to practice law in States A and B, with Lawyer's office located in State B. Client residing in State A hires Lawyer to complete litigation in State A. Prior counsel on this matter forged the Client's signature on a document that was filed with the tribunal, which has prejudiced the rights of Client going forward in this matter.

State A requires Lawyer to report professional misconduct of another lawyer to State A's disciplinary authority even if doing so requires Lawyer to disclose information relating to the representation without the consent of the client. State B follows Model Rule 8.3, which requires Lawyer to report professional misconduct of another lawyer, but if Lawyer would have to reveal information relating to the representation in making such a report, the

---

14. As noted above, if the tribunal does not have a rule designating the rules of professional conduct that apply to a lawyer appearing before the tribunal, the applicable rules will be those of the jurisdiction where the tribunal sits.

Lawyer only may report the misconduct if Client provides informed consent to make the disclosure.

Which State's version of Rule 8.3 governs Lawyer's reporting obligations? State A or State B?

Because Lawyer is representing a State A client and Lawyer's work for Client is in connection with a matter pending before a State A tribunal, Rule 8.5(b)(1) would require Lawyer to follow the Rules of State A and report prior counsel in accordance with State A's version of Rule 8.3. Even though Lawyer's office is in State B, and even if prior counsel of the Client was admitted only in State B, or even if the *Client* was only a resident of State B, State A's version of Rule 8.3 applies because the matter is pending before the tribunal in State A and Lawyer's conduct—reporting prior counsel—is conduct in connection with a matter pending before a tribunal in State A.

Scenario 4: Confidentiality Duties

Lawyer is licensed in State A and State B, and practices from an office in State A. State A is a Model Rules state and Model Rule 1.6, Confidentiality of Information, permits, but does not require, a lawyer to disclose information relating to the representation to the extent the lawyer reasonably believes necessary "to prevent reasonably certain death or substantial bodily harm."[15] State B's confidentiality rule requires a lawyer to reveal such information, using the term "must reveal," client confidential information to prevent death or substantial bodily harm to another person.

Lawyer is representing a Client/Buyer, who resides in State B, in a transactional matter to purchase residential real estate in State A from Seller in State A. The matter is not before a tribunal. The transaction has become contentious because Buyer and Seller are having a difficult time coming to terms on the agreement. Buyer and Seller have been engaging in negotiations on the transaction at Buyer's place of business in State B. At a recent meeting, Client/Buyer privately made a specific threat to Lawyer to gravely physically harm the Seller at their next meeting if Seller refuses to accept Buyer's terms. Lawyer reasonably believes that the Client will carry out the threat. Is Lawyer required to disclose the threat by Client/Buyer to Seller?

Rule 8.5(b)(2) will determine which jurisdiction's version of Rule 1.6 applies to the situation because the matter is not before a tribunal. Paragraph (b)(2) tells Lawyer to look to the "rules of the jurisdiction in which the lawyer's conduct occurred, or, if the predominant effect of the conduct is in a different jurisdiction, the rules of that jurisdiction."

Although the Lawyer's conduct, informing the Seller of the Client/Buyer's threat, could take place from any number of locations, the Committee believes that the predominant effect of Lawyer's conduct is in State B. In as-

---

15. MODEL RULES OF PROF'L CONDUCT R. 1.6(b)(1).

sessing where the predominant effect of Lawyer's conduct occurs, a lawyer should consider where the client is located, where the client's actions might occur, which jurisdiction's substantive law would be applied to the client's actions and where the lawyer is admitted. In this scenario both State A and State B are involved because the Client/Buyer is residing in State B, but the Seller and transaction are in State A. However, the threatened harm would most likely occur in State B because Client/Buyer made a specific threat to Lawyer to harm the Seller at their next meeting and prior meetings have been held in State B at Client/Buyer's place of business.

The Lawyer may reasonably conclude that the predominant effect for the matter involving the Client's/Buyer's threat is in State B due to the Client's location and the location where the threat is specified to occur. Therefore, State B's version of Rule 1.6 will applicable and Lawyer must disclose the Client's threat.

Scenario 5: Screening for Laterals Lawyers

A law firm with multiple U.S. offices would like to hire a Lawyer A who is currently associated with another firm. Lawyer A is licensed in State A and would practice law from the firm's office in State A. The firm's hiring of Lawyer A would impute a former client conflict of interest to another lawyer at the firm, Lawyer B. Lawyer B is licensed in State B and practices law from the firm's office in State B.

As prescribed in Model Rule 1.10(a)(2), State A allows the law firm to screen Lawyer A without obtaining the consent of the affected clients (Lawyer A's soon-to-be former client and Lawyer B's current client). State B, however, does not follow Model Rule 1.10(a)(2) and would impute Lawyer A's conflict to Lawyer B unless Lawyer A's soon-to-be former client and Lawyer B's current client gives informed consent, confirmed in writing. To prevent imputing Lawyer A's conflict to Lawyer B, may the law firm screen Lawyer A without obtaining the consent of the affected clients?

This is a common scenario where the hiring law firm wants to hire a lawyer who is practicing at a different firm, commonly called a "lateral hire," but the lateral is currently working on a client matter adverse to a client of a lawyer at the hiring firm. The hiring firm wants to avoid imputation of the new lawyer's conflicts to the hiring firm. Most states have adopted a screening rule similar to Model Rule 1.10(a)(2), which permits the screening of a lateral irrespective of the lateral's level of involvement with the soon-to-be former client's matter. Some states have adopted rules where the availability of screening depends on the lateral's level of knowledge or participation in the soon-to-be-former client's matter. Other states do not permit screening to avoid the imputed conflict, and therefore require the hiring firm to obtain the informed consent of the affected clients.

The choice of law analysis for screening laterals will initially pivot on whether the imputed conflict of interest affects a pending lawsuit or a transactional matter. If the conflict that would be imputed from Lawyer A to Lawyer B concerns litigation filed in State B, then State B's screening rules would govern unless the tribunal's rules provide otherwise.[16] Similarly, if the imputed conflict arises in a matter that Lawyer B is litigating before a tribunal located in State C, then State C's screening rules would govern unless the tribunal's rules provide otherwise.[17]

The analysis is more complicated if the conflict that would be imputed from Lawyer A to Lawyer B involves a transactional matter. The location of Lawyer B's conduct—handling a potentially conflicted representation from the law firm's office in State B—is but one consideration.

Under this non-litigation scenario, Lawyer B's client and the client on the opposite side of the transaction—Lawyer A's soon-to-be former client—will shoulder any harm associated with the imputed conflict. Considering the factors referenced above to assess where the "predominant effect" will be, if the affected parties to the transaction have their principal places of business or reside in State A, then the predominant effect of the imputed conflict will be in State A even though Lawyer B practices from an office in State B.[18] State B's screening rules would apply if both parties to the transaction are in State B.

When the parties to the potentially conflicted transaction are in different states, additional factors such as the location of the subject of the transaction (e.g., the location of real property, business operations, or services to be performed), the substantive law governing the transaction, and the location of deposited funds may point the predominant effect to one state over another. For instance, if Lawyer B's client resides in State B and is purchasing real estate located in State B (which means State B's law would govern the transaction), then the predominant effect of Lawyer B's conduct remains in State B even if the selling client (Lawyer A's soon-to-be former client) is in State A and the selling client will deposit the transaction's funds in a bank account in State A.

In non-litigated matters with significant contacts to more than one state, it may be unclear where the predominant effect of Lawyer's B representation will occur. For those situations, it would be prudent for Lawyer B to follow the more restrictive rule in State B (which is also the location of Lawyer B's conduct and Lawyer B's state of licensure) and obtain the informed consent of each affected client, confirmed in writing. Lawyer B, however, will not be subject to professional discipline for violations of Model Rules 1.9 and 1.10 so long as Lawyer B acts in accordance with the rules of the jurisdiction in

---

16. MODEL RULES OF PROF'L CONDUCT R. 8.5(b)(1).
17. *Id.*
18. MODEL RULES OF PROF'L CONDUCT R. 8.5(b)(2).

which Lawyer B reasonably believes the predominant effect of Lawyer B's representation will occur.[19]

Conclusion

Model Rule 8.5 provides guidance for determining which jurisdiction's rules of professional conduct apply to a lawyer's conduct. When a lawyer's conduct is in connection with a matter pending before a tribunal, the lawyer must comply with the ethics rules of the jurisdiction in which the tribunal sits, unless otherwise provided. For all other conduct, including conduct in anticipation of litigation not yet filed and conduct not involving litigation, a lawyer must comply with the ethics rules of the jurisdiction where the lawyer's conduct occurs or, if different, where the predominant effect of the lawyer's conduct occurs. Factors to assess where that "predominant effect" occurs may include the client's location, where a transaction occurs, which jurisdiction's substantive law applies to the transaction, the location of the lawyer's principal office, where the lawyer is admitted, the location of the opposing party, and the jurisdiction with the greatest interest in the lawyer's conduct. A lawyer will not be subject to discipline if the lawyer's conduct conforms to the rules of a jurisdiction in which the lawyer reasonably believes the predominant effect of the lawyer's conduct will occur.

---

19. MODEL RULES OF PROF'L CONDUCT R. 8.5(b)(2). Another alternative when the predominant effect is uncertain is for a lawyer and client to agree that the lawyer's representation will be governed by a particular state's conflicts of interest rules. MODEL RULES OF PROF'L CONDUCT R. 8.5 cmt. [5]. The specified state must have a reasonable relationship to the client representation.

AMERICAN BAR ASSOCIATION
STANDING COMMITTEE ON ETHICS AND PROFESSIONAL RESPONSIBILITY
321 N. Clark Street, Chicago, Illinois 60654-4714 Telephone (312) 988-5328
CHAIR: Lynda Shely, Scottsdale, AZ
■ Mark A. Armitage, Detroit, MI ■ Melinda Bentley, Jefferson City, MO ■ Matthew Corbin, Olathe, KS
■ Robinjit Kaur Eagleson, Lansing, MI ■ Doug Ende, Seattle, WA
■ Hon. Audrey Moorehead, Dallas, TX ■ Wendy Muchman, Chicago, IL
■ Keith Swisher, Scottsdale, AZ ■ Charles Vigil, Albuquerque, NM

CENTER FOR PROFESSIONAL RESPONSIBILITY
Mary McDermott, Lead Senior Counsel
©2023 by the American Bar Association. All rights reserved.

AMERICAN BAR ASSOCIATION
STANDING COMMITTEE ON ETHICS AND PROFESSIONAL RESPONSIBILITY

Formal Opinion 505   May 3, 2023
Fees Paid in Advance for Contemplated Services

Under the Model Rules of Professional Conduct, a fee paid to a lawyer in advance for services to be rendered in the future must be placed in a client trust account and may be withdrawn only as earned by the performance of the contemplated services. This protects client funds and promotes client access to legal services in the event the representation terminates before all contemplated services have been rendered. All fees must be reasonable, and unearned fees must be returned to the client. Therefore, it is not accurate to label a fee "nonrefundable" before it actually has been earned, and labels do not dictate whether a fee has been earned.

This opinion examines a lawyer's obligations under the ABA Model Rules of Professional Conduct with respect to fees paid in advance for legal work to be performed by the lawyer in the future.[1] In particular, this opinion seeks to clarify the proper handling and disposition of fees paid in advance for legal work to be performed in the future, including where the lawyer must deposit and maintain the funds and when the lawyer may treat them as earned. The opinion also explains when a lawyer must refund all or a portion of fees paid in advance and discusses whether such a payment may be, or can even be labeled, "nonrefundable." The answers are derived from the application of several Model Rules, including: 1.5(a), 1.5(b), 1.15(a), 1.15(c), 1.15(d), and 1.16(d).

Fees for services may be paid after completion of the services, of course. However, for certain matters, many lawyers request or require that funds in a certain amount be paid to the lawyer at the outset of the representation to secure payment for the lawyer's later work. Under the Model Rules such fees must be placed in a Rule 1.15-compliant trust account, to be disbursed to the

---

1. This opinion is based on the American Bar Association Model Rules of Professional Conduct as amended by the ABA House of Delegates through August 2022. The laws, court rules, regulations, rules of professional conduct, and opinions promulgated in individual jurisdictions are controlling. This is especially noteworthy for this opinion as jurisdictions have adopted substantially different rules relating to the management of client property including fees paid in advance for legal work to be performed in the future.

lawyer only after the fee has been earned. This is to protect the client from the risk that the lawyer may not be able to refund the prepaid fee in the event the representation terminates before the contemplated work is completed. The Model Rules protect the lawyer from the risk of nonpayment by allowing advance fees to be received and protect the client by requiring that the funds are kept safe and separate from the funds of the lawyer or firm.

I. Terminology

As a preliminary matter, it is useful to define terms commonly used to label certain client-lawyer fee arrangements: advances, retainers, flat or fixed fees, and "nonrefundable" or "earned-on-receipt" fees.

A. Advances v. Retainers

Fees paid by a client to a lawyer in advance for legal work to be performed by the lawyer in the future are sometimes referred to as an "advance fee," an "advanced fee," an "advance fee payment," an "advance fee deposit," a "fee advance," or simply an "advance." Advances are also sometimes called "special retainers," "security retainers," or simply "prepaid fees." To be consistent and clear, this opinion will use the term "advance" when discussing fees paid to the lawyer for legal work to be performed in the future.

When a client pays an advance to a lawyer, the lawyer takes possession—but not ownership—of the funds to secure payment for the services the lawyer will render to the client in the future.

This opinion will also refer to the term "retainer" fee. Neither the term "retainer" nor "retainer fee" is found in the Model Rules of Professional Conduct. Regrettably, many lawyers use the term loosely to mean any sum of money paid to the lawyer at or near the commencement of representation.[2] Whereas an advance is a deposit of money with the lawyer to pay for services to be rendered in the future, there is another type of payment that is not for services. Rather, "[t]he purpose of [a retainer] is to assure the client that the lawyer will be contractually on call to handle the client's legal matters."[3] This type of agreement and payment is variously referred to as a "general retainer," "classic retainer," "true retainer," "availability retainer," or an "engagement retainer."[4] Because all of these terms mean the same thing, this

---

2. There is widespread agreement that the word "retainer" has been used so inconsistently that is has practically lost all definable meaning. BLACK'S LAW DICTIONARY (11th ed. 2019) ("Over the years, lawyers have used the term 'retainer' in so many conflicting senses that it should be banished from the legal vocabulary.") (quoting Mortimer D. Schwartz & Richard C. Wydick, PROBLEMS IN LEGAL ETHICS 100, 101 (2d ed. 1988)).

3. CHARLES W. WOLFRAM, MODERN LEGAL ETHICS 506 (West 1986).

4. Some jurisdictions have commendably sought to define terms and draw distinctions in their court rules. *See* Ariz. Rules of Prof'l Conduct R. 1.5 cmt. [7] ("The 'true' or 'classic' retainer is a fee paid . . . merely to insure the lawyer's availability to represent the client and to preclude the lawyer from taking adverse representation. What is often called a retainer but is in fact merely an advance fee deposit involves a security deposit to insure the pay-

APPENDIX F: FORMAL ETHICS OPINIONS

opinion will use the term "general retainer" to refer to this arrangement.[5] A general retainer is paid—and deemed earned—upon the promise of availability to represent a client, whether or not services are actually needed or requested by the client.[6] Thus, a general retainer has been conceptualized as a form of an option contract.[7] In other words, hourly time is not billed against a general retainer and a general retainer is not a flat fee for a specific amount of the lawyer's time—it is solely to reserve the lawyer's availability. An important result of these related features is that the money paid by the client in connection with a general retainer should not be placed in a trust account since it is considered earned upon the commencement of the contract.[8]

---

ment of fees when they are subsequently earned, either on a flat fee or hourly fee basis. A flat fee is a fee of a set amount for performance of agreed work, which may or may not be paid in advance but is not deemed earned until the work is performed. . . ."). *See also* Fla. State Bar R. 4-1.5(e)(2) (defining "retainer," "flat fee," and "advance fee") and Iowa R. Civ. P. 45.8-10 (defining "general retainer," "special retainer, and "flat fee").

5. It is sometimes said that retainers come in two varieties: "general retainers" and "special retainers." A special retainer is simply an advance going by another, unfortunately misleading, name. *See* Lester Brickman & Lawrence A. Cunningham, *Nonrefundable Retainers Revisited*, 72 N.C. L. Rev. 1, 5-6 (1993) ("A special retainer is an agreement between lawyer and client in which the client agrees to pay the lawyer a specified fee in exchange for specified services to be rendered. The fee may be calculated on an hourly, percentage or other basis and may be payable either in advance or as billed.") (footnotes omitted). The Committee is of the opinion that a special retainer is the same thing as an "advance." To be consistent and clear, this opinion will use the term "advance" when referring to such arrangements, although some of the cited sources and authorities may use the term "special retainer."

6. "Because the general retainer is not a payment for the performance of services, but rather is compensation for the lawyer's promise of availability, the fee is earned by the lawyer at the time the retainer is paid and thus should not be deposited into a client trust account. The general retainer is not an advance deposit against future legal services, which instead would be separately calculated and charged should the lawyer actually be called upon by the client to perform the legal services in the future." Gregory C. Sisk, *Duties to Effectively Represent the Client*, § 4-4.4(b) (A Retainer for Lawyer Availability), *in* LEGAL ETHICS, PROFESSIONAL RESPONSIBILITY, AND THE LEGAL PROFESSION (West 2016).

7. Lester Brickman, *The Advance Payment Dilemma: Should Payments be Deposited to the Client Trust Account or to the General Office Account*, 10 CARDOZO L REV. 647, 649 n.13 (1989). *See also In re* O'Farrell, 942 N.E.2d 799, 803 (Ind. 2011).

8. This opinion does not attempt to exhaustively discuss general retainers. Though they can and do have legitimate uses, for years they have been criticized, disfavored, and narrowly construed based on contract law, public policy, and contemporary ethics principles. *See, e.g.*, Charles J. McClain, Jr., *The Strange Concept of the Legal Retaining Fee*, 8 J. LEGAL PROF. 123 (1983) (common law of retainers "rests on rather shaky conceptual foundations" full of "inconsistencies and contradictions" and "contributing yet another irritant to the already strained relations between the legal profession and the public at large"); Pamela S. Kunen, *No Leg to Stand on: The General Retainer Exception to the Ban on Nonrefundable Retainers Must Fall*, 17 CARDOZO L. REV. 719 (1996) (discussing "historical and descriptive misconceptions" and arguing that, in many instances, such retainers generate the fiduciary obligations attending other lawyer-client fee agreements); and Joseph M. Perillo, *The Law of Lawyers' Contracts Is Different*, 67 FORDHAM L. REV. 443, 449-453 (1998).

Some authorities treat the term "general retainer" or "true retainer," etc., as synonymous with "nonrefundable." This is not correct. A general retainer may, by custom, be considered earned when paid, but this does not mean that it is forever exempt from scrutiny under the Rules. It may be determined to be an unreasonable fee, or even unearned if the lawyer does not make himself or herself available. For example, if a company retains a lawyer to handle a hostile takeover bid should one arise and the lawyer does not, in fact, accept the engagement, then the fee, which may have been paid many months earlier and treated as the lawyer's own property, may be determined to be unreasonable and/or unearned and therefore the subject of an order requiring it to be returned, refunded, or repaid to the client. Other circumstances requiring refund might include the death, disability, suspension, or disbarment of the lawyer. Like all fees, a general retainer must be reasonable under the circumstances.[9]

General retainers "are quite rare,"[10] and have "largely disappeared from the modern practice of law."[11] However, attempts to cast what is actually an advance payment of fees for services to be performed later as a general retainer are very much present today. Given the rarity and unusual nature of a general retainer, and the fact that very few clients would actually need or benefit from one, the nature of the fee and lawyer's obligations and client's benefits under such an agreement must be explained clearly and in detail, including the fact that fees for legal services performed will be charged in addition to the general retainer,[12] and use of the term should be restricted to its traditional definition.

This opinion focuses on advance fees paid by individual clients, usually for a single legal matter (or related matters) that will not recur on a regular basis. Examples include a divorce, defense of criminal charges, and discharge from employment or other civil matters not handled on a contingent fee basis. However, some clients may need legal services of a certain type on a repeat basis and may contract for such services. For example, the client and lawyer may enter into a renewable one-year agreement providing for a monthly payment to handle any or all collections arising out of one or more of the client's businesses. Some lawyers and clients may use the term "retainer" or "general retainer" to refer to such an arrangement. Such arrangements may be perfectly appropriate although they may not meet the definition of a general retainer even if "availability" is said to be a part of the arrangement. Perhaps the arrangement may best be understood as a fixed fee

---

9. MODEL RULES OF PROF'L CONDUCT R. 1.5(a); RESTATEMENT (THIRD) OF THE LAW GOVERNING LAWYERS § 34 (2001) [hereinafter RESTATEMENT].

10. Douglas R. Richmond, *Understanding Retainers and Flat Fees*, 34 J. LEGAL PROF. 113, 116 (2009). *See also In re* O'Farrell, 942 N.E.2d at 804 n.5.

11. Provanzano v. Nat'l Auto Credit, Inc., 10 F. Supp. 2d 44, 51 (D. Mass. 1998).

12. MODEL RULES OF PROF'L CONDUCT R. 1.5(b); RESTATEMENT, *supra* note 9, § 38.

APPENDIX F: FORMAL ETHICS OPINIONS

agreement, except that instead of handling one matter for a set fee no matter what services end up being required, the lawyer is handling several matters (subject to whatever limitations the parties place on the number, type, geography, etc., of the matters).[13]

B. Flat or Fixed Fees

Some lawyers prefer to charge their clients a flat or fixed fee for discrete legal services they provide. Examples include closing the purchase of a single-family home, incorporating a small business, drafting a will, or providing a defined, limited-scope service, such as drafting a motion. A flat fee is one that "embraces all work to be done, whether it be relatively simple and of short duration, or complex and protracted."[14]

If a flat or fixed fee is paid by the client in advance of the lawyer performing the legal work, the fees are an advance. Use of the term "flat fee" or "fixed fee" does not transform the arrangement into a fee that is "earned when paid." "Flat" or "fixed" does not even mean that the fee must be paid at the commencement of the representation, although most lawyers who do not have an existing relationship with a client may want to ensure payment and may, therefore, ask for the fee to be paid in advance before committing to the representation. If they do, as will be emphasized below, then that fee must be placed in a Rule 1.15-compliant trust account, to be disbursed to the lawyer only after the fee has been earned.

Several courts and ethics opinions endorse the option of dividing the representation into segments such that certain portions of a flat fee advance are considered earned before completion of all the contemplated work.[15]

---

13. As we have noted, courts scrutinize purported general retainers to ensure that the lawyer is not attempting to circumvent the ethics rules requiring refund of unearned fees upon termination of the representation. The same is true with what are sometimes called "hybrid" fees or retainers. Such a fee is "a putative general retainer that is denominated as both for availability and for services," and it is likely to be considered by courts to be "fully refundable to the extent not earned by services rendered." Lester Brickman & Lawrence A. Cunningham, *Nonrefundable Retainers: A Response to Critics of the Absolute Ban*, 64 U. CIN. L. REV. 11, 22 (1995). *See also*

N.Y. City Bar Formal Op. 2015-2 (Nonrefundable Monthly Fee in a Retainer Agreement) (2015), *citing* Agusta & Ross v. Trancamp Contracting Corp., 193 Misc.2d 781, 785-86 (N.Y. Civ. Ct. 2002) for the proposition that "enforcement of a hybrid retainer 'should be subject to close scrutiny, governed by a rebuttable presumption that any moneys retained by counsel are for services, rather than availability.'"

14. ABA Comm. on Ethics and Professional Responsibility, Informal Op. 1389 (1977).

15. *See, e.g.*, New Hampshire Bar Assoc. Ethics Committee Practical Ethics Article, *Practical Suggestions for Flat Fees or Minimum Fees in Criminal Cases* (Jan. 17, 2008). *See also In re Mance*, 980 A.2d 1196, 1202, 1204-1205 (D.C. 2009), *citing* Alec Rothrock, *The Forgotten Flat Fee; Whose Money is it and Where Should it be Deposited?*, 1 FLA. COSTAL L.J. 293, 323 (1999) for the proposition that some opinions "allow the lawyer to withdraw fees according to milestones 'based upon passage of time, the completion of certain tasks, or any other basis mutually agreed upon between the lawyer and client.'"

Some jurisdictions have codified this approach in their rules.[16] Thus, if agreed to, the lawyer may remove such earned portions of a flat fee advance from trust prior to the completion of the full scope of the legal services to be performed as certain "milestones" or stages of the representation are reached or completed. This approach allows the lawyer to be paid in part before the end of the representation and provides some assistance in determining the refund amount in case of early termination. Of course, "extreme 'front-loading' of payment milestones in the context of the anticipated length and complexity of the representation" may not be reasonable.[17]

C. So Called "Nonrefundable" and "Earned Upon Receipt" Fees

Some lawyers use labels like "nonrefundable retainer," "nonrefundable fee," or "earned on receipt" in the body or title of a fee agreement. These are not actual types of fees. And use of these descriptors does not, in and of itself, make a fee arrangement a general retainer. In fact, these terms are most often used in an attempt to make an advance fee nonrefundable.

The Model Rules of Professional Conduct do not allow a lawyer to sidestep the ethical obligation to safeguard client funds with an act of legerdemain: characterizing an advance as "nonrefundable" and/or "earned upon receipt." This approach does not withstand even superficial scrutiny. A lawyer may not charge an unreasonable fee. See Model Rule 1.5(a) ("A lawyer shall not make an agreement for, charge, or collect an unreasonable fee or an unreasonable amount for expenses."). Comment [4] to Rule 1.5 provides this additional guidance: "A lawyer may require advance payment of a fee, but is obliged to return any unearned portion. See Rule 1.16(d)." See also, Model Rule 1.15(c) and others discussed in connection with Hypothetical 1 below. Therefore, under the Model Rules, an advance fee paid by a client to a lawyer for legal services to be provided in the future cannot be nonrefundable. Any unearned portion must be returned to the client. Labeling a fee paid in advance for work to be done in the future as "earned upon receipt" or "nonrefundable" does not make it so.[18]

---

16. *See, e.g.*, Colo. Rules of Prof'l Conduct R. 1.5(h) (defining a flat fee, explaining proper handling, setting forth required contents of the agreement, and appending an authorized form agreement).

17. *In re* Mance, *supra* note 15.

18. *See, e.g., In re* O'Farrell, 942 N.E.2d 799, 803 (Ind. 2011) ("Regardless of the term used to describe a client's initial payment, its type is determined by its purpose, i.e., what it is intended to purchase."); Mo. Sup. Ct. Advisory Comm. Formal Op. 128 (Amended 2018) (labels not conclusive); *In re* Wintroub, 277 Neb. 787, 801; 765 N.W.2d 482 (2009) (citing cases from several jurisdictions for the proposition that "a lawyer may not retain an unearned fee, even if the fee agreement clearly provides that the fee is nonrefundable"); Iowa Sup. Ct. Att'y Disciplinary Bd. v. Turner, 918 N.W.2d 130, 147 (Iowa 2018) (simply labeling payment of advance fees as "nonrefundable" does not relieve attorney from obligation to deposit them into trust accounts).

Hypothetical scenarios illustrating these concepts and applying the Model Rules are discussed in Section IV below.

II. Model Rule of Professional Conduct 1.15: The Anti-commingling Rule and the Need to Protect Client Funds, Including Advances

Rules of professional conduct exist for the protection of the public. That purpose is well served when the rules are designed and enforced to prevent concrete financial harm to clients. The anti-commingling principle, embodied in Rule 1.15, is a longstanding and effective component in the client protection arsenal. This is why, since their inception in 1908, the American Bar Association's model codes and rules of ethics have prohibited lawyers from commingling their property (including funds) with the property of clients and third parties.[19]

Under the general anti-commingling rule, Model Rule 1.15(a), client property, which includes unearned fees paid in advance, must be held in an account separate from the lawyer's own property.[20] In 2002, Model Rule 1.15 was amended to address specifically the issue of advance fees in a new paragraph (c): "A lawyer shall deposit into a client trust account legal fees and expenses that have been paid in advance, to be withdrawn by the lawyer only as fees are earned or expenses incurred." Therefore, advances must be placed into a lawyer's trust account until those fees are earned.

The Commission on Evaluation of the Rules of Professional Conduct ("Ethics 2000 Commission"), which recommended the addition of this paragraph, did so in response to reports "that the single largest class of claims made to client protection funds is for the taking of unearned fees."[21] Accord-

---

19. See ABA CANONS OF PROFESSIONAL ETHICS, Canon 11 (1908); ABA MODEL CODE OF PROF'L RESPONSIBILITY, DR 9-102 (1969); ABA MODEL RULES OF PROF'L CONDUCT R. 1.15 (1983, revised 2002). One treatise explains the nature and breadth of this key obligation:

One of the core fiduciary duties of a lawyer is to safeguard the property that the lawyer receives from the client or from other sources but that belongs to the client or third persons. Property received from a client may include funds to be applied to a transaction, a payment in satisfaction of a judgment or settlement, an advance deposit against lawyer's fees, valuable documents to be analyzed, or property of evidentiary value. Under Rule 1.15(a) of the Model Rules of Professional Conduct, "[a] lawyer shall hold property of clients or third persons that is in a lawyer's possession in connection with a representation separate from the lawyer's own property." The lawyer therefore must keep the property in a secure location and segregate those assets from the lawyer's own property. Gregory C. Sisk, Duties to Effectively Represent the Client, § 4-5.6 (The Duty to Safeguard Client Funds and Property), in Legal Ethics, Professional Responsibility, and the Legal Profession (West Academic Publishing, 2016).

20. *In re* Kendall, 804 N.E.2d 1152, 1161 (Ind. 2004). Also, Rule 1.15(a)'s predecessor was applied to advance fees. Iowa Sup. Ct. Bd. of Prof'l Ethics & Conduct v. Frerichs, 671 N.W.2d 470, 477 (Iowa 2003) (failure to place advance fee in a trust account violated DR 9-102(A)).

21. A LEGISLATIVE HISTORY: THE DEVELOPMENT OF THE ABA MODEL RULES OF PROFESSIONAL CONDUCT, 1982–2005 342 (ABA 2006).

ingly, paragraph (c) "provides needed practical guidance to lawyers on how to handle advance deposits of fees and expenses."[22] Stated simply, under the Model Rules advance fees must be placed in a Rule 1.15-compliant trust account, to be disbursed to the lawyer only after the fee has been earned.

Some jurisdictions have authorized lawyers to treat advances as the lawyer's property upon payment, so long as the client signs a fee agreement designating the sum as "nonrefundable" or "earned on receipt" or some other variation on this theme.[23] This approach departs from the safekeeping policy of the Model Rules described herein and creates unnecessary risks for the client.[24]

---

22. Id.

23. See, e.g., Or. Rules of Prof'l Conduct R. 1.5(c)(3). That jurisdiction's version of Rule 1.15(c) contains an exception to the anti-commingling rule for advance fees when "the fee is denominated as 'earned on receipt,' 'nonrefundable' or similar terms and complies with Rule 1.5(c)(3)." Or. Rules of Prof'l Conduct R. 1.15-1(c). A considerable minority of U.S. jurisdictions have authorized this variant approach to advances by rule, ethics opinion, or judicial decree. See, e.g., State Bar of Ariz. Op. 99-02 (1999) (non-refundable, earned-upon-receipt fee is ethical if reasonable under Rule 1.5 and client is fully informed about and expressly agrees to such a fee, preferably in writing; such a fee does not go into a lawyer's trust account); Fla. Rules of Prof'l Conduct R. 4-1.5(e)(2)(B) and Comment (nonrefundable flat fee is the property of the lawyer and should not be held in trust); Wash. State Rules of Prof'l Conduct R. 1.5(f)(2) (if agreed to in advance in a writing signed by the client, a flat fee is the lawyer's property on receipt and shall not be deposited into a trust account); and N.Y. St. Bar. Assn. Comm. Prof'l Ethics Op. 816 (2007) (reaffirming 1985 opinion concluding that "fees paid to a lawyer in advance of services rendered are not necessarily client funds and need not be deposited in client trust account"). Such jurisdictions typically provide, via rule or otherwise, that advance fees must be refunded if unreasonable or work remains to be done even if language to the contrary is used and the funds have been taken by the lawyer pursuant to a rule and/or agreement.

24. See In re Long, 368 Or. 452, 455–56, 474-75, 491 P.3d 783, 788–89, 798-99 (2021), cert. denied 142 S. Ct. 2685 (2022), in which the court candidly discussed the rule and its fallout:

Respondent's limited financial resources also led to his extensive use of fee agreements that allowed him to access advance fees before completing the promised services. . . . The [Oregon] Rules of Professional Conduct allow for alternative fee agreements, under which advance fees become the lawyer's property at the time the fees are received—that is, before the lawyer has performed the promised services. RPC 1.5(c)(3). In those instances, the advance fees are not placed in the lawyer's trust account and are sometimes referred to as "earned on receipt." Fees may be "earned on receipt" only pursuant to a written fee agreement disclosing that "the funds will not be deposited into the lawyer trust account" and that "the client may discharge the lawyer at any time and in that event may be entitled to a refund of all or part of the fee if the services for which the fee was paid are not completed." Id. [¶] According to respondent, because he frequently had pressing personal and business costs, he would not have been able to operate his legal practice if he could access a client's fees only after he completed the promised services. . . . [¶] Although respondent's handling of those advance fees did not itself violate a Rule of Professional Conduct, it nevertheless left respondent's clients vulnerable. "Earned on receipt" fee agreements shift the risk of loss to the client. If the client relationship ends before the law-

APPENDIX F: FORMAL ETHICS OPINIONS

III. Model Rule of Professional Conduct 1.16: Declining or Terminating Representation

Model Rule 1.16(d) requires that, upon termination of representation, a lawyer shall refund "any advance payment of fee or expense that has not been earned or incurred." This Rule, and Rule 1.15, work in tandem to achieve the regulatory objective of protection of the public from financial harm caused by inattentive or unscrupulous lawyers.[25]

Advances are unearned because they are payment today for work to be performed in the future. They were unearned upon receipt and remain unearned until the work is performed. The Model Rules mandate that advances belong to the client, must be preserved until they are actually earned, and must be refunded if the representation terminates before the fees are earned.

As a practical matter it may be somewhat more difficult to determine what has been earned and what is unearned when a representation ends before completion of the contemplated services when the client pays a flat or fixed fee instead of an hourly rate. However, courts routinely apportion the services completed and sum earned when a representation terminates before a lawyer has completed all of the contemplated work.[26]

---

yer has performed the services needed to keep the advance fees, then the lawyer is required to return the fees for the uncompleted work. If the lawyer has already spent the advance fees and has no other financial resources upon which to draw, then the lawyer may be unable to provide the client with the required refund. [¶] That is what happened to many of respondent's clients. . . . [¶] Respondent's misconduct caused extensive injuries, which were not merely financial. Many of respondent's clients had limited financial means and needed their advance fees returned before they could afford to hire new lawyers. When respondent failed to return those advance fees, some clients simply went without legal representation.

25. Nothing tarnishes the profession's reputation like a lawyer who takes an advance fee for legal services to be performed in the future, does not complete the work contemplated by the fee arrangement, and does not refund the money, perhaps because he or she cannot. Once the money has been spent by the lawyer, it may never be recovered by the client (or by the client protection fund which may have reimbursed the client). Even if a civil judgment or disciplinary order of restitution is entered it may do little good if the lawyer is impecunious, judgment-proof, or bankrupt. Discipline in that case may offer a measure of public protection through deterrence, but it does not recompense the client. That client's access to justice may also be impeded. The client may be unable to pay another advance fee and may, therefore, be unrepresented if legal aid or pro bono assistance is unavailable. Model Rules 1.15 and 1.16 exist to protect a client from these consequences.

26. *See, e.g., In re* O'Farrell, 942 N.E.2d 799, 808 (Ind. 2011) (quantum meruit available upon client termination of flat fee agreement). *Cf.* Plunkett & Cooney, PC v. Capitol Bancorp Ltd, 212 Mich. App. 325, 331; 536 N.W.2d 886 (1995) (discharged lawyer with fixed-fee agreement entitled to compensation for services rendered calculated by percentage of services required under contract, unless lawyer and client have agreed to other terms for valuing work completed).

IV. Hypothetical Scenarios Involving Client Payments at the Commencement of a Specific Representation.

Hypothetical 1 ("Nonrefundable Retainer")

A lawyer is consulted by a client seeking to terminate her marriage. The lawyer informs the client that the lawyer requires a $6,000 "retainer" to cover the filing of a divorce complaint, preparing a motion to enjoin the transfer of assets and a possible motion for a protective order, attending hearings relative to those motions, and any negotiations or related work until the lawyer expends 20 hours. The client was also informed that additional "retainers" may be required to complete the matter, and that the retainers will be credited toward payment for the lawyer's services at the reasonable rate of $300 per hour. The lawyer's fee agreement states, in pertinent part:

> Client agrees to pay Lawyer a nonrefundable retainer fee of $6,000. Client understands that no portion of this fee shall be refunded or returned to Client for any reason.

> Client further agrees that should Lawyer expend more than 20 hours on Client's matter, Client shall pay additional retainers as requested by Lawyer which shall be applied to Lawyer's billing for this matter at a rate of $300 per hour and to any costs or expenses incurred in the representation.

Three weeks after signing the agreement and paying the $6,000, Client notified Lawyer that she wanted to reconcile with her husband and asked for an itemization of Lawyer's time and expenses and a refund of any unearned fees. Lawyer had filed the complaint, but it had not been served. Lawyer had also prepared but had not filed a motion to enjoin the transfer of certain assets. Lawyer had spent 5.5 hours on the file and $150 to file the complaint, but responded to the Client that no refund was due because the $6,000 was a nonrefundable fee.

Question: Does Lawyer owe Client a refund for any of the $6,000 paid to Lawyer and are any rule violations established by this scenario?

Answer: Yes, Lawyer owes Client a refund. First, the $6,000 paid by Client to the Lawyer are fees paid in advance not a general retainer. Under this agreement, Lawyer is rendering legal services at the rate of $300 per hour. This is true from the outset as is established by simply reading the portion of the agreement quoted above and performing some simple math. The $6,000 entitles Client to 20 hours of Lawyer's work on the matter.

APPENDIX F: FORMAL ETHICS OPINIONS

Second, lawyer was required to have placed the $6,000 of advanced fees into the Lawyer's client trust account. Model Rule 1.15(c) provides that: "A lawyer shall deposit into a client trust account legal fees and expenses that have been paid in advance, to be withdrawn by Lawyer only as fees are earned or expenses incurred." The so-called nonrefundable fee here is an advance payment of fees that may only be withdrawn from the client trust account as earned by Lawyer. The facts of this hypothetical are silent as to whether Lawyer placed the $6,000 in the trust, operating, or personal account and as to whether it was spent in whole or in part. Lawyers may be disciplined for treating advance fees as their own property before the fees are earned, i.e., before the contemplated legal services are rendered.[27] Commingling and perhaps misappropriation may have occurred here if Lawyer deposited the $6,000 into an account other than a client trust account and spent it.

In this scenario, assuming that the legal work performed was appropriate and useful, Lawyer has earned $1,650.00 in legal fees. Lawyer also spent $150 for the expense of filing the complaint. Failure to return the balance of $4,200 is a violation of Model Rule 1.16(d) (upon termination of representation, a lawyer shall refund any advance payment of fee or expense that has not been earned or incurred). Comment [4] to Rule 1.16(d) explains the fundamental legal principle underlying this requirement: "A client has a right to discharge a lawyer at any time, with or without cause, subject to liability for payment for the lawyer's services." Lawyer's failure to provide an accounting for the fees paid in advance also constitutes a violation of Rule 1.15(d).

Model Rule 1.5(a) provides: "A lawyer shall not make an agreement for, charge, or collect an unreasonable fee or an unreasonable amount for expenses." Comment [4] to Rule 1.5 states: "A lawyer may require advance payment of a fee, but is obliged to return any unearned portion. See Rule 1.16(d)." Thus, keeping the balance ($4,200) violates Rule 1.5(a) on these facts. Because Rule 1.5 precludes a lawyer from agreeing to an unreasonable fee, it is also violated by the Lawyer's inclusion of the following provision in the fee agreement: "Client agrees to pay Lawyer a nonrefundable fee of $6,000. Client understands that no portion of this fee shall be refunded or returned to Client for any reason."[28]

---

27. "A lawyer misappropriates client funds in violation of DR 1–102(A)(3), (4), (5), and (6)DR 1–102(A)(3), (4), (5), and (6) when special retainers and flat fees paid in advance are treated as money belonging to the lawyer and not maintained in a trust account until the fee has been earned." Iowa Sup. Ct. Bd. of Pro. Ethics & Conduct v. Frerichs, 671 N.W.2d 470, 475 (Iowa 2003). *See also In re* Fazande, 290 So. 3d 178, 185 (La. 2020) (lawyer violated Rule 1.15(c) by failing to deposit into his client trust account advance fees and costs).

28. *In re* Kendall, 804 N.E.2d 1152, 1160 (Ind. 2004) ("We hold that the assertion in a lawyer fee agreement that such advance payment is nonrefundable violates the requirement of Prof. Cond. R. 1.5(a) that a lawyer's fee 'shall be reasonable.'"). *See also* N.Y. City Bar Ass'n Formal Opinion 1991-3 (in light of reasonableness requirement, duty to refund un-

Finally, because a lawyer may, in fact, be required to refund an advance payment of fees in various situations, characterizing such an advance as "nonrefundable" may also amount to a violation of Rule 1.4 (communication) and Rule 8.4(c) (misrepresentation) as the mischaracterization of the funds may have a chilling effect on a client seeking a refund of unearned fees upon termination of the representation.[29]

Lawyer and the fee agreement use the words "retainer" and "fee" interchangeably. In this hypothetical it appears that the word "retainer" is used incorrectly to refer to the advance payment of legal fees at the initiation of a matter, or, really, at any time during the representation as is suggested by the agreement's provision that additional "retainers" may be required.

Hypothetical 2 (Purported General Retainer)

The facts are the same as in Hypothetical 1, except that the lawyer's standard fee agreement states, in pertinent part:

> Client agrees to pay Lawyer a non-refundable engagement fee of $6,000 which shall be deemed earned upon receipt by Lawyer. This engagement fee is for the purpose of retaining Lawyer and assuring the availability of Lawyer in this matter. Client understands that no portion of the engagement fee shall be refunded or returned to Client for any reason.
>
> Client further agrees that should Lawyer expend more than 20 hours, Client shall pay upon request an additional retainer in an amount determined by Lawyer which shall be applied to Lawyer's billing for this matter at a rate of $300 per hour and to any costs or expenses incurred in the representation.
>
> Again, the facts are the same: Lawyer spent 5.5 hours and a filing fee for the complaint, and Client reconciles and seeks a refund. Lawyer declines to refund any portion of the fee, claiming it is nonrefundable.

---

earned fees, and client's "essentially absolute" right to discharge counsel, "a lawyer may not properly denominate or characterize a fee as 'nonrefundable' or otherwise use words that could reasonably be expected to convey to the client the understanding that a fee paid before the services are performed will not be subject to refund or adjustment under any possible circumstance").

29. *See, e.g., In re* Sather, 3 P.3d 403, 415 (Colo. 2000) (knowing use of misleading language, i.e., describing flat advance fee as "nonrefundable," violated Colo. RPC 8.4(c)) and Ala. State Bar Op. RO-93-21 (1993) ("Any indication by the lawyer that the fee is non-refundable is inaccurate and inherently misleading and would violate Rule 1.4(b) Communication; Rule 1.5(b) Fees; and Rule 8.4(c) Misrepresentation."). *See also* Mo. Sup. Ct. Advisory Comm. Formal Op. 128 (Amended 2018) (in various situations "the description of the fee as 'nonrefundable' is misleading").

APPENDIX F: FORMAL ETHICS OPINIONS

Question: Does Lawyer owe Client a refund for any of the $6,000 paid to Lawyer and are any rule violations established by this scenario?

Answer: Yes. The answer and analysis for Hypothetical 1 apply here as well. The only difference ("retainer" and "engagement fee" language) makes no difference at all. The fee arrangement still has the same basic structure and, for the reasons discussed above, the $6,000 is clearly an advance payment for the future performance of legal services, not an actual "retainer" because the lawyer contemplates billing time against the advance.[30] Accordingly, the $6,000 must be held in trust until earned and any unearned portion properly refunded to the client.

Under the Model Rules, there are no magic words that a lawyer can use to change what is actually an advance payment for fees into a general retainer: "an attorney cannot treat a fee as 'earned' simply by labeling the fee 'earned on receipt' or referring to the fee as an 'engagement retainer.'"[31] Notwithstanding the use of the terms "engagement fee," "retainer," and "availability," the fee in Hypothetical 2 is still not a general retainer fee and is, therefore, not deemed earned on receipt. The purpose of the fee dictates its character and treatment irrespective of labels or terminology used.

Courts examine the transaction and agreement very carefully to ensure that the purported general retainer is not an attempt to charge and retain unearned advance fees.[32] Accordingly, a lawyer claiming to have a general retainer must be prepared to demonstrate a valuable benefit to the client and/ or an actual detriment to the lawyer.[33] It is easy to recite that the lawyer is prioritizing the client's work, turning away other work, keeping up on the relevant law, etc. However, it must be shown that such things were not only

---

30. *Cf. In re* Lais, No. 91-O-08572, 1998 WL 391171, at *14-15 (Cal. Bar Ct. July 10, 1998) (characterization as "'fixed, non-refundable retaining fee' paid 'for the purpose of assuring the availability of [respondent] in this matter'" was "not determinative" and the fee was not a "true" (general) retainer, but actually payment for the first 10 hours of lawyer's services).

31. *In re* Sather, 3 P.3d 403, 412 (Colo. 2000). *See also* note 18, *supra*.

32. Richmond, *supra* note 10, at 116: "As a practical matter, general retainers are rare. . . . The types of representations that justify or require general retainers are also scarce. Courts hearing fee related controversies are therefore properly skeptical of general retainer claims." *See also* RESTATEMENT, *supra* note 9, § 34 ("Engagement-retainer fees agreed to by clients not so experienced should be more closely scrutinized to ensure that they are no greater than is reasonable and that the engagement-retainer fee is not being used to evade the rules requiring a lawyer to return unearned fees.")

33. Att'y Grievance Comm'n of Maryland v. Stinson, 428 Md. 147, 183-185, 50 A.3d 1222, 1244-1245 (2012) (purported engagement fee for "willingness and availability" to represent client not a true general retainer where no benefit to client or detriment to lawyer established and lawyer "produced no useable work").

actually done, but that they were necessary for the representation and not part of the lawyer's basic responsibilities.[34]

Hypothetical 3 (Flat Fee)

A client seeks to hire a lawyer for representation in a criminal matter. The fee agreement provides: "Client shall pay Lawyer the sum of $15,000 for representation in the matter of State v Client, and that no part of the flat fee shall be refunded for any reason. Client understands that the flat fee is the agreed upon amount due Lawyer regardless of the time expended on the matter or how it is resolved." Client signed the agreement and paid the full $15,000. Lawyer deposited the $15,000 into his firm's operating account. Lawyer reviewed the police report, left a message for the prosecutor and law enforcement officer, appeared on behalf of the defendant at the arraignment, and filed an appearance with the court. A few weeks after the arraignment, Client discharged Lawyer and requested an accounting and partial refund. Lawyer refused, stating that the flat fee was earned when it was paid.

As we noted above, flat fees paid in advance of performing the work are subject to Rule 1.15(c) and the other rules set forth in the analyses in Hypotheticals 1 and 2. In other words, the foregoing rules regarding safekeeping, refundability, and reasonableness apply.

Flat fees are not general retainers and must not be treated as such. That the price set for the representation is not based on hours worked but is instead based on the completion of certain described services does not mean that the fee must be considered earned on receipt or nonrefundable when there is work yet to be done. Of course, if the flat fee is paid *after* the work is completed, the funds are earned and are not deposited into the trust account.

V. Conclusion

The Model Rules protect a client's right to terminate the fiduciary relationship with a lawyer and have the money to which the client is entitled available to obtain successor counsel if desired. Rule 1.15 requires that fees paid in advance must be held in a trust account until the services for which the fees will be paid are actually rendered, thereby allocating various risks to lawyer and client. The lawyer does not have to bear the risk of nonpayment after the work is completed; Rule 1.15 provides a process for withdrawal of earned fees and even for disputes, should they arise. And the client does not have to bear the risk that the funds will be spent, attached by the lawyer's

---

34. *See Stinson*, 50 A.3d at 1243 (benefits offered to the client in exchange for the nonrefundable fee were "nothing more than the ethical obligation imposed on all lawyers when they agree to provide legal services to a client. . . . A lawyer who agrees to perform legal services also necessarily agrees to be available to perform those services."), *citing* Lester Brickman & Lawrence A. Cunningham, *Nonrefundable Retainers Revisited*, 72 N.C. L. Rev. 1, 24 (1993), and Iowa Sup. Ct. Bd. of Pro. Ethics & Conduct v. Frerichs, 671 N.W.2d 470, 477 (Iowa 2003).

APPENDIX F: FORMAL ETHICS OPINIONS

creditors, or otherwise dissipated before the legal work is performed due to a lawyer's unwillingness or inability to do so.

Other ethics opinions and resources discuss good billing practices and fee agreement drafting tips. However, we offer the following suggestions in relation to the matters addressed in this opinion. Use plain language. Thus, instead of "retainer" say "advance" and explain that it is a "deposit for fees."[35] Explain that the sum deposited will be applied to the balance owed for work on the matter, and how and when this will happen. For example, the fee agreement could provide that on a monthly basis the client will be invoiced for the time expended by the lawyer and state when the sum reflected in the invoice will be withdrawn from the trust account. When the arrangement is for hourly billing, explain that if the deposit exceeds the final billing any balance will be remitted to the client. If the advance fee is fixed and the representation may continue for some time or involve several stages, consider dividing the representation into reasonable segments and providing for withdrawal of a reasonable portion of the deposited fee as the representation progresses and the fee becomes partially earned.[36] Finally, it may be wise to recognize the reality that many relationships do not last and include a provision explaining what will happen if the representation is terminated before the matter is completed.[37]

---

35. GEOFFREY C. HAZARD, JR., PETER R. JARVIS, TRISHA THOMPSON & W. WILLIAM HODES, THE LAW OF LAWYERING §9.07 (4th ed. 2022-2 Supp. 2014). Of course, the applicable Rules of Professional Conduct must be consulted, and it may be prudent or required to use certain terms. However, accurately translating legal terms of art is not only helpful to the client but also assists with interpretation and enforcement. So, if the term "advance" or "special retainer" is used in the applicable rules, the lawyer will want to use it in the fee agreement. However, consider also adding an explanation that it is functionally a deposit to cover fees for work in the future.

36. *See supra* notes 15 & 16.

37. Again, see Colo. R. Prof'l Conduct R. 1.5(h) and accompanying flat fee form providing helpful language for dividing a representation into increments and explaining a method of calculating the fees the lawyer has earned should the representation terminate prior to completion of the tasks or events specified in the agreement.

AMERICAN BAR ASSOCIATION
STANDING COMMITTEE ON ETHICS AND PROFESSIONAL RESPONSIBILITY
321 N. Clark Street, Chicago, Illinois 60654-4714 Telephone (312) 988-5328
CHAIR: Lynda Shely, Scottsdale, AZ
■ Mark A. Armitage, Detroit, MI ■ Melinda Bentley, Jefferson City, MO ■ Matthew Corbin, Olathe, KS
■ Robinjit Kaur Eagleson, Lansing, MI ■ Doug Ende, Seattle, WA
■ Hon. Audrey Moorehead, Dallas, TX ■ Wendy Muchman, Chicago, IL
■ Keith Swisher, Scottsdale, AZ ■ Charles Vigil, Albuquerque, NM

CENTER FOR PROFESSIONAL RESPONSIBILITY
Mary McDermott, Lead Senior Counsel
©2023 by the American Bar Association. All rights reserved.

AMERICAN BAR ASSOCIATION
STANDING COMMITTEE ON ETHICS AND PROFESSIONAL RESPONSIBILITY

Formal Opinion 506 June 7, 2023
Responsibilities Regarding Nonlawyer Assistants

A lawyer may train and supervise a nonlawyer to assist with prospective client intake tasks including obtaining initial information about the matter, performing an initial conflict check, determining whether the assistance sought is in an area of law germane to the lawyer's practice, assisting with answering general questions about the fee agreement or process of representation, and obtaining the prospective client's signature on the fee agreement provided that the prospective client always is offered an opportunity to communicate with the lawyer including to discuss the fee agreement and scope of representation. Because Model Rule 5.5 prohibits lawyers from assisting in the unauthorized practice of law, whether a nonlawyer may answer a prospective client's specific question depends on the question presented. If the prospective client asks about what legal services the client should obtain from the lawyer, wants to negotiate the fees or expenses, or asks for interpretation of the engagement agreement, the lawyer is required to respond to ensure that the non-lawyer does not engage in the unauthorized practice of law and that accurate information is provided to the prospective client so that the prospective client can make an informed decision about whether to enter into the representation.[1]

I. Introduction

Nonlawyers[2] provide tremendous client and lawyer support for law firms. This Formal Opinion addresses a lawyer's ethical obligations when

---

1. This opinion is based on the ABA Model Rules of Professional Conduct as amended by the ABA House of Delegates through February 2023. The laws, court rules and opinions, regulations, and rules of professional conduct, promulgated in individual jurisdictions are controlling.

2. The term "nonlawyer" is used in this Opinion, consistent with the term as used in Rule 5.3, to include all law firm employees, agents, contractors, and vendors who are not licensed lawyers (or otherwise authorized to practice law) but work under the supervision of a licensed lawyer including, for instance, paralegals, legal assistants, case managers, firm administrators, intake staff, and clerks. This term does *not* refer to professionals who are licensed by a jurisdiction to provide legal services in that jurisdiction, such as Arizona Legal Paraprofessionals, Utah Regulatory Sandbox participants, Minnesota Legal Paraprofessional Pilot Project, New York Court Navigators, or Washington Limited License Legal Technicians.

the lawyer delegates to a nonlawyer specific prospective client-intake tasks. Lawyers may train and supervise nonlawyers to assist with initial client intake tasks if the lawyers have met their obligations for management and supervision of the nonlawyers pursuant to ABA Model Rule of Professional Conduct 5.3 and prospective clients are given the opportunity to consult with the lawyers to discuss the matter.[3]

II. Analysis

A. Rule 5.3 Responsibilities Regarding Nonlawyer Assistants ABA Model Rule of Professional Conduct 5.3 addresses a lawyer's responsibilities regarding nonlawyer assistants.[4] Rule 5.3(a) provides that lawyers who are partners or managers in a firm must ensure that the firm has policies that assure a nonlawyer's conduct is "compatible" with the professional obligations of the lawyer. Paragraph (b) of the Rule requires that lawyers who directly supervise nonlawyer assistants must "make reasonable efforts to ensure that the person's conduct is compatible with the professional obligations of the lawyer." Comment [2] notes, "A lawyer must give such assistants appropriate instruction and supervision concerning the ethical aspects of their employment...."[5]

A lawyer's delegation of prospective client intake tasks to a nonlawyer or the lawyer's use of technology to assist with the initial intake of clients provides significant benefits and increased efficiency to lawyers. For example, nonprofit legal services organizations frequently train, supervise, and rely on nonlawyers to perform initial screening of prospective clients to determine whether there are conflicts of interest and whether the prospective clients are requesting services that fall within the organization's practice areas. Similarly, for-profit law firms have offered limited scope online legal services that provide website intake questions, a menu of available limited scope legal document completion services (such as simple powers of attorney, LLC formation, property deed transfers, and name changes), a conflict checking algorithm, and then "click-to-accept-terms" engagement agreements.[6] Delegating initial client intake to nonlawyers also is common in mass

---

3. Because this Committee does not opine on substantive legal questions, this Formal Opinion assumes that the assistance provided by the nonlawyer does not violate applicable unauthorized practice of law regulations or statutes. Different jurisdictions may have different views on what constitutes the practice of law.

4. MODEL RULES OF PROF'L CONDUCT R. 5.3, cmt. [2] "Lawyers generally employ assistants in their practice, including secretaries, investigators, law student interns, and paraprofessionals. Such assistants, whether employees or independent contractors, act for the lawyer in rendition of the lawyer's professional services."

5. For an extensive analysis of Rule 5.3, see ABA Comm. on Ethics & Prof'l Responsibility, Formal Op. 467 (2014).

6. *See* ABA Comm. on Ethics & Prof'l Responsibility, Formal Op. 10-457 & MODEL RULES OF PROF'L CONDUCT R. 1.18, cmt. [2] for guidance regarding lawyer websites and when an individual becomes a prospective client.

tort and class action practices. There, trained intake personnel may check for conflicts of interest, collect basic information from prospective plaintiffs or class members for lawyers to ascertain their eligibility to make a claim, and explain how fees and costs are charged in such cases. If the prospective client meets the eligibility criteria and specifics set forth by the lawyers, then the intake personnel send the prospective clients the standard fee agreement for consideration.

While the benefits of using nonlawyer assistants are many, without proper policies, training, and supervision in place, this delegation could lead to ethical violations and unfortunate consequences for clients and lawyers.[7] The practice must be "carefully and astutely managed."[8]

B. Establishing the Client-Lawyer Relationship

When a prospective client contacts a lawyer for help in solving a legal matter, the lawyer and the prospective client discuss the scope of representation including the client's objectives for the representation and the actions the lawyer will take to achieve the client's goal.[9] Rule 1.5(b) requires a lawyer to communicate to the client the "scope of the representation and the basis or rate of the fee and expenses for which the client will be responsible ... preferably in writing, before or within a reasonable time after commencing the representation, except when the lawyer will charge a regularly represented client on the same basis or rate."[10] Essentially, the client must know what the client bargained for.[11]

Rule 1.4(b) mandates that a lawyer communicate with clients and provide the clients, to the extent reasonably necessary, with explanations that allow the clients to make informed decisions regarding their representation. Some of the communication duties set forth in Rules 1.5(b) and 1.4(b) also apply in the context of explaining fee agreements to prospective clients. We note that Rule 1.4(b) does not expressly apply to prospective clients. Indeed, some of Rule 1.4(a)'s requirements—such as providing updates, consulting about means being employed to address objectives, and responding

---

7. See *In re* Phillips, 226 Ariz. 112, 244 P.3d 549 (2010) (setting forth guidelines for use of nonlawyers in intake process, including applicability of Rule 5.3 and prohibiting nonlawyers from having clients sign engagement agreements without attorney involvement); *In re* Pinkins, 213 B.R. 818 (Bankr. E.D. Mich. 1997) (relying, in part, on State Bar of Mich. Informal Op. RI-128 (1992), superseded by RI-349).
8. State Bar of Mich. Informal Op. RI-349 (2010).
9. MODEL RULES OF PROF'L CONDUCT R. 1.2(a).
10. Though the Model Rule states this obligation in the passive context, jurisdictions have interpreted the obligation to communicate this information to be a lawyer's obligation. *See, e.g., In re* Freeman, 835 N.E.2d 494, 498 (Ind. 2005). That interpretation logically flows from the conclusion that the Model Rules govern the conduct of lawyers.
11. GEOFFREY C. HAZARD, W. WILLIAM HODES & PETER R. JARVIS, THE LAW OF LAWYERING § 9.02, 9-8 (4th ed. 2002); MODEL RULES OF PROF'L CONDUCT R. 1.5(b) ("requires" discussion of fees).

promptly to requests for information regarding a representation—would not make sense in that context. But it would seem imprudent to wait until after engagement for a lawyer to "explain a matter to the extent reasonably necessary to permit the client to make informed decisions regarding the representation" as required by Rule 1.4(b). ABA Formal Opinion 02-425 (2002) applied Rule 1.4(b) to lawyers who "ask prospective clients to execute retainer agreements that include provisions mandating the use of arbitration to resolve fee disputes and malpractice claims." This interpretation has been extended to explaining "certain implications of the joint representation" by at least one ethics committee.[12] Therefore, we apply Rule 1.4(b) to lawyers when they communicate with both current and prospective clients.

A lawyer may develop policies, train, and supervise a nonlawyer so that the lawyer may delegate to the nonlawyer client intake tasks assuming those tasks do not constitute the practice of law in the applicable jurisdiction. For example, a lawyer may delegate to the nonlawyer obtaining initial information about the matter,[13] performing an initial conflict check,[14] determining whether the assistance sought is in an area of law germane to the lawyer's practice,[15] answering general questions about the fee agreement or process of representation, and even obtaining the prospective client's signature on the fee agreement as long as the prospective client is offered an opportunity to communicate with the lawyer to discuss the matter.

While many client-intake tasks lawyers perform may be delegable with proper policies in place, training, and supervision, lawyers who delegate do not relinquish their responsibilities under the Model Rules. Once the attorney-client relationship is formed, lawyers still have the responsibility to reasonably consult with the client regarding the client's objectives and how to achieve them.[16] Lawyers also have the responsibility to "promptly comply with reasonable requests for information" and consult with clients who have engaged them regarding limits on the lawyers' conduct given applica-

---

12. N.Y.C. Bar Ass'n Comm. on Prof'l Ethics, Formal Op. 2017-7 (2017).

13. Nonlawyers can be trained to obtain the names of all relevant parties, the date(s) of the incident(s) involved, and the nature of the legal matter.

14. Nonlawyers can be trained to run conflict checks with the firm's systems and to filter for not just parties, but witnesses, opposing counsel, vendors, and other individuals who may create a potential conflict of interest for the firm. However, when a relevant or closely related name comes up in the conflict checking process, the lawyer must be the one to review the similarities and make the final determination of whether or not a conflict exists and whether any such conflict or not it is a waivable conflict.

15. Where the lawyer's services would involve a single transaction, such as helping companies register their corporation filing documents with the state, with the appropriate training, a nonlawyer would likely be able to explain the type of services provided for a set fee. Allowing a nonlawyer to answer general questions related to the lawyer's services in such a situation would not require them to provide independent legal advice. However, the nonlawyer must be trained to recognize when the client's questions venture from discussing general services.

16. MODEL RULES OF PROF'L CONDUCT R. 1.2(a) & 1.4(a)(2).

ble laws and ethical duties.[17] And, Rules 1.2, 1.4, and 1.5(b) require a lawyer to communicate with clients about fees, the scope of representation, and any limitations thereon.

Whether a nonlawyer may answer a prospective client's *specific question* depends on the question presented and what would be considered to be the practice of law in the jurisdiction. That is important because Model Rule 5.5(a) prohibits lawyers from assisting others in practicing law in a jurisdiction in violation of the regulation of the legal profession in that jurisdiction. As Comment [2] notes, the definition of the practice of law is established by law and varies from one jurisdiction to another. Lawyers should understand how it is defined in their jurisdiction and take care that the supervised nonlawyers understand that definition and how it limits what nonlawyers may do. For example, whether a nonlawyer may answer a question relating to fee or cost calculation or how payments can be made may depend on whether the question requires the application of law to the facts of the case, as opposed to a question that merely asks about a firm procedural matter. When the question presented would require the application of law to facts, a nonlawyer also may convey a client question to the lawyer, have the lawyer determine the answer to the question, and then relay the lawyer's answer to the client, again, depending on the complexity of the question posed. The lawyer will be responsible for determining if the inquiry is best answered by the lawyer communicating directly with the client, so the lawyer can gather more information to make an informed recommendation.

Nonlawyers may provide general information about how the firm charges legal fees, such as explaining that fees are charged hourly, or on a contingency basis, or the matter is billed at a fixed rate. Or, if the question merely relates to how payments can be processed or other administrative matters, then the nonlawyer may provide information to answer the inquiry. However, if the prospective client asks about what legal services the client should obtain from the lawyer to address the client's objectives, wants to negotiate the fees or expenses, or asks for an interpretation of the rights and responsibilities set forth in the engagement agreement, Model Rules 1.4(b), 1.5, and 5.5[18] require the lawyer to respond. Ultimately, the scope of what the nonlawyers may do in this context will depend on whether the services in question constitute the practice of law in the jurisdiction where they are being provided.[19] Because Model Rule 5.5(a) precludes lawyers from assisting others in engaging in the unauthorized practice of law, and Model Rule

---

17. Model Rules of Prof'l Conduct R. 1.2 & 1.4(a)(4), (a)(5).

18. Once the prospective client becomes a client, then Rules 1.2 and 1.4(a) would also be implicated.

19. Indeed, the question of which jurisdiction's definition of the practice of law should be applied may be subject to a legal analysis. *See* ABA Comm. on Ethics & Prof'l Responsibility, Formal Op. 504 (2023).

5.3(b) requires lawyers to reasonably ensure the supervised nonlawyers conduct themselves compatibly with the lawyer's professional obligations, the lawyers are responsible for making sure this line is not crossed.

As noted above, delegation of prospective client intake must be carefully and astutely managed. What appears to be a simple question about how long the lawyer will spend on the matter, may actually be a question about the representation itself and cannot be accurately answered without the lawyer's personal knowledge and expertise.[20] Therefore, a lawyer must provide nonlawyers who are performing client-intake tasks with policies, training, and supervision regarding which questions the nonlawyer may answer, how to respond to those questions, and which questions should be presented to the lawyer.

Conclusion

Nonlawyers provide significant client and lawyer support for law firms. A lawyer may train and supervise a nonlawyer to assist during prospective client intake screening by obtaining initial information about the matter, performing an initial conflict check, determining whether the assistance sought is in an area of law germane to the lawyer's practice, assisting with answering general questions about the fee agreement or process of representation, and even by obtaining the prospective client's signature on the fee agreement provided that these tasks do not constitute the practice of law in the applicable jurisdiction and that the prospective client always is offered an opportunity to discuss the fee agreement and scope of representation with the lawyer.

---

20. THE LAW OF LAWYERING, *supra* note 11, at §9.04; *see also* ABA MODEL GUIDELINES FOR UTILIZATION OF PARALEGAL SERVICES, Guideline 3(b), at 9, *available at* https://www.americanbar.org/content/dam/aba/administrative/paralegals/aba-model-guidelines-for-utilization-of-paralegal-services-2021-web.pdf ("Many state guidelines prohibit paralegals from "setting fees" or "accepting cases. . . . NALA Ethics Canon 3 states that a paralegal must not establish attorney-client relationships or set fees.").

AMERICAN BAR ASSOCIATION
STANDING COMMITTEE ON ETHICS AND PROFESSIONAL RESPONSIBILITY
321 N. Clark Street, Chicago, Illinois 60654-4714 Telephone (312) 988-5328
CHAIR: Lynda Shely, Scottsdale, AZ
■ Mark A. Armitage, Detroit, MI ■ Melinda Bentley, Jefferson City, MO ■ Matthew Corbin, Olathe, KS ■ Robinjit Kaur Eagleson, Lansing, MI ■ Doug Ende, Seattle, WA ■ Hon. Audrey Moorehead, Dallas, TX ■ Wendy Muchman, Chicago, IL ■ Keith Swisher, Scottsdale, AZ ■ Charles Vigil, Albuquerque, NM

CENTER FOR PROFESSIONAL RESPONSIBILITY
Mary McDermott, Lead Senior Counsel
©2023 by the American Bar Association. All rights reserved.

ABA MODEL RULES

AMERICAN BAR ASSOCIATION
STANDING COMMITTEE ON ETHICS AND PROFESSIONAL RESPONSIBILITY

Formal Opinion 507 July 12, 2023
Office Sharing Arrangements with Other Lawyers

It is generally permissible for lawyers to participate in office sharing arrangements with other lawyers under the ABA Model Rules of Professional Conduct. At the same time, office sharing lawyers should appreciate that such arrangements will require them to take appropriate measures to comply with their ethical duties concerning the confidentiality of information, conflicts of interest, supervision of non-lawyers, and communications about their services. The nature and extent of any additional safeguards will necessarily depend on the circumstances of each arrangement.

I. Introduction[1]

Office sharing among lawyers comes in many forms—lawyers with separate law practices sharing office space, support staff, and equipment; law firms renting unused office space to unaffiliated lawyers; or even lawyers sharing an office suite, receptionist, and conference room as part of a virtual law practice or on a temporary basis. Lawyers participating in these arrangements must take appropriate steps to secure client information and clearly communicate the nature of the relationship to the public and their clients.[2] In addition, there are potential conflicts of interest issues that office sharing lawyers must appreciate, including imputed conflicts for lawyers "associated in a firm," representing clients with adverse interests, and consultations be-

---

1. This opinion is based on the ABA Model Rules of Professional Conduct as amended by the ABA House of Delegates through February 2023. The laws, court rules and opinions, regulations, and rules of professional conduct, promulgated in individual jurisdictions are controlling.

2. Compliance with the obligations imposed by the Model Rules of Professional Conduct, as discussed in this opinion, depends on a lawyer's role, level of authority, and responsibility in the law firm's operations. ABA Comm. on Ethics & Prof'l Responsibility, Formal Op. 483, at n. 6 (2018). See generally ABA Comm. on Ethics & Prof'l Responsibility, Formal Op. 467 (2014). See MODEL RULES OF PROF'L CONDUCT R. 5.1 (2022) (Responsibilities of Partners, Managers, and Supervisory Lawyers); MODEL RULES OF PROF'L CONDUCT R. 5.2 (Responsibilities of a Subordinate Lawyer); and MODEL RULES OF PROF'L CONDUCT R. 5.3 (Responsibilities Regarding Nonlawyer Assistance).

tween lawyers. This opinion addresses some minimum ethical requirements and suggested practices arising in the office sharing context, particularly in the areas of confidentiality, conflicts of interest, supervision, and communications concerning a lawyer's services.

II. Discussion

A. Protecting Client Information

Confidentiality is central to the practice of law.[3] Maintaining the confidentiality of client information is therefore imperative for lawyers in an office sharing arrangement.[4] The mere sharing of office space does not automatically equate with the disclosure of client information.[5] The physical arrangement of the shared office space, however, must not expose client information to other office-sharing lawyers and their staff. Everyone should also avoid discussing cases in or near common areas, which could lead to the disclosure of client information.[6]

Depending on the specific circumstances of the office sharing arrangement, lawyers may need to consider additional confidentiality safeguards. This could include separate lobby or waiting areas; refraining from leaving client files out on workspaces, conference rooms, or kitchen tables; installing privacy screens on computer monitors and locking down computers when not actively in use; clean desk policies; and regular training and reminders to staff of the need to keep all client information confidential.[7] Office sharing lawyers can also restrict access to client-related information by securing

---

3. *See* MODEL RULES OF PROF'L CONDUCT R. 1.6(a) (providing that "[a] lawyer shall not reveal information relating to the representation of a client unless the client gives informed consent, the disclosure is impliedly authorized in order to carry out the representation or the disclosure is permitted by paragraph (b)").

4. State Bar of Cal. Comm. on Prof'l Responsibility & Conduct Op. 1997-150, 1997 WL 240818, at *3–4 (1997); Conn. Bar Ass'n Prof'l Ethics Comm. 2014-04, 2014 WL 12823983, at *1 (2014); D.C. Bar Ass'n Op. 303, at 1 (2001) [hereinafter D.C. Bar Op.]; La. State Bar Ass'n Rules of Prof'l Conduct Comm. Op. 07-RPCC-013, at 1 (2007); Mich. State Bar Comm. on Prof'l & Judicial Ethics Op. RI-249, 1996 WL 381521, at *2 (1996) [hereinafter Mich. State Bar Op. RI-249]; Mo. Bar Informal Op. 950169, at 1 (1995); N.J. Sup. Ct. Advisory Comm. on Prof'l Ethics Op. 498, 1982 WL 117856, at *1 (1982); Ohio Bd. of Prof'l Conduct Advisory Op. 2022-11, 2022 WL 10219976 (2022); Ohio Bd. of Prof'l Conduct Advisory Op. 2017-05, 2022 WL 10219976, at *1 (2017).

5. Ill. St. Bar Ass'n Comm. on Prof'l Ethics Advisory Op. 85-14, 1986 WL 378934, at *4 (1986).

6. State Bar of Cal. Comm. on Prof'l Responsibility & Conduct Op. 1997-150, 1997 WL 240818, at *3–4 (1997); Colo. Bar Ass'n Ethics Comm. Op. 89, at 5 (2018); Mich. State Bar, Comm. on Prof'l & Judicial Ethics Op. RI-313, 1999 WL 406884, at *1 (1999); N.Y. State Bar Ass'n Comm. on Prof'l Ethics Op. 794, 2006 WL 1386607, at *4 (2006).

7. *See, e.g.*, ABA Comm. on Ethics & Prof'l Responsibility, Formal Op. 498, at 3–7 (2021) [hereinafter ABA Formal Op. 498] (discussing technologies and related strategies to protect the confidentiality of client information in a virtual practice).

physical client files in locked cabinets or offices and using separate telephone lines and computer systems.[8] Lawyers, however, may overcome confidentiality concerns with shared telephone and computer systems with appropriate security measures, staff training, and client disclosures.[9]

Lawyers in an office sharing arrangement may decide to share support staff, such as receptionists, administrative assistants, and paralegals. In these situations, maintaining the confidentiality of client information is tested. Instructing all lawyers and employees, and particularly shared employees, on their confidentiality obligations and the office procedures in place to guard sensitive client documents and communications are examples of reasonable measures to protect client confidentiality.[10] Of course, appropriate supervision of shared personnel is also required under Model Rule 5.3.[11]

B. Clear Communication About the Relationship

Lawyers who share offices but do not practice together as a law firm must take appropriate steps to clearly communicate the nature of their relationship to the public and to their clients.

Model Rule 7.1 prohibits any "false or misleading communication about the lawyer or the lawyer's services."[12] Comment [7] to the Rule further ex-

---

8. Colo. Bar Ass'n Ethics Comm. Op. 89, *supra* note 6, at 4–7; Ind. State Bar Ass'n Legal Ethics Comm. Op. 8, at 2–3 (1985); D.C. Bar Op. 303, *supra* note 4, at 1; Mo. Bar Informal Op. 980220, at 1 (1998); N.Y. State Bar Ass'n Comm. on Prof'l Ethics Op., 2012 WL 6087183, at *1–2 (2012); Ohio Bd. of Prof'l Conduct Advisory Op. 91-9, 1991 WL 717479, at *2 (1991); Va. State Bar Legal Ethics Comm. Op. 754, 1986 WL 1180470, at *1 (1986).

9. Colo. Bar Ass'n Ethics Comm. Op. 89, *supra* note 6, at 1, 5; D.C. Bar Op. 303, *supra* note 8, at 1; Mo. Bar Informal Op. 970192 (1997); Ohio Bd. of Prof'l Conduct Advisory Op. 92-13, 1992 WL 739290, at *3 (1992); Or. St. Bar Ass'n Op. 2005-50, 2005 WL 5679839, at *1 (2005). *See also* ABA Formal Op. 498, *supra* note 7, at 3–5 (discussing virtual practice technologies and other security measures to safeguard client information); Ohio Bd. of Prof'l Conduct Adv. Op. 2022-11, 2022 WL 10219976, at *2 (2022) (recommending that computers connected to a shared network "be secured by individual credentials and other security measures to prevent lawyers or staff from accessing the data and files on a network belonging to others").

10. State Bar of Cal. Comm. on Prof'l Responsibility & Conduct Op. 1997-150, *supra* note 4, at *3–4; D.C. Bar Op. 303, *supra* note 4, at 1; Mich. State Bar Op. RI-249, *supra* note 4, at *2; Mo. Bar Informal Op. 950169, *supra* note 4, at 1; Neb. Jud. Ethics Comm. Op. 89-2, 1989 WL 1803035, at *4 (1989); Ohio Bd. of Prof'l Conduct Advisory Op. 2022-11, *supra* note 4, at *3. *But see* Utah State Bar Advisory Op. 125, 1994 WL 631269, at *2 (1994) (finding it "difficult to see how it would be possible for shared secretarial arrangements not to put confidential information at risk").

11. Model Rule 5.3 addresses both partner and supervisor responsibilities for ensuring that nonlawyer assistants' behavior is compatible with lawyers' professional obligations. MODEL RULES OF PROF'L CONDUCT R. 5.3. *See* ABA Comm. on Ethics & Prof'l Responsibility, Formal Op. 498, at 3–4 (examining lawyers' supervisory obligations for nonlawyer assistants in a virtual practice); Ohio Bd. of Prof'l Conduct Advisory Op. 2022-11, *supra* note 4, at *3 (discussing the sharing of nonlawyer staff).

12. MODEL RULES OF PROF'L CONDUCT R. 7.1.

plains that lawyers "may not imply or hold themselves out as practicing together in one firm when they are not a firm, as defined in Rule 1.0(c), because to do so would be false and misleading."[13] Accordingly, office-sharing lawyers must ensure that the public is not misled about the nature of their relationship, such as confusion about whether the lawyers are part of a law firm, partnership, or professional corporation when no such affiliation exists.[14]

Lawyers in an office sharing arrangement should use separate business cards, letterhead, and directory listings, as well as office signs, firm names, and advertisements that describe their distinct practices and do not suggest a close association between professionals operating within the same space.[15] It is desirable for lawyers sharing office space to have separate telephone lines, but a receptionist may answer a common telephone line with a generic salutation such as "Law Offices" to avoid implying that the lawyers are practicing together in the same firm.[16]

It may not be possible to have separate signage where a law firm subleases excess space to unaffiliated lawyers or to lawyers with whom the firm works on a matter-by-matter basis, or where lawyers work in rented temporary space such as WeWork or Regus™ offices. Nevertheless, unaffiliated lawyers sharing space must take reasonable measures to ensure that clients are not confused about their associations with the other lawyers practicing in the immediate area. Office sharing lawyers must understand the need to clarify for their clients these distinct professional relationships. Any communications to the public should also signal that the law practices are not affiliated with one another, other than in their resource-sharing arrangement.[17]

---

13. *Id.* at cmt. 7. *See also* MODEL RULES OF PROF'L CONDUCT R. 1.0(c) (defining "firm" or "law firm" as "a lawyer or lawyers in a law partnership, professional corporation, sole proprietorship or other association authorized to practice law; or lawyers employed in a legal services organization or the legal department of a corporation or other organization").

14. MODEL RULES OF PROF'L CONDUCT R. 1.4 & 7.1; State Bar of Cal. Comm. on Prof'l Responsibility & Conduct Op. 1997-150, *supra* note 4, at *1; Colo. Bar Ass'n Ethics Comm. Op. 89, *supra* note 6, at 2; D.C. Eth. Op. 303, *supra* note 4, at 1.

15. State Bar of Cal. Comm. on Prof'l Responsibility & Conduct Op. 1997-150, *supra* note 4, at *1; Colo. Bar Ass'n Ethics Comm. Op. 89, *supra* note 6, at 6; Conn. Bar Ass'n Prof'l Ethics Comm. Op. 97-9, 1997 WL 700580, at *2 (1997); D.C. Eth. Op. 303, at 1; Mich. State Bar Op. RI-249, *supra* note 4, at * 3; Mo. Bar Informal Adv. Op. 980220, *supra* note 8, at 1; N.Y. City Bar Ass'n Prof'l Ethics Comm. Advisory Op. 680, 1990 WL 677022, at *1 (1990); Ohio Bd. of Comm'rs on Grievances & Discipline Advisory Op. 89-36, 1989 WL 535040, at *2 (1989); Va. State Bar Legal Ethics Comm. Op. 874, 1987 WL 1379105, at *1 (1987).

16. State Bar of Ariz. Op. 01-09 (2001); Conn. Bar Ass'n Prof'l Ethics Comm. Op. 97-9, *supra* note 15, at *2; D.C. Bar Op. 303, at 1; Mich. Eth. Op. RI-249, 1996 WL 381521, at *3; Ohio Adv. Op. 95-1, 1995 WL 813784, at *4 (Ohio Bd. of Comm'rs on Grievances & Discipline 1995); Wash. Adv. Op. 1304, at 1 (Wash. State Bar, Comm on Prof'l Ethics 1989).

17. Conn. Eth. Op. 2014-04, 2014 WL 12823983, at *1; D.C. Bar. Op. 303, *supra* note 4, at 1; Mich. State Bar Op. RI-249, *supra* note 4, at *2; Mo. Bar Informal Op. 950169, *supra* note 4, at 1.

C. Conflicts of Interest Considerations

Lawyers in shared office arrangements should pay particular attention to (1) avoiding the imputation of conflicts of interest, (2) taking on potential new matters that are adverse to clients represented by other office sharing lawyers, and (3) consulting with fellow office sharing lawyers.

1. Imputation of Conflicts

Model Rule 1.10(a) imputes conflicts of interest to all lawyers "associated in a firm."[18] Thus, imputation of a lawyer's conflict of interest to other lawyers in an office-sharing arrangement will pivot on whether the lawyers are, or appear to the public or their clients as, "associated in a firm."[19]

Under the Model Rules, office sharing lawyers are not automatically treated as a single law firm for conflicts of interest purposes.[20] This determination will depend on the facts and circumstances of each arrangement.[21] Office sharing lawyers who do not protect the confidentiality of their respective clients, regularly consult with each other on matters, share staff who have access to client information, mislead the public about their identity and services, or otherwise fail to keep their practices separate, are more likely to be treated as "associated in a firm" for conflict imputation purposes.[22]

---

18. MODEL RULES OF PROF'L CONDUCT R. 1.10(a).
19. MODEL RULES OF PROF'L CONDUCT R. 1.10(a) & cmt. 1; Colo. Bar Ass'n Ethics Comm. Op. 89, *supra* note 6, at 1; Mich. State Bar Op. RI-249, *supra* note 4, at *5.
20. Mich. State Bar Op. RI-249, *supra* note 4, at *1; N.Y. State Bar Ass'n Comm. on Prof'l Ethics Op. 794, *supra* note 6, at *1 (2011); *see* MODEL RULES OF PROF'L CONDUCT R. 1.0(c) & cmt. 2 (stating that "two practitioners who share office space and occasionally consult or assist each other ordinarily would not be regarded as constituting a firm," but "if they present themselves to the public in a way that suggests that they are a firm or conduct themselves as a firm, they should be regarded as a firm" under the Model Rules).
21. *See* ABA Comm. on Ethics & Prof'l Responsibility, Formal Op. 88-356, at 2–4 (1988) (explaining that whether a temporary lawyer should be treated as "associated in a firm" for conflicts imputation purposes requires "a functional analysis of the facts and circumstances involved in the relationship," with a particular focus on the temporary lawyer's access to information relating to the representation of other firm clients).
22. *In re* Sexson, 613 N.E.2d 841, 843 (Ind. 1993); MODEL RULES OF PROF'L CONDUCT R. 1.0(c) & cmt. 2; Ariz. State Bar Comm. on the Rules of Prof'l Conduct Op. 01-09, at 1 (2001); Colo. Bar Ass'n Ethics Comm. Op. 89, *supra* note 6, at 1, 4; D.C. Bar Op. 303, *supra* note 4, at 1; Ky. Bar Ass'n Ethics Comm. Op. E-418, at 4 (2001); Ind. State Bar Ass'n Legal Ethics Comm. Op. 8, *supra* note 8, at 3; La. State Bar Ass'n Rules of Prof'l Conduct Comm. Op. 07-RPCC-013, *supra* note 4, at 3; Mo. Bar Informal Op. 950169, *supra* note 4, at 1; N.Y. State Bar Ass'n Comm. on Prof'l Ethics Op. 794, *supra* note 6, at *4; N.Y. City Bar Ass'n Prof'l Ethics Comm. Advisory Op. 680, *supra* note 15, at *2; Ohio Bd. of Prof'l Conduct Advisory Op. 2022-11, *supra* note 4, at *2; S.C. Bar Ethics Advisory Comm. Op. 08-11, 2008 WL 8089795, at *2 (2008); Utah State Bar Advisory Op. 125, *supra* note 10, at *2; Vt. Bar Ass'n Prof'l Responsibility Comm. Op. 79-22, at 1 (1979).

APPENDIX F: FORMAL ETHICS OPINIONS

2. Representing Clients with Adverse Interests

Where lawyers in an office sharing arrangement properly shield the confidentiality of their respective clients and do not hold themselves out to the public as members of the same firm, it may be permissible under the Model Rules to represent clients with adverse interests—even in the same lawsuit or transaction.[23] Although this determination will ultimately turn on specifics of the office sharing arrangement and the nature of the proposed representations, Model Rules 1.4 and 1.7 may obligate lawyers to disclose the details of the office sharing arrangement to their respective clients, including their efforts to maintain confidentiality, and to obtain each clients' informed consent, confirmed in writing.[24]

In addition, any staff shared by the lawyers should not possess or otherwise have access to information from both adverse clients.[25] Implementing an adequate ethical screen between shared staff members can be an effective measure in this regard, and to avoid the sharing of client information more generally.[26]

Notwithstanding the ability of office sharing lawyers to represent clients with adverse interests, some state ethics opinions understandably advise

---

23. ABA Comm. on Ethics & Prof'l Responsibility, Informal Op. 1486, at 1 (1982) [hereinafter ABA Informal Op. 1486] (lawyers who share space and represent adverse interests in pending lawsuits should explain fully the relationship to, and obtain the consent of, clients to continue to represent adverse interests).; Md. State Bar Ass'n Op. 1987-43, at 1 (1987); Mo. Bar Informal Adv. Op. 970192, *supra* note 9, at 1; N.J. Sup. Ct. Advisory Comm. on Prof'l Ethics Op. 515, 1983 WL 106225, at *1–2 (1983); Ohio Bd. of Prof'l Conduct Advisory Op. 89-005, 1989 WL 535010, at *1 (1989); Or. St. Bar Ass'n Op. 2005-50, *supra* note 9, at *1; S.C. Bar Ethics Advisory Comm. Op. 08-11, *supra* note 22, at *2 (2008); S.C. Bar Ethics Advisory Comm. Op. 91-37, 1992 WL 810417, at *1–2 (1992); Vt. Bar Ass'n Prof'l Responsibility Comm. Op. 80-15, at 1–2 (1980); Va. State Bar Legal Ethics Comm. Op. 943, 1987 WL 1378998, at *1 (1987); Va. State Bar Legal Ethics Comm. Op. 799, 1986 WL 1180507, at *1 (1986); Wash. State Bar Comm. on Prof'l Ethics Op. 1793, at 1 (1997); Wash. State Bar Comm. on Prof'l Ethics Op. 1559, at 1 (1994).

24. ABA Informal Op. 1486, *supra* note 23, at 1; Colo. Bar Ass'n Ethics Comm. Op. 89, *supra* note 6, at 4; Md. Eth. Op. 1987-43, at 1; Mich. Eth. Op. RI-249, 1996 WL 381521, at *3; N.J. Eth. Op. 515, 1983 WL 106225, at *1–2; Ohio Adv. Op. 89-005, 1989 WL 535010, at *2 (Ohio Bd. of Comm'rs on Grievances & Discipline 1989); S.C. Bar Ethics Advisory Comm. Op. 91-37, *supra* note 23, at *1–2; Vt. Bar Ass'n Prof'l Responsibility Comm. Op. 80-15, *supra* note 23, at 1–2; Va. State Bar Legal Ethics Comm. Op. 943, *supra* note 23, at *1; Wash. State Bar Comm. on Prof'l Ethics Op. 1793, *supra* note 23, at 1.

25. Ky. Bar Ass'n Ethics Comm. Op. E-406, at 3 (1998); Me. Bd. of Overseers of the Bar Prof'l Ethics Comm'n Op. 41, at 1 (2019); Or. St. Bar Ass'n Op. 2005-50, *supra* note 9, at *1; S.C. Bar Ethics Advisory Comm. Op. 91-37, *supra* note 23, at *1–2. The Committee does not believe it is possible for lawyers in an office sharing arrangement to maintain this kind of separation when representing clients with adverse interests if the lawyers together share only one staff member.

26. *See generally* Cal. Lawyers Ass'n Ethics Comm. Formal Op. 2021-1 (2021) (discussing elements of effective ethical screens).

lawyers to avoid these situations entirely.[27] Potential pitfalls range from inadvertent disclosures of client information in a shared office to opposing parties coincidentally scheduling meetings at the same time. Before entering an office sharing arrangement, it is prudent for a lawyer to examine the nature of the other lawyers' practices to determine whether conflicts of interest are likely to arise.[28]

3. Consultations Between Office Sharing Lawyers

It is natural for lawyers in office sharing arrangements to informally consult one another about their respective client matters. Merely engaging in informal consultations from time to time, however, does not result in the lawyers being "associated in a firm" under Model Rule 1.10(a).[29] At the same time, lawyers who occasionally consult with other lawyers in shared office arrangements should not disclose "client information that may reveal the identity of a client or privileged information."[30] Lawyers may instead discuss issues using hypothetical facts. As comment [4] to Model Rule 1.6 explains, "[a] lawyer's use of a hypothetical to discuss issues relating to the representation is permissible so long as there is no reasonable likelihood that the listener will be able to ascertain the identity of the client or the situation involved."[31]

Consultations between office sharing lawyers can also trigger unanticipated conflicts of interest, restricting a consulted lawyer's ability to represent a current or future client under Model Rule 1.7(a)(2).[32] For instance, if Lawyer A and Lawyer B share office space, and Lawyer A divulges client information to Lawyer B during an informal consultation to help Lawyer A prepare a case for trial, then Lawyer B may assume a responsibility not to use or reveal the information, which could materially limit Lawyer B's ability to represent a current or future client.[33] This situation parallels the confidentiality

---

27. Colo. Bar Ass'n Ethics Comm. Op. 89, *supra* note 6, at 3; S.C. Bar Ethics Advisory Comm. Op. 08-11, *supra* note 22, at *2; Va. State Bar Legal Ethics Comm. Op. 943, *supra* note 23, at *1; *see also* ABA Comm. on Ethics & Prof'l Responsibility, Informal Op. 1474, at 1 (1982) (concluding that "representation of opposing sides by lawyers working in the same military office and sharing common secretarial and filing facilities should be avoided").
28. Colo. Bar Ass'n Ethics Comm. Op. 89, *supra* note 6, at 3.
29. Ohio Bd. of Prof'l Conduct Advisory Op. 2022-11, *supra* note 4, at *1.
30. *Id.*
31. Model Rules of Prof'l Conduct R. 1.6 cmt. 4.
32. Model Rules of Prof'l Conduct R. 1.7(a)(2); ABA Comm. on Ethics & Prof'l Responsibility, Formal Op. 98-411, at 7 (1998) [hereinafter ABA Formal Op. 98-411].
33. Model Rules of Prof'l Conduct R. 1.7(a)(2); ABA Formal Op. 98-411, at 9. *See also* Liebnow v. Boston Enterprises, 296 P.3d 108, 115 (Colo. 2013) (citing ABA Formal Op. 98-411, at 7) (concluding that where "one lawyer has consulted another lawyer and has revealed confidential information about her case, including her theory of the case and trial strategy, that could materially limit the consulted attorney's ability to represent the opposing party ... due to the consulted attorney's potential responsibility to keep the information confidential").

duties that lawyers owe to prospective clients under Model Rule 1.18 and the conflicts problems that can surface if a lawyer receives too much information from a prospective client during an initial consultation.[34]

To prevent these issues, Lawyer B can conduct a standard conflict check prior to any informal consultation or collaboration with Lawyer A.[35]

III. Conclusion

The ABA Model Rules of Professional Conduct permit lawyers to participate in office sharing arrangements, but those doing so must fully consider and comply with their applicable ethical responsibilities, including confidentiality, conflicts of interest, supervision, and communications concerning a lawyer's services.

---

34. MODEL RULES OF PROF'L CONDUCT R. 1.18. *See also* ABA Comm. on Ethics & Prof'l Responsibility, Formal Op. 492 (2020) (discussing lawyers' obligations to prospective clients and the conflicts issues that can surface if lawyers receive "significantly harmful" information from a prospective client).

35. *See generally* Conn. Bar Ass'n Prof'l Ethics Comm. Op. 98-11, 1998 WL 993681, at *1–2 (1998).

AMERICAN BAR ASSOCIATION
STANDING COMMITTEE ON ETHICS AND PROFESSIONAL RESPONSIBILITY
321 N. Clark Street, Chicago, Illinois 60654-4714 Telephone (312) 988-5328
CHAIR: Lynda Shely, Scottsdale, AZ
■ Mark A. Armitage, Detroit, MI ■ Melinda Bentley, Jefferson City, MO ■ Matthew Corbin, Olathe, KS
■ Robinjit Kaur Eagleson, Lansing, MI ■ Doug Ende, Seattle, WA
■ Hon. Audrey Moorehead, Dallas, TX ■ Wendy Muchman, Chicago, IL
■ Keith Swisher, Scottsdale, AZ ■ Charles Vigil, Albuquerque, NM

CENTER FOR PROFESSIONAL RESPONSIBILITY
Mary McDermott, Lead Senior Counsel
©2023 by the American Bar Association. All rights reserved.

AMERICAN BAR ASSOCIATION
STANDING COMMITTEE ON ETHICS AND PROFESSIONAL RESPONSIBILITY

Formal Opinion 508   **August 5, 2023**

The Ethics of Witness Preparation

A lawyer's role in preparing a witness to testify and providing testimonial guidance is not only an accepted professional function; it is considered an essential tactical component of a lawyer's advocacy in a matter in which a client or witness will provide testimony. Under the Model Rules of Professional Conduct1 governing the client-lawyer relationship and a lawyer's duties as an advisor, the failure adequately to prepare a witness would in many situations be classified as an ethical violation. But, in some witness-preparation situations, a lawyer clearly steps over the line of what is ethically permissible. Counseling a witness to give false testimony or assisting a witness in offering false testimony, for example, is a violation of at least Model Rule 3.4(b). The task of delineating what is necessary and proper and what is ethically prohibited during witness preparation has become more urgent with the advent of commonly used remote technologies, some of which can be used to surreptitiously "coach" witnesses in new and ethically problematic ways.

Introduction

> **Jack McCall:** Well, I'm a hard case for you, counselor. And no mistake, everyone in there saw me shoot him.
>
> **Lawyer:** If you'll let me set our strategy, I don't think we'll dispute what people saw.
>
> **Jack:** Now, I guess you're here to break me out.
>
> (*Lawyer chuckles*)
>
> **Lawyer:** Son, did James Butler Hickok ever kill a -- relative of yours?

---

1. This opinion is based on the ABA Model Rules of Professional Conduct as amended by the ABA House of Delegates through 2023. The laws, court rules, regulations, rules of professional conduct, and opinions promulgated in individual jurisdictions are controlling.

APPENDIX F: FORMAL ETHICS OPINIONS

Jack: James Butler Hickok?

Lawyer: Wild Bill Hickok. Did he ever kill a brother of yours or—or the like?

Jack: A brother?

Lawyer: I'm asking you if what happened in that saloon was vengeance, for the death of a family member? Possibly a brother in Abilene. Or the like.

Jack: *(Jack smirks, cocks head pensively)* A brother in Abilene . . . .

(Lawyer smiles, pats Jack twice on the knee, and exits).[2]

Preparing a witness or a client to testify in advance of a deposition or adjudicative proceeding—or in some situations providing a client or witness with midstream guidance during the testimonial process – is such a familiar component of a lawyer's trial-advocacy repertoire that it needs little introduction or explanation. Many would condemn a lawyer's failure to prepare a client or witness.[3] Failure to do so competently and diligently can constitute an ethics violation.[4]

But, in some witness-preparation situations, a lawyer clearly steps over the line of what is ethically permissible. Certain categories of lawyer activity are firmly established as unethically interfering with the integrity of the justice system and unethically obstructing another party's access to evidence. Among the rules applicable to such conduct are Rule 1.2 (Scope of Representation and Allocation of Authority between Client and Lawyer), Rule 3.3 (Candor Toward

---

2. THE TRIAL OF JACK MCCALL, DEADWOOD, season 1, episode 5 (Home Box Office, Inc. 2010).

3. William Hodes, *The Professional Duty to Horseshed Witnesses Zealously Within the Bounds of the Law*, 30 TEXAS TECH. L. REV. 1343 (1999) ("Journey not far enough, and a lawyer deserves sanction for failing to carry out the most basic duties encompassed by the client-lawyer relationship.") (footnote omitted); Roberta K. Flowers, *Witness Preparation: Regulation of the Profession's Dirty Little Secret*, 38 HASTINGS CONST. L.Q. 1007, 1009 (2011) ("Witness preparation is considered by most criminal attorneys—prosecutors and criminal defense attorneys alike—to be an essential part of trial advocacy.") (footnote omitted); Adam Liptak, *Crossing a Fine Line on Witness Coaching*, N.Y. TIMES (Mar. 16, 2006) ("[L]awyers often spend hours preparing witnesses to testify, a practice that is not only accepted but also generally considered necessary. Lawyers have been punished for incompetent representation for failing to interview and prepare witnesses.").

4. *See* MODEL RULES OF PROF'L CONDUCT R. 1.1 (Competence) & cmt. [5]; MODEL RULES OF PROF'L CONDUCT R. 1.3 (Diligence).

the Tribunal), Rule 3.4 (Fairness to Opposing Party and Counsel), Rule 4.4 (Respect for Rights of Third Persons), and Rule 8.4 (Misconduct).

The distinction between legitimate witness preparation and guidance versus unethical efforts to influence witness testimony, a practice sometimes known as coaching, horseshedding, woodshedding, or sandpapering,[5] can be ambiguous owing in large part to the concurrent ethical duties to diligently and competently represent the client and to refrain from improperly influencing witnesses.[6] For purposes of this opinion, the term coach is used to signify unethical or ethically questionable conduct. The task of delineating what is necessary and proper and what is ethically prohibited during witness preparation has become more urgent with the advent of commonly used remote technologies, some of which can be used to surreptitiously "coach" witnesses in new and ethically problematic ways.

Analysis

Some quantum of client and witness preparation is appropriate and an affirmative ethical responsibility. But lawyers "must respect the important ethical distinction between discussing testimony and seeking improperly to influence it."[7] There is, in general, a distinction between manipulative conduct during client/witness preparation and active interference with or attempts to influence testimony while a witness is testifying. This opinion addresses both, because either can implicate a lawyer's ethical duties.

With remote proceedings having become commonplace, the sense that brazen witness-coaching behaviors are occurring or could easily occur

---

5. BLACK'S LAW DICTIONARY 885 (11th ed. 2019) (defining horseshedding as "The instruction of a witness favorable to one's case (esp. a client) about the proper method of responding to questions while giving testimony."). To be sure, a witness can be coached to tell the truth, which would not ordinarily be unethical. The practice of emphasizing continuously the importance of telling the truth, and that truthfully and accurately recounting facts is ultimately the witness's responsibility, is a useful guardrail to avoid coaching. *See* Resolution Tr. Corp. v. Bright, 6 F.3d 336, 341 (5th Cir. 1993) (district court's disbarment of two lawyers for aggressively pushing witness regarding choice of words was an abuse of discretion where there was no evidence that conduct was in bad faith or testimony was false; evidence that lawyers told witness to read the affidavit carefully before signing it undermined allegation that lawyers' conduct was an attempt to cause witness testify falsely under oath).

6. Many commentators have underscored this tension. *See, e.g.*, Tom Barber, *Restrictions on Lawyers Communicating with Witnesses During Testimony: Law, Lore, Opinions, and the Rule*, 83 FLA. BAR JOURNAL 58 (July-Aug. 2009) (noting that "there is considerable disagreement as to the definition of 'coaching' as opposed to legitimate preparation").

7. *See* Geders v. United States, 425 U.S. 80, 90 n.3 (1976) (citing Ethical Consideration 7-26 of the ABA Code of Professional Responsibility (1975)); *see also* Hall v. Clifton Precision, 150 F.R.D. 525, 528 (E.D. Pa. 1993) ("The goal of obtaining the facts of a case is defeated when the lawyer and not the witness is answering questions or influencing the answers to them.").

APPENDIX F: FORMAL ETHICS OPINIONS

has been validated by a number of reported instances of misconduct.[8] This development should guide the manner in which courts and lawyers are superintending the use of remote technology.

A. What Preparatory Conduct is Ethical?

Providing a witness with effective preparatory guidance is undoubtedly a component of the "thoroughness and preparation" element of Model Rule 1.1.[9] It is accepted that lawyers can engage in, for example, the following activities:

- remind the witness that they will be under oath
- emphasize the importance of telling the truth
- explain that telling the truth can include a truthful answer of "I do not recall"[10]
- explain case strategy and procedure, including the nature of the testimonial process or the purpose of the deposition
- suggest proper attire[11] and appropriate demeanor and decorum
- provide context for the witness's testimony
- inquire into the witness's probable testimony and recollection

---

8. The risk of witness-preparation misconduct is not particularly augmented in a remote environment because such interactions still occur "behind closed doors," so to speak. Technology-driven efforts to influence in-progress witness testimony—signaling or messaging a witness testifying remotely, out of the sight of opposing counsel and the adjudicative officer—has generated increased scrutiny.

9. *See* MODEL RULES OF PROF'L CONDUCT R. 1.1 (Competence) & cmt. [5]. Other germane rules include MODEL RULES OF PROF'L CONDUCT R. 1.3 (Diligence), 1.4 (Communication), and 2.1 (Advisor). *See, e.g.*, Hall v. Clifton Precision, 150 F.R.D. 525, 528 (E.D. Pa. 1993) (an attorney has right and duty to prepare a client for deposition); Maryland v. Earp, 571 A.2d 1227, 1234 (Md. 1990) ("[a]ttorneys have not only the right but also the duty to fully investigate the case and to interview persons who may be witnesses."); John S. Applegate, *Witness Preparation*, 68 TEX. L. REV. 277, 287-88 (1989), ("The practical literature uniformly views the failure to interview witnesses prior to testimony as a combination of strategic lunacy and gross negligence.").

10. Telling a witness that a truthful answer of "I do not recall" is an acceptable response and ethically distinguishable from telling a witness, "The less you recall the better." The latter is a statement that affirmatively encourages a witness to "forget" information, i.e., to lie under oath about what is remembered. It is the ethical equivalent of telling a witness affirmatively to testify to something that is contrary to fact. *See* MODEL RULES OF PROF'L CONDUCT R. 3.4(b) (a lawyer shall not counsel or assist a witness to testify falsely).

11. Vanessa Friedman, *Caroll, Clothes and Credibility*, N.Y. TIMES (May 9, 2023) (noting that witness's attire and demeanor were so effective that people wondered if someone was stage-managing the style: "Well, her lawyers, duh. It has long been understood that appearance is part of any courtroom drama.").

- identify other testimony that is expected to be presented and explore the witness's version of events in light of that testimony
- review documents or physical evidence with the witness, including using documents to refresh a witness's recollection of the facts
- identify lines of questioning and potential cross-examination
- suggest choice of words that might be employed to make the witness's meaning clear[12]
- tell the witness not to answer a question until it has been completely asked
- emphasize the importance of remaining calm and not arguing with the questioning lawyer
- tell the witness to testify only about what they know and remember and not to guess or speculate
- familiarize the witness with the idea of focusing on answering the question, i.e., not volunteering information.[13]

When it comes to preparation of a client or witness for a testimonial event such as a trial or deposition, there is a fair amount of latitude in the types of lawyer-orchestrated preparatory activities that are recognized as permissible.[14]

B. Unethical Pre-Testimony Coaching

Within the broad class of lawyer conduct directed at a client's or witness's future testimony, certain categories of lawyer activity are firmly established as unethically interfering with the integrity of the justice system and unethically obstructing another party's access to evidence. A lawyer violates ethical obligations by counseling a witness to give false testimony, assisting a witness in offering false testimony, advising a client or witness to disobey

---

12. THE RESTATEMENT (THIRD) OF THE LAW GOVERNING LAWYERS, § 116, cmt. b (2000), emphasizes that in suggesting choice of words "a lawyer may not assist the witness to testify falsely as to a material fact," which would constitute knowingly counseling or assisting a witness to testify falsely or otherwise to offer false evidence. *Id.* (citing RESTATEMENT § 120(1)(a)).

13. Many of these techniques are expressly referenced in the RESTATEMENT (THIRD) OF THE LAW GOVERNING LAWYERS §116, cmt. b.

14. *See generally* JONATHAN L. ROSNER, PREPARING WITNESSES (2022-23 ed.); DANIEL I. SMALL, PREPARING WITNESSES: A PRACTICAL GUIDE FOR LAWYERS AND THEIR CLIENTS (5th ed. 2020); Video: Jan Mills Spaeth, *Become a Strong and Credible Witness: Witness Preparation for Deposition and Trial* (2019) (streaming HD video); JAMES M. MILLER, FROM THE TRENCHES II: MASTERING THE ART OF PREPARING WITNESSES (2019); KENNETH R. BERMAN, REINVENTING WITNESS PREPARATION: UNLOCKING THE SECRETS TO TESTIMONIAL SUCCESS (2018).

APPENDIX F: FORMAL ETHICS OPINIONS

a court order regulating discovery or trial process, offering an unlawful inducement to a witness, or procuring a witness's absence from a proceeding.[15]

Prominent among the ethics rules in this area is Model Rule 3.4(b), which prohibits a lawyer from advising or assisting a witness—whether a client or not—to give false testimony.[16] Instigating a witness to lie can occur in ways beyond an outright instruction to fabricate testimony. For example, it is unethical to tell a witness to "downplay" the number of times a witness and a lawyer met to prepare for trial[17] or to encourage a client to misrepresent a location of a slip and fall accident to have a viable claim.[18] Other representative examples of unacceptable witness coaching and influencing behaviors

---

15. *See, e.g., In re* Stroh, 97 Wash. 2d 289, 300, 644 P.2d 1161, 1167 (1982) (disbarring lawyer following conviction for tampering with a witness; "Under no circumstances may false testimony knowingly be introduced into a hearing by an officer of the court.").

16. MODEL RULES OF PROF'L CONDUCT R. 3.4(b). Such conduct might also constitute assisting the client to engage in conduct that the lawyer knows is criminal, i.e., perjury, in violation of Model Rule 1.2(d), as well as offering false evidence in violation of Model Rule 3.3(a)(3). MODEL RULES OF PROF'L CONDUCT R. 1.2(d) & 3.3(a)(3). For examples of discipline for transgressing these rules, *see, e.g., In re* Peasley, 90 P. 3d 764 (Ariz. 2004) (lawyer who coached witness to lie disbarred); *In re* Paul Stormont, 873 S.W.2d 227 (Mo. 1994) (lawyer disbarred in Missouri and reciprocally suspended for two-years in Illinois for advising client during recess to deny material facts of another witness's testimony that lawyer knew were true and prompting client on redirect to testify to known false testimony); *see also In re* Attorney Discipline Matter, 98 F.3d 1082 (8th Cir. 1996) (affirming reciprocal disbarment of same Missouri lawyer); *In re* Mitchell, 244 Ga. 766, 262 S.E.2d 89 (1979) (disbarring lawyer who had instructed six witnesses to say that a fictitious man by the name of "David Thompson" was the real father of a child whose paternity was disputed); *In re* Oberhellmann, 873 S.W.2d 851, 852 (Mo. 1994) (disbarring lawyer who, during client's deposition, instructed client to lie about a number of things, including client's place of residence).

17. *In re* Meltzer, 21 N.Y.S.3d 63, 64 (2015) (accepting lawyer's resignation and ordering disbarment in matter arising from lawyer's instructions that witness "downplay" the number of times they met to discuss testimony to prepare for trial in the event witness was asked such a question on cross-examination).

18. *In re* Rios, 965 N.Y.S.3d 418, 421, 423-24 (2013) (lawyer disciplined for violation of New York RPC 8.4(c)).

include programming a witness's testimony,[19] knowingly violating sequestration orders,[20] and encouraging a witness to present fabricated testimony.[21]

It is also unethical to compensate a lay witness for the substance of their testimony or to condition such payment on the content of the witness's

---

19. *In re* Brooke P. Halsey, Jr., Case No. 02-O-10195-PEM (State Bar of California Hearing Dep't, Aug. 1, 2006) (prosecutor's secret pre-trial coaching of forensic pathologist who had performed autopsy of victim was so intrusive and extensive that it "tampered with the heart of [the witness's] testimony"). Except in extreme cases of witness programming such as *Halsey*, the extent to which a lawyer can "script" or "prefabricate" otherwise truthful witness testimony has not been definitively resolved. Compare United States v. Welton, 2009 U.S. Dist. Lexis 138113 (C.D. Cal. 2009) ("While directing a witness to use (or avoid using) particular words when phrasing an answer is unacceptable conduct, particularly for a prosecutor . . . there is no evidence that [the witness] testified falsely . . . as a result of the advice she received from the [prosecuting attorney]") with Resolution Tr. Corp. v. Bright, 6 F.3d 336 (5th Cir. 1993) (drawing distinction between asking witness to swear to facts which are knowingly false and placing statements in draft affidavit that have not been previously discussed with witness). *See generally* Matthew Hector, *The Beau Brindley Case: Witness Preparation v. Coaching*, 103 ILL. BAR JOURNAL 11, 11 (2015) (analyzing federal district court for the Northern District of Illinois's decision that use of question-and-answer scripts to prepare witnesses for trial was not prohibited coaching, and noting that there is "no bright line" between rigorous witness preparation and improper witness coaching).

20. Transcript of Evidentiary Hearing Before the Honorable Leonie M. Brinkema, U.S. District Court Judge, United States v. Zacarias Moussaoui, No. 01-692 (E.D. Va. Mar. 14, 2006) (lawyer representing Transportation Security Administration emailed trial transcripts to a group of potential witnesses who were under a sequestration order; the court barred the government from introducing that evidence, and the lawyer was referred to the Pennsylvania Disciplinary Board). *See also* Miller v. Universal City Studios, Inc., 650 F.2d 1365 (5th Cir. 1981) (court ordered exclusion of witness testimony *where* lawyer violated sequestration order by allowing an expert witness to view the transcripts of other witness contrary to an order based on Fed. R. Evid. 615). *But see* State v. Blakeney, 137 Vt. 495, 408 A.2d 636 (1979) (sequestration order excluding witnesses from courtroom in no way restricted the right of counsel to confer with their clients or witnesses; purpose of the order was not to segregate witnesses from counsel who called them, although issuance of such an order would be within the sound discretion of the trial judge in an appropriate case).

21. *In re* Edson, 108 N.J. 464, 471-73 (1987) (lawyer disbarred after providing an undercover detective posing as a client with a memo fabricating facts to be used as the detectives' testimony, in violation of New Jersey RPC 1.2(d), RPC 8.4(a), (b), (c), and (d)). Even merely permitting a client to testify to fabricated evidence is sanctionable as offering false evidence. *See* Attorney Griev. Comm'n v. Elmendorf, 404 Md. 353, 946 A.2d 542 (2006) (leaving person with the impression that they could mislead the court in a divorce action by attesting to compliance with 6-month waiting period violated Rule 8.4(d)); Patsy's Brand, Inc. v. I.O.B. Realty, Inc., No.98 CIV 10175(JSM), 2002 WL 59434 (S.D.N.Y. Jan 16, 2002) (citing Rule 3.3(a)(3), court sua sponte sanctioned law firm for permitting client to submit false affidavit; although client insisted affidavit was true, where "no reasonable lawyer would believe it" in light of other evidence known to law firm).

testimony,[22] even if that payment is for "truthful" testimony.[23] Other types of unlawful inducements are similarly unethical.[24] For example, donating money to a witness's favorite charity was held to be an improper attempt to influence testimony.[25] In addition, offering a witness money or other incentives *not* to testify is a species of witness tampering and flatly prohibited by the Model Rules.[26]

C. Unethical Conduct During Witness Testimony

While the methods of advance witness preparation are variable and there is a broad range of acceptable methods, the equation changes when a lawyer's efforts to refine witness testimony happen during a trial or deposition. Overtly attempting to manipulate testimony-in-progress would in most situations constitute at least conduct prejudicial to the administration of justice in violation of Model Rule 8.4(d). Violation of a court rule or order restricting such coaching behaviors would be knowing disobedience of the rules of a tribunal in violation of Model Rule 3.4(c).[27]

---

22. MODEL RULES OF PROF'L CONDUCT R. 3.4, Comment [3] ("The common law rule in most jurisdictions is that it is improper to pay an occurrence witness any fee for testifying and that it is improper to pay an expert witness a contingent fee."). Most states permit "reasonable" compensation to occurrence witnesses for time and expenses in preparing to testify, although some jurisdictions place restrictions on testimony for actual courtroom time. ABA Comm. on Ethics & Prof'l Responsibility, Formal Op. 96-402 (1996) (nonexpert witness may be compensated for time spent attending trial or deposition or preparing for testimony if payment is not conditioned upon the content of testimony and does not violate any law). *See generally* ABA ANNOTATED MODEL RULES OF PROFESSIONAL CONDUCT, Rule 3.4, at 425-27 (10th ed. 2023) (discussion of Witness Fees).

23. *In re* Discipline of Callister, No. 70901 (Nev. 2017) (lawyer suspended for offering to pay a witness $7,000 for his "honest testimony" in support of certain facts and threatening the witness with personal liability and "the legal implications of perjury" if he testified the other way).

24. *E.g.*, People v. Gifford, 76 P.3d 519 (Colo. O.P.D.J. 2003) (advising client to offer ex-wife real estate in exchange for favorable testimony in criminal case). *See generally* ABA ANNOTATED MODEL RULES OF PROFESSIONAL CONDUCT, Rule 3.4, at 424 (10th ed. 2023) (discussion of Offering Illegal Inducement to Witness).

25. Christopher v. DePuy Orthopaedics, Inc., 888 F.3d 753 (5th Cir. 2018) (granting relief from judgment under FED. R. CIV. P. 60(b) where lawyer had represented that experts were non-retained and serving "pro bono," but lawyer had secretly donated $10,000 to one expert's private school alma mater before trial and collectively paid the two experts $65,000 after trial).

26. *See, e.g.*, *In re* Discipline of Kronenberg, 155 Wash.2d 184, 198 (2005) (disbarment appropriate for lawyer who gave victim-witness $3,000 and a one-way bus ticket to Oklahoma so witness would not testify against defendant in a criminal case, in violation of Washington State RPC 8.4(a)-(d) bribing and tampering with a witness and 8.4(c) for deceiving prosecutors about procuring the witness's absence; lawyer also deemed unfit to practice law).

27. In some cases, such conduct may also be a violation of MODEL RULES OF PROF'L CONDUCT R. 3.4(a) (unlawfully obstructing another party's access to evidence). *See generally* ABA ANNOTATED MODEL RULES OF PROFESSIONAL CONDUCT, Rule 3.4, at 422 & 427-29 (10th ed. 2023) (discussions of Obstructing Another Party's Access to Evidence and Obeying Obligation to Tribunal).

Winking at a witness during trial testimony, kicking a deponent under the table, or passing notes or whispering to a witness mid-testimony are classic examples of efforts to improperly influence a witness's in-progress testimony.[28] Other more subtle types of signaling also implicate ethical obligations and at times result in court-ordered sanctions. A familiar type of covert coaching is the so-called "speaking objection," or "suggestive objection." These are "statements that go beyond just stating the objection or the basis for the objection and are intended—or at least suspected of being intended—to coach the witness and impede the deposing attorney's discovery."[29] The rules in many state and federal jurisdictions prohibit objections that have the effect of coaching a witness, and may also prohibit lawyers from instructing a witness not to answer a question unless specifically authorized to do so.[30] Some jurisdictions have enacted rules for the conduct of depositions that expressly restrict speaking objections.[31]

---

28. *See, e.g.*, Vnuk v. Berwick Hospital Co., No. 3:14-CV-01432, 2016 WL 907714, at *4 (M.D. Pa. Mar. 2, 2016) (finding lawyer violated court rules by conferring with witness over break, passing notes and whispering during deposition). One commentator likened lawyer-to-witness gesturing to the catcher's signal to the pitcher in a baseball game advising what pitch to throw. Holland & Hart, *Witnesses: Don't Rely on 'Catcher Signals'*, JDSupra (Apr. 26, 2021), available at https://www.jdsupra.com/legalnews/witnesses-don-t-rely-on-catcher-signals-5364552/.

29. Michael Roundy, *Speaking Objections Risk Sanctions*, ABA Litigation Section Practice Points, *available at* https://www.americanbar.org/groups/litigation/committees/pretrial-practice-discovery/practice/2019/speaking-objections-risk-sanctions/?login (May 31, 2019). Openly asking a witness to correct an inadvertent misstatement when the witness obviously misunderstood a question or simply misspoke is not a coaching concern. In some circumstances involving false witness testimony, a lawyer may have an ethical duty to take reasonable remedial measures to correct the testimony. *See* Model Rules of Prof'l Conduct R. 3.3, cmt. [10]. *See generally* ABA Annotated Model Rules of Professional Conduct, Rule 3.3, at 412-13 (10th ed. 2023) (discussion of Remedial Measures).

30. *E.g.*, Fed. R. Civ. P. 30(c)(2) ("An objection must be stated concisely in a nonargumentative and nonsuggestive manner. A person may instruct a deponent not to answer only when necessary to preserve a privilege, to enforce a limitation ordered by the court, or to present a motion under Rule 30(d)(3)."); Sec. Nat. Bank of Sioux City, Iowa v. Day, 800 F.3d 936, 942 (8th Cir. 2015) (lawyers should not use an objection to instruct the witnesses how to answer or not answer a question); Deville v. Givaudan Fragrances Corp., 419 F. App'x 201, 209 (3d Cir. 2011) (affirming imposition of sanctions upon finding that attorney "testified on behalf of witness by way of suggestive speaking objections"); Goode v. Ramsaur, No. 20-cv-00947-DDD-KLM, 2023 U.S. Dist. LEXIS 80236 *13-24 (D. Colo. May 8, 2023) (finding sanctionable counsel's conduct involving countless speaking objections during deposition); Sec. Nat. Bank of Sioux City, Iowa v. Abbott Laboratories, 299 F.R.D. 595, 604 (N.D. Iowa 2014) (objections must be stated in a non-suggestive manner).

31. Brightman v. Corizon, Inc., 2021 NY Slip Op 50735(U), ¶ 2, 72 Misc. 3d 1213(A), 150 N.Y.S.3d 233 (Sup. Ct. 2021) (referencing New York's Uniform Rules for the Conduct of Depositions, which expressly limit speaking objections: "Speaking objections are thus singled out as undesirable: they are not necessary to preserve an objection to form, they disrupt and impede the conduct of the deposition, and they risk coaching the deponent on how to answer a pending question.").

APPENDIX F: FORMAL ETHICS OPINIONS

Relatedly, when a witness's testimony is underway, lawyers sometimes attempt to exercise midcourse testimonial influence and undertake damage control during a break or recess and may even seek or insist upon such breaks while a question is pending for the apparent purpose of coaching the witness in a private conference. Although there is no express ethical prohibition on communications between witness and counsel during a break in testimony, adjudicative officers have, at times, exercised control over these circumstances, including entering specific orders and imposing deposition guidelines and/or sanctions.[32]

Lawyers should both refrain from efforts to physically signal witnesses when testimony is in progress and attend closely to the strictures imposed by court rule, local rule, or court order.

1. Misconduct in Remote Settings

The use of remote communications platforms and other technologies in adjudicative proceedings and depositions, provides opportunities and temptations for lawyers to surreptitiously tell or signal witnesses what to say or not say in the proceedings of a tribunal.

This is not a novel phenomenon. When the ubiquity of cell phone technology made it convenient to communicate with another person covertly, some lawyers began to abuse it. In a troubling example of text-message-based coaching, a Florida lawyer, in a worker's compensation case, was disciplined for sending text messages to a witness regarding the witness's testimony while a deposition was in progress, which texts included coaching and spe-

---

32. *See, e.g.,* Hall v. Clifton Precision, 150 F.R.D. 525, 528 (E.D. Pa. 1993) (holding that a lawyer and client "do not have an absolute right to confer during the course of the client's deposition"; noting that deposition guidelines restricting private conferences would be undermined "by a lawyer's making of lengthy objections which contain information suggestive of an answer to a pending question," i.e., speaking objections); Brightman v. Corizon, Inc., 2021 NY Slip Op 50735(U), ¶ 2, 72 Misc. 3d 1213(A), 150 N.Y.S.3d 233 (Sup. Ct. 2021) (discussing prohibition in Uniform Rules for the Conduct of Deposition on a lawyer interrupting the deposition for the purpose of communicating with the deponent, as well as the trial court's discretion to bar consultation between a party and counsel while the party is testifying to the extent consistent with the party's constitutional rights). *See also Deville v. Givaudan Fragrances Corp.*, 419 F. Appx. 201, 207 (3rd Cir. 2011) (upholding sanctions for abusive, unprofessional and obstructive conduct during deposition); *Specht v. Google, Inc.*, 268 F.R.D. 596, 598-599, 603 (N.D. Ill. 2010) (imposing sanctions for speaking objections that obstructed deposition); *BNSF Ry. Co. v. San Joaquin Valley RR Co.*, 2009 WL 3872043, *3 (E.D. Cal. Nov. 17, 2009) (imposing sanctions for inappropriate and burdensome objections).

cific directions on how to respond to questions.[33] Similarly, it is improper for a lawyer to text a witness who is testifying at trial.[34]

The logistics of trials and depositions using remote meeting technologies are such that a lawyer and a witness may be in one location, with the opposing lawyer at another location, and, in trial situations, an adjudicative officer in yet another. In these circumstances, many things can happen that cannot readily be monitored by participants in the other remote locations.[35] It would be relatively easy for an off-camera lawyer or someone acting at the lawyer's behest to signal a witness with undetectable winks, nods, thumbs up or down, passed notes, or the like. Surreptitious off-camera activities such as texting the witness or other real-time electronic messaging are possible and easily done.

Allegations of misconduct in remote proceedings have been addressed by regulators and the judiciary. A lawyer has been disciplined for providing a client with answers to questions while off camera during a remote proceeding.[36] Another example involved a lawyer representing the defendant in a federal lawsuit, who, during a remote deposition, was overheard by opposing counsel providing the client with an answer to a question, after which the client repeated the answer as the client's own. After reviewing the deposition

---

33. When confronted about the text messages by counsel taking the deposition, the lawyer falsely denied texting the witness and stated he was only receiving a text from his daughter. Then, after agreeing to put his cellphone away, the lawyer continued sending texts, and inadvertently sent text messages intended for the witness to deposing counsel. The Florida Bar v. James, 329 So.3d 108, 109-112 (Fla. 2021) (finding violation of Florida Bar Rules 3-4.3 (commission of any act that is unlawful or contrary to honesty and justice), 4-3.4(a) (obstructing another party's access to evidence), Rule 4-8.4(d) (conduct prejudicial to the administration of justice)).

34. *See* Sky Dev. Inc v. Vistaview Dev. Inc., 41 So. 3d 918 (Fla. Dist. Ct. App. 2010) (lawyer who texted witness while witness was testifying at trial constituted a "blatant showing of fraud, pretense, collusion or other similar wrongdoing"); Wei Ngai v. Old Navy, No. 07-5653 (KSH) (PS), 2009 U.S. Dist. LEXIS 67117, at 4 (D.N.J. July 31, 2009) (during remote video-conference deposition with lawyer in one state while deponent was in another, lawyer and deponent exchanged five text messages; because lawyer also accidentally sent a text meant for deponent to opposing counsel, the texting came to light; in ordering production of the text messages, court rejected assertion of attorney-client privilege for the texts, which violated Fed. R. Civ. P. 30(c) ("depositions are to be conducted in the same manner as trial examination") because texts were equivalent to passing notes to client with the intent "to influence the fact finding goal of the deposition process").

35. *See* Wei Ngai v. Old Navy, Civil Action No. 07-5653 (KSH) (PS), 2009 U.S. Dist. LEXIS 67117, at *2 (D.N.J. July 31, 2009) (in dispute over defense counsel's sending of text messages to witness during remote deposition, plaintiff's counsel noted that the deponent and defense counsel were only visible from the "chest up" and that she was unable to observe defense counsel's hands during the deposition).

36. *In re* Claridge, PDJ 2021-9088 (Ariz. Jan. 21, 2022) (suspending lawyer for 60 days by consent where lawyer used chat feature to instruct client during cross-examination at trial using GoToMeeting platform, in violation of Arizona Ethics Rule 3.4(a) ER 8.4(c), and ER 8.4(d)).

footage, opposing counsel found 50 additional circumstances where the lawyer had provided the client with answers to questions while off-camera during the remote deposition.[37]

Lawyers have a duty to comply with the rules of professional conduct and rules of court that prohibit witness coaching, in all testimonial contexts regardless of the format of the deposition, hearing, or trial. Remote coaching, like its historical antecedents, puts the perpetrating lawyer at risk of adjudicative rebukes and court-ordered sanctions,[38] as well as disciplinary sanctions.[39]

2. Systemic Precautions for Addressing Such Misconduct

All lawyers have an ethical obligation to understand how relevant technology works.[40] Some degree of sophistication regarding the nature of the technology used in remote proceedings will help avoid inadvertent missteps.[41] An understanding of the coaching-related risks of remote technology will also enable lawyers and adjudicative officers concerned about potential surreptitious coaching to structure remote proceedings in ways that will deter its occurrence and enhance the ability to detect it.

---

37. Barksdale School Portraits, LLC v. Williams, 339 F.R.D. 341 (D. Mass. 2021) (disqualifying lawyer from case, ordering that jurors be allowed to hear both the deposition witness's testimony and the lawyer's coaching and draw their own conclusions regarding the credibility of the testimony, and referring matter to another federal district court judge to evaluate potential discipline); *see also In re* Jeffrey Rosin, No. 21-mc-91571-LTS (U.S. Dist. Ct. for the Dist. of Mass., Jan. 19, 2022) (ordering lawyer in *Barksdale School Portraits* case to contact a group called Lawyers Concerned for Lawyers "for the limited purpose of receiving and completing counseling on better management of emotions and judgment in the face of adversity").

38. *See, e.g., Barksdale School Portraits, supra* note 37; Johnson v. Statewide Investigative Services Inc., No. 20-C-114 (N.D. Ill., March 4, 2021) (magistrate judge accepted lawyer's explanations of questionable conduct during Zoom deposition, finding that what happened during deposition was the result of a lack of professionalism and collegiality rather than an unethical attempt to coach witness).

39. The most severe sanctions to date were the disciplinary suspensions in the *James* and *Claridge* cases, discussed *supra* at notes 33 & 36. *See* Zack Needles, *Ethics Authorities Go Relatively Easy on Virtual Witness Coaching—For Now*, LAW.COM (Feb. 2, 2022) (noting that "ethics authorities have shown a fair amount of mercy to the offending lawyers, perhaps in recognition of the fact that virtual litigation is still pretty weird for everyone involved.").

40. MODEL RULES OF PROF'L CONDUCT R. 1.1, cmt. [8].

41. In Johnson v. Statewide Investigative Services Inc., No. 20-C-114 (N.D. Ill., March 4, 2021), a dispute over what appeared to be remote coaching, the trial judge firmly rejected a lawyer's proffered explanation that the problems occurred because he was not "technologically savvy," noting that at the time of the deposition, lawyers across the country had been primarily conducting their practices using technology for ten months: "This has included a host of different videoconferencing platforms for court hearings, depositions, and appellate arguments. Thus, while [a lawyer's] lack of technology expertise may have sufficed as an explanation at one point in time, it is no longer valid or credible."

What systemic precautions will prove useful in helping to prevent and detect incidences of problematic remote coaching and empower adjudicators to intervene as appropriate to control questionable lawyer conduct during remote trials and depositions? The following suggested approaches—though not ethically required under the Model Rules—provide a starting point:

- Skillful cross-examination[42]
- Court orders directing uninterrupted testimony[43]
- Motions to terminate or limit a deposition or for sanctions[44]
- Inclusion of protocols in remote deposition orders, scheduling orders, and proposed discovery plans[45]

---

42. This remedy was recommended by the United States Supreme Court. *See* Geders v. United States, 425 U.S. 80, 89-90 (1976) ("The opposing counsel in the adversary system is not without weapons to cope with 'coached' witnesses. A prosecutor may cross-examine a defendant as to the extent of any 'coaching' during a recess, subject, of course, to the control of the court. Skillful cross-examination could develop a record which the prosecutor in closing argument might well exploit by raising questions as to the defendant's credibility, if it developed that defense counsel had in fact coached the witness as to how to respond on the remaining direct examination and on cross-examination.").

43. This remedy also was recommended by the United States Supreme Court as a component of the judge's power to control the progress and shape of the trial. *See* Geders v. United States, 425 U.S. 80, 90 (1976) ("[T]he trial judge, if he doubts that defense counsel will observe the ethical limits on guiding witnesses, may direct that the examination of the witness continue without interruption until completed. If the judge considers the risk high he may arrange the sequence of testimony so that direct- and cross-examination of a witness will be completed without interruption. That this would not be feasible in some cases due to the length of direct- and cross-examination does not alter the availability, in most cases, of a solution that does not cut off communication for so long a period as presented by this record. Inconvenience to the parties, witnesses, counsel, and court personnel may occasionally result if a luncheon or other recess is postponed or if a court continues in session several hours beyond the normal adjournment hour. In this day of crowded dockets, courts must frequently sit through and beyond normal recess; convenience occasionally must yield to concern for the integrity of the trial itself.").

44. *See* FED. R. CIV. P. 30(d); STEVEN BAIKER-MCKEE & WILLIAM M. JANSSEN, FEDERAL CIVIL RULES HANDBOOK 871 (2022 ed.) (a party may move to terminate a deposition if it is being conducted in bad faith or in an unreasonably annoying, embarrassing, or oppressive manner; a court may impose an "appropriate sanction" on a person engaging in obstructive behavior). *See* ADVISORY COMMITTEE NOTES TO THE FEDERAL RULES OF CIVIL PROCEDURE, 1980 AMENDMENT TO FED. R. CIV. P. 26, Subdivision (f) (1980) ("In the judgment of the Committee abuse can best be prevented by intervention by the court as soon as abuse is threatened.").

45. Such protocols can be agreed to as part of a stipulation to a deposition by remote means or ordered by the court when authorizing that a deposition be taken by remote means. *See* FED. R. CIV. P. 30(b)(4). Protocols could also be included in a proposed discovery plan. *See* FED. R. CIV. P. 26(f). A number of courts routinely require that depositions be conducted in accordance with the stringent procedures set forth in *Hall v. Clifton Precision*, 150 F.R.D. 525, 528 (E.D. Pa. 1993). *E.g.*, Kelleher v. Wells Fargo Ins. Servs., No. 10-6247-NLH-KMW, 2011 U.S. Dist. LEXIS 13074, at *2 (D.N.J. Feb. 10, 2011). For an example of a re-

APPENDIX F: FORMAL ETHICS OPINIONS

- Administrative orders governing the conduct of remote depositions[46]
- Inclusion of remote protocols in trial plans and pretrial orders[47]
- Development of guidelines and best practices for conduct in remote proceedings[48]
- Professionalism/Civility/Courtesy Codes[49]

Structuring remote proceedings in advance by way of agreement, court order, or collectively adopted behavioral norms will create greater transparency and provide helpful guardrails to guide lawyers away from unethical conduct.

Conclusion

Under the Model Rules of Professional Conduct, a lawyer's failure to prepare and guide a witness would in many situations violate the ethical duties of competence and diligence. Witness preparation becomes unethical when the conduct transgresses Model Rules governing prohibiting interference with the integrity of the justice system and obstructing another party's access to evidence. The use of technology in the profession, particularly

---

mote deposition protocol, see Uniform Civil Rules for New York State Trial Courts, Rule 202.70(g), Appendix G, STIPULATION AND PROPOSED ORDER CONCERNING PROTOCOL FOR CONDUCTING REMOTE DEPOSITIONS, *available at* https://www.nycourts.gov/LegacyPDFS/RULES/trialcourts/202.70(g)%20-%20Rule%2037-Appendix%20G.pdf (last visited Aug. 25, 2023).

46. *See, e.g.*, SUPREME JUDICIAL COURT OF MASSACHUSETTS UPDATED ORDER REGARDING REMOTE DEPOSITIONS (Oct. 23, 2020), *available at* https://www.mass.gov/supreme-judicial-court-rules/supreme-judicial-court-updated-order-regarding-remote-depositions.

47. *See* FED. R. CIV. P. 16(c) & (e). *See, e.g.*, STATE OF NEW YORK UNIFIED COURT SYSTEM, VIRTUAL BENCH TRIAL PROTOCOLS AND PROCEDURES (including Proposed Stipulation and Order for Virtual Bench Trial Protocols and Procedures), *available at* https://www.nycourts.gov/whatsnew/pdf/VirtualBenchTrial-Protocols-2112021.pdf (last visited Aug. 25, 2023).

48. *See* NATIONAL CENTER FOR STATE COURTS, REMOTE PROCEEDINGS TOOLKIT 47-50 (Proceedings Conduct) (2002), *available at* https://www.ncsc.org/__data/assets/pdf_file/0027/82377/Remote-Proceeding-Toolkit-Final.pdf; WASHINGTON STATE SUPREME COURT, REMOTE JURY TRIALS WORK GROUP BEST PRACTICES IN RESPONSE TO FREQUENTLY ASKED QUESTIONS (FAQ) (June 2021) (including links to resources such as sample orders for remote/virtual jury trials), *available at* https://www.courts.wa.gov/newsinfo/index.cfm?fa=newsinfo.remotejurytrialsworkgroup.

49. *See, e.g.*, COLORADO PRINCIPLES OF PROFESSIONALISM, PRINCIPLE 7.2.5 (2011) ("We will refrain from coaching deponents by objecting, commenting, or acting in any other manner that suggests a particular answer to a question."), *available at* https://www.cobar.org/For-Members/Committees/Professionalism-Coordinating-Council/Principles-of-Professionalism#9712573-colorado-principles-of-professionalism (2011). A compilation of Professionalism Codes from around the United States can be found on the ABA Center for Professional Responsibility Resources page of the ABA website, *available at* https://www.americanbar.org/groups/professional_responsibility/resources/professionalism/professionalism_codes/.

remote-meeting technologies, presents distinct opportunities for surreptitious witness coaching. But the Model Rules that constrain unethical witness coaching extend to all testimonial contexts, regardless of format. It is prudent for lawyers and adjudicators to consider prophylactic measures designed for use in remote proceedings to prevent and detect incidences of unethical coaching conduct.

AMERICAN BAR ASSOCIATION
STANDING COMMITTEE ON ETHICS AND PROFESSIONAL RESPONSIBILITY
321 N. Clark Street, Chicago, Illinois 60654-4714 Telephone (312) 988-5328
CHAIR: Lynda Shely, Scottsdale, AZ
■ Mark A. Armitage, Detroit, MI ■ Melinda Bentley, Jefferson City, MO ■ Matthew Corbin, Olathe, KS
■ Robinjit Kaur Eagleson, Lansing, MI ■ Doug Ende, Seattle, WA
■ Hon. Audrey Moorehead, Dallas, TX ■ Wendy Muchman, Chicago, IL
■ Keith Swisher, Scottsdale, AZ ■ Charles Vigil, Albuquerque, NM

CENTER FOR PROFESSIONAL RESPONSIBILITY
Mary McDermott, Lead Senior Counsel
©2023 by the American Bar Association. All rights reserved.